For None Can Rank Above Thee

A History of Cal-Mum Red Raiders Football

Thomas E. Pullyblank

Square Circle Press
Voorheesville, New York

For None Can Rank Above Thee:
A History of Cal-Mum Red Raiders Football

Published by
Square Circle Press LLC
137 Ketcham Road
Voorheesville, NY 12186
www.squarecirclepress.com

© 2012 by Thomas E. Pullyblank.

All rights reserved. No part of this publication may be reproduced or transmitted in any form or by any means, electronic or mechanical, except brief quotes extracted for the purpose of book reviews or similar articles, without permission in writing from the publisher.

First paperback edition 2012.
Printed and bound in the United States of America on acid-free, durable paper.
ISBN 13: 978-0-9856926-1-2
ISBN 10: 0-9856926-1-8
Library of Congress Control Number: 2012950243

Publisher's Acknowledgments
Cover ©2012 by Square Circle Press; design by Richard Vang. Epigraph: Caledonia *alma mater* by Margaret McCabe, 1926. Illustration sources: map illustration ©2012 by Barry Robinson; front cover, 1, 2, 3, 15 (all), 19, 22, 23 (all), 24, 25 (all), back cover (left) - Author and Pullyblank family collections; 4, 5 - Rochester *Democrat and Chronicle*; 7, 8, 11, 12, 13, 14, 16, 17, 20, 21, 26, 27, 30, 31, 35 - *Ainodelac* (Caledonia High School and Caledonia-Mumford Central School yearbooks); 6, 9, 10, 18 (all) - Ed Coots collection; 28, 29, 32, 33, 34, 36, back cover (right): Mike Monacelli collection (photos by Mark Riggi).

Front cover photo: The Soldier's Monument, November 14, 1980, following Cal-Mum's 26-21 Section V championship victory over LeRoy.

Back cover photos: The 1929 undefeated, untied and unscored-upon team (left) and the 2003 New York State champions (right).

Caledonia, hear us praise thee;
all hail to thy dear name;
Oh may we ne'er disgrace thee
or cause thee any shame,
We will honor thee and love thee,
obey thy law and rule,
For none can rank above thee,
Caledonia, our dear school.

You have taught us to be steadfast,
to be faithful, good and true;
To be honest in our dealings
and always loyal too.
These aren't all the priceless lessons
we've learned at thy footstool,
And for all of them we thank thee,
Caledonia our dear school.

When we have left the classrooms,
when we are far away,
Fond memories will linger
to cheer us every day.
Though we roam in foreign countries,
our love will ne'er grow cold,
But we will still adore thee,
Caledonia, our dear school.

Margaret McCabe (1926)

Contents

Acknowledgments vii
Map of "No. 1 Country" 2

Chapter One: Who's Number One? 3
Chapter Two: 1929 10
Chapter Three: Football Families 24
Chapter Four: The Big Mac Attack 37
Chapter Five: Monumental Meetings, 1978-1981 48
Chapter Six: Under Pressure 65
Chapter Seven: Monacelli Moments 94
Chapter Eight: 1995 110
Chapter Nine: Destroy LeRoy 119

Sources/References 133

Appendix A: Game-by-Game Scores, 1925-2011 140
Appendix B: Season Records, 1925-2011 185
Appendix C: Cumulative Coaching Records, 1925-2011 189
Appendix D: The Undefeated Teams 190
Appendix E: 25 Memorable Victories, 10 Forgettable Losses 194
Appendix F: The Cal-Mum Red Raider Football Hall of Fame 196
Appendix G: Cal-Mum Versus LeRoy, 1900-2011 198

Index to Players and Coaches 202
About the Author 207

Illustrations follow page 75.

Acknowledgments

For None Can Rank Above Thee: A History of Cal-Mum Red Raiders Football was generations in the making. My grandfather, Eugene Pullyblank, played on the legendary undefeated, untied and unscored-upon team. My father, Robert Pullyblank, and my uncle, Donald Pullyblank, played on the undefeated, untied 1950 team coached by my grandfather's teammate, Robert Freeman. My oldest brother Mike played on the undefeated, untied 1973 and 1974 teams, and again in 1975, when he was selected an All-American at quarterback. My brother Steve played along side my cousin Mark on the 1976 and 1977 teams. My brother Jim played on the 1980 and 1981 teams. Finally, my cousin Rob played on the 1983 and 1984 teams, and thereafter handed the mantle of starting left end to me, having received it from two of my brothers in turn.

The family story doesn't end there: numerous nephews have played Cal-Mum football since I graduated in 1986. They are still playing, working their way through the system from modified to junior varsity to varsity, when I and their parents and aunts and uncles and grandparents can cheer for them against the same teams with whom we competed in our youths.

This book is dedicated to them, my kin past and present, for giving me the privilege of being part of something great that extends both backwards and forwards in time. Someday, when we're all in heaven, the Pullyblank clan will have one heck of a team!

This book is also dedicated to the Pullyblank women, who, throughout the years, cheered us on and made cookies and washed our uniforms and offered hugs of celebration after victory and tears of condolence after defeat. My mother Betty Jane Pullyblank and my sisters Ann and Amy are at the top of this list.

Finally, this book is dedicated to all the coaches who helped teach us Pullyblank boys how to play the game well, how to be good teammates to our fellow Raiders and good sports to our opponents, and how to conduct ourselves with dignity. My father says that it's an honor and a privilege to wear the maroon and white. In large part this was due to the lessons taught and the examples given by our coaches.

For me, those coaches were Bill McAlee, Roger House, Ed Matthews, Mike Monacelli and Gary Fredericks. I could easily sit down at the Iroquois and tell you several fond stories about each of them, and I'm sure that many of you could reciprocate. When it came to writing this book, Ed Matthews provided some initial inspiration, Bill McAlee provided regular encouragement, and Mike Monacelli provided expertise, knowledge and more than a little coaching wisdom.

There are others who need thanking. To Shannon Martin for generously sharing her late husband Rob Martin's incredible collection of Cal-Mum Red Raider football articles. Rob's collection spans the decades from 1970 to 2003. His meticulously organized scrapbooks made research a pleasure. To Jim Pullyblank for his own scrapbook, which I inherited when Jim went off to college and which I practically memorized as I tried, with varying success, to fill his and my older brothers' shoes. To Carol Matthews for sharing her late husband Ed Matthews' football collection. While not as exhaustive as Rob Martin's, Coach Matthews' material included some precious gems from the early years of Cal-Mum football. To Pat Garrett at the Big Springs Historical Association in Caledonia. Not only did she help me tremendously with my research into the undefeated teams, she also gave me a guided tour of the Big Springs' collection that provided much of the imaginative framework for the type of lives the farm boys from Caledonia lived when they went to Rochester to play and beat the city slickers from Aquinas. To Jim Vokes for sharing his memories and knowledge. His family traveled a similar multi-generational path through Cal-Mum football history as the Pullyblanks, and I know that Jim is just as thankful as I am for all our blessings. To Barry Robinson for the map, and to Matt Robinson for getting the word out to the Rochester media. To Stephanie Pullyblank, assisted by her father and my brother Steve, whose help putting this manuscript together, especially the historically significant lists in the appendices, was invaluable. And finally to Kristin and Bradon, who patiently listened to the stories from my own Cal-Mum Red Raider glory days, asked good questions about them and, most importantly, continue to provide me with the love and support that makes for a well-lived life.

For None Can Rank Above Thee

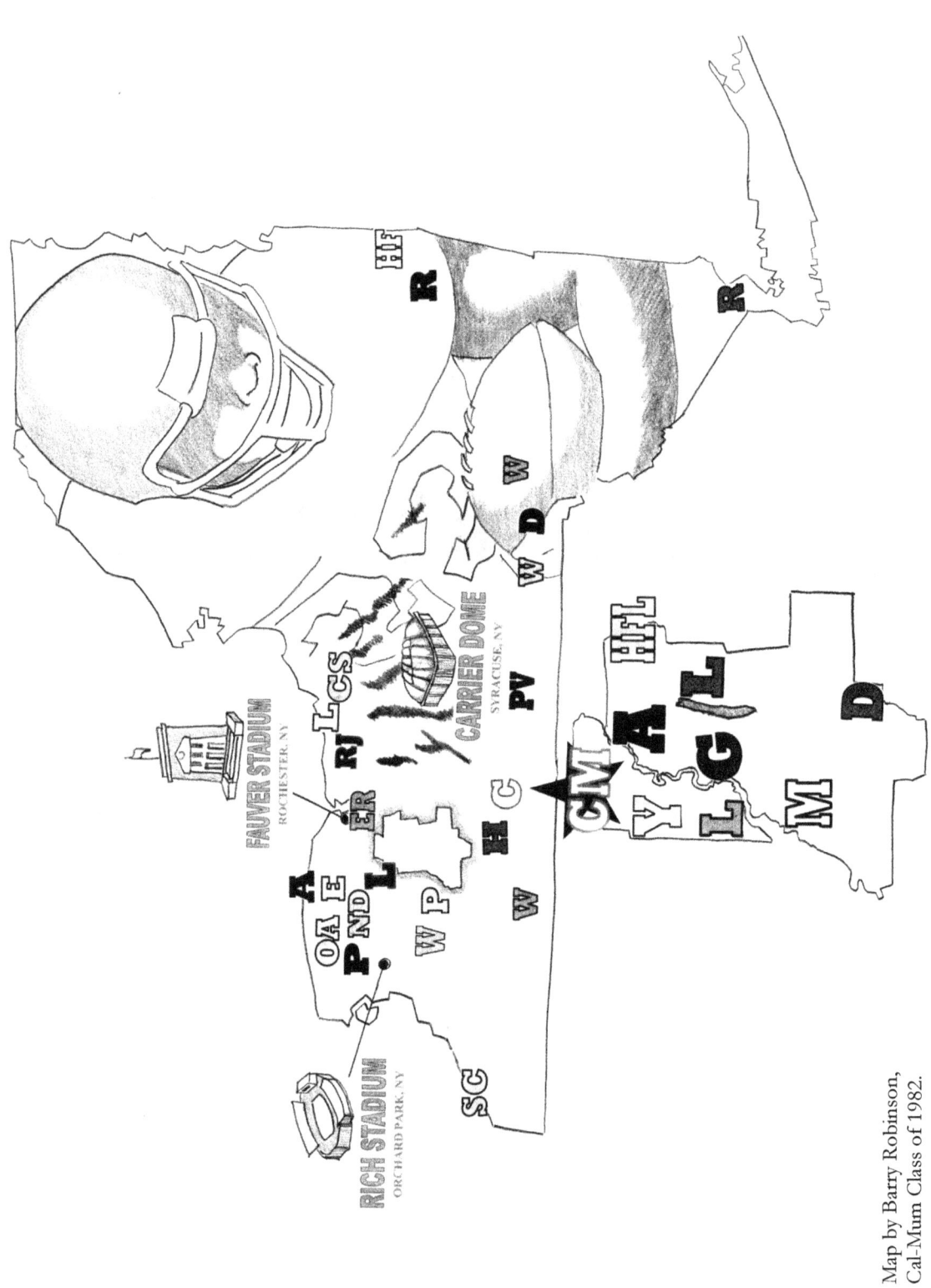

Map by Barry Robinson, Cal-Mum Class of 1982.

Chapter One:
Who's Number One?

MAYBE IT'S THE MOON that came full two nights before. We western New Yorkers know well what strange happenings the Hunter's Moon can bring, especially when it waxes full so close to Halloween.

Maybe it's the teams' combined histories. The first game between Caledonia and LeRoy was played in 1900. In the twenty years before 1977, there have been only three losing records between them, all Cal-Mum's. Both teams have cheerleaders who date boys from the other school. Both teams' rosters include young men whose fathers and grandfathers lined up against their opponent's fathers and grandfathers. For these schools, gridiron memories are in the blood.

Possibly it's the teams' styles of play, one the mirror image of the other. Both teams boast a hard-nosed, straight-ahead, run-up-the-gut type of game. Both teams play smash-mouth football.

Cal-Mum saw the LeRoy Oatkan Knights demolish Honeoye Falls-Lima a few weeks before. "We thought we could run on them" despite the score, said Raider running back Jeff Sweet.

A contingent of LeRoy players watched the Cal-Mum Red Raiders squeak by Livonia the previous Saturday. "Their players were laughing at us from behind the end zone," Cal-Mum's Junior Poles explained. "Laughing at us!"

LeRoy averaged 38 points per game to this point of the season. Cal-Mum averaged 30. The numbers justify both teams' confidence.

Possibly, too, it's the coaches' contrasting styles, also reflecting each other, but in this case like a fun-house-mirror. On the home sideline is LeRoy's Frank Ruane, tall, lean and dignified with a shock of remarkable white hair, his black overcoat billowing in the late October breeze. On the visitor's side is Cal-Mum's Bill McAlee, short and squat, outfitted at game time in his usual maroon and white checkered sport coat. McAlee's equally remarkable brush cut is hidden underneath a maroon fedora.

Definitely it's the articles in competing Rochester dailies profiling both teams and predicting that something special will be in the air come Friday.

"This is the best backfield I've seen at one school," boasts LeRoy "super-fan" Joe Macaluso in the Rochester *Democrat and Chronicle* when asked about the trio of running backs who had already scored twenty touchdowns that season.

Adds another fan: "If I had to defense this backfield, I don't know what I'd do." The implication, of course, is that Cal-Mum won't know what to do either.

A third Oatkan Knight supporter displays cardboard tombstones of conquered opponents on his front lawn. A special tombstone, bigger than the rest, is on the porch, awaiting the victory over Cal-Mum.

Cal-Mum's pre-game state of mind is different. "We do the same things now we did on August 24," says a calm and confident Bill McAlee in the Rochester *Times-Union*. "We'll do the same thing tomorrow that we did the last Tuesday. And the Tuesday before that."

If Cal-Mum loses? "Hey, that game is over. You can't turn back time. You can just look for a new day tomorrow."

And if one of his players were to make a mistake that cost the Red Raiders the game? "Maybe we expect too much of our children because we think they are ready for something they're not ready for," McAlee muses. "A 17-year old is a 17-year old. If a kid fumbles and it costs you the game—the kid doesn't WANT to fumble. Life is too complicated for him to have to carry that fumble around with him."

LeRoy boasts. Cal-Mum plays it down. Each approach has been successful. Each approach has brought many football victories to these small upstate New York towns over the years.

Add to all this—the moon, the history, the styles, the coaches, the hype—add to all of it a simple numerological fact. LeRoy, 5-0, is the number-one-ranked small school football team in New York State, while Cal-Mum, 6-0, is ranked number seven. There's an inherent intensity in a battle of unbeaten teams, an intensity that's heightened when both teams are so good. Yet a cruel fact lurks in the not-too-distant future, awaiting one of them. Barring a tie, someone will not be unbeaten for long.

All the possibilities and the certainties line up tonight. Almost five thousand people, far more than the population of either village, are at Hartwood Park, in LeRoy, on October 28, 1977. They are here to watch Cal-Mum and LeRoy play a game that will decide the best football team in Livingston County, and likely among small schools in the state.

One simple question will be answered tonight: Who's number one?

MORE IMMEDIATELY for Cal-Mum, the 1977 game is about revenge. A year before, on Hamilton Field, the Red Raiders were trounced by visiting LeRoy. Cal-Mum had led 7-6 at the half, but it was a precarious lead as penalties and missed opportunities denied LeRoy several scores that would have given the Oatkan Knights the advantage, perhaps a comfortable one. Halftime came and went. As the teams returned to the field for their second-half warm ups, an ominous sign appeared—or caused things to disappear into the dark, rather, as the stadium lights suddenly blew out.

Power to three banks of bulbs was eventually restored after an hour's anxious delay, but the Raiders might just as well have played in the dark. The offense sputtered. Giveaways cost Cal-Mum two scores. The home team defense was good, but the Oatkan Knights were clearly quicker and stronger, more eager perhaps. Despite the best efforts of the cheerleaders, the crowd remained lackadaisical throughout the second half. When it was all over LeRoy walked away with a 28-7 victory. The Raider faithful walked away with their heads down. They did not yet know that what they saw would not be seen again for another five years, another 49 games.

Yet the loss hurt the Raider faithful. Any loss to LeRoy does, more than most. As they walked to their cars, or as they sipped their first glass of Genny draft at the Iroquois Hotel later that night, they consoled each other with the mantra that all sports fans turn to in the aftermath of defeat: wait 'til next year.

1977, AS IT TURNED OUT, was a year worth waiting for. The world's first computer was demonstrated and Apple, Inc. was founded. Jimmy Carter was inaugurated and a massive blizzard crippled much of western New York. Americans by the millions watched *Roots* on TV, bought Fleetwood Mac's *Rumours* and mourned the death of Elvis. The Oakland Raiders won the Super Bowl, the Portland Trailblazers the NBA championship and the Yankees, powered by Reggie "Mr. October" Jackson, defeated the Dodgers in the World Series. The Toronto Blue Jays and Seattle Mariners played their first games. The Tampa Bay Buccaneers won their first game.

But in the last full week of October, everyone's attention in Mumford, Caledonia, Lime Rock and LeRoy, perhaps everyone's attention in Livingston County, is directed towards "the war."

Rick Woodson of the Rochester *Times Union* explains it best:

> This is the week of the war.
> Caledonia-Mumford vs. LeRoy.
> In Livingston County [Division] I, it is the high school game of the week. In the communities involved, it is the game of the year. A happen-

ing… Cal-Mum and LeRoy want to beat each other just because they're there.

The uncertainties of athletic competition are beginning to sort themselves out as the 1977 iteration of "the war" approaches. Unlike 1976, when Cal-Mum, LeRoy and Livonia ended the season tied atop the division standings, 1977 has two clear cut favorites in Livingston County, so much so that both teams are ranked among the top ten small school football teams in New York State. Cal-Mum versus LeRoy—the war is about to resume.

The first quarter of the game is eerily similar to the 1976 contest, as neither team does much against the other. A few yards here, a third down conversion there, but no drives that impress and certainly no indication of the same offensive firepower both teams have demonstrated so far this season. The tension is palpable as the first quarter ends in a scoreless tie.

Maybe it's the moon?

Then, early in the second quarter, Cal-Mum breaks out for the first big play of the game. Jeff D'Angelo runs a deep post pattern out of the backfield and gets half a step on LeRoy defensive back Macky Thiele. Quarterback Chris Wyatt floats the ball over Thiele, but almost over D'Angelo as well. D'Angelo, however, dives and catches the ball. It's a 31-yard gain that puts the Raiders at the LeRoy 4-yard line. On the next play, a good old-fashioned off-tackle behind the blocks of the Pullyblank cousins, Mark and Steve, fullback Pat Harrigan takes the ball in for the game's first score.

Cal-Mum comes close again when the Raiders move the ball to the LeRoy 2 towards the end of the second quarter. But this time LeRoy stops Harrigan on fourth down. As they had in 1976, the Raiders go into the locker room with a slim halftime lead. They know, in the context of this rivalry, that a slim lead is the equivalent to no lead at all.

Fans on both sidelines reminisce about last year's halftime and the blown fuse that darkened Cal-Mum's Hamilton Field. The grounds crew at Hartwood Park laughs as one of their number suggests that they should cut the lights on purpose to give their team a boost, as happened the year before. But the teams return to the field, and the second-half kickoff proceeds under full illumination.

Merely joking about it seems to work, though, as LeRoy's offense shows all indications of a revival in the third quarter. The Oatkan Knights run the ball play after play, finally getting some yardage against Cal-Mum's unorthodox 6-2 defense. But at the Cal-Mum 24, linebacker Steve Burger, with help from defensive tackle Junior

Poles, stops LeRoy running back Tracy Pike on a fourth-and-inches run up the gut. Cal-Mum holds. It would be the most important defensive play of the night.

Cal-Mum takes full advantage of the momentum swing that the big defensive stop provides. Nine plays and 67 yards into the drive, the Raiders pull a pre-Halloween trick out from McAlee's bag of treats, a catch and lateral from Jeff Sweet to Mark Seefried, who takes the ball into the end zone without a touch from an Oatkan Knight defender. Seefried had already caught a key 34-yard pass on third down during the drive. This lateral, an easier catch and a much, much bigger play, gives Lady Momentum a song to sing.

A good roast deserves gravy. A good cake deserves icing. With Lady Mo' on their side, Jeff Sweet and his Red Raider teammates provide the finishing touch in the fourth quarter when Sweet intercepts a Dave Bonacquisti pass, and then rushes for 38 yards and catches passes for 28 more. Sweet naturally takes the ball into the end zone for Cal-Mum's final score. Despite Coach Frank Ruane's best attempts at keeping LeRoy's spirits up, the home fans' cheering falls to a hush, the home players' heads start to sag. Victory belongs to the visiting Red Raiders.

The 19-0 shutout is preserved with Jim Wood's pick as time runs out, a fitting end to a defensive performance that surprises even the most confident Cal-Mum fans.

"I knew we'd score, but I wasn't so sure how the defense would be," says a jubilant Chris Wyatt after the game. "The defense had to do it tonight or we weren't going to be in it."

Jeff Sweet puts the victory into a community perspective. "Everybody takes credit for this one. This was a town effort and a school effort. All week long the teachers and the other kids at school treated us special. They had signs all over and you couldn't walk down the hall without thinking about the game. I think that was the difference. We wanted it more."

Bill McAlee's final comments as he steps onto the team bus are also about the community. "We're going home to Caledonia," he says. "We'll stop on the way if there's anyone waiting at the monument."

It won't be the last time that the Red Raider defense comes up big. It won't be the last time that Cal-Mum wins because it wants victory more. It won't be the last time that the team bus stops at the monument. And yes, Coach McAlee, there will always be somebody waiting.

A VICTORY THAT SIGNIFICANT needs dissection. Early the next morning, at the Moonwinks and Cozy Kitchen, the scalpels are out and ready.

Some say it was Jeff Sweet's doing. The 5'8" 150 pound senior ran the ball 26 times for 115 yards, caught several important passes and made several crucial plays in the defensive backfield. His masterpiece was the final touchdown drive that turned the win into a blowout.

Others say it was the entire offense. A 354 to 163 advantage in yards gained certainly provided good evidence for this argument. With the line blocking well, with Sweet and Pat Harrigan running the ball, with Chris Wyatt throwing passes that were exactly where they had to be, with Jeff D'Angelo and Mark Seefried catching everything that was thrown their way, the Raider offense certainly proved it could move the ball on anybody.

Still others claim it was the defense. Earlier in the week, McAlee and his defensive coach, Roger House, had decided to play the whole game in a 6-2 formation instead of in the usual 4-4 scheme that Cal-Mum had used in its previous six games. The change was risky. If LeRoy quarterback Dave Bonacquisti was able to throw the ball behind the crowded first wave of Cal-Mum defenders, or if any of LeRoy's three star running backs were able to get even a few yards past the line of scrimmage, then 19-0 easily could have become 19-14 or even 21-19.

But, as Chris Wyatt had put it immediately after the game, the Raiders defense came through. Junior Poles, Bob Loomis and, especially, linebacker Steve Burger shadowed and hounded the Oatkan Knights backfield all game. They never allowed the halfbacks to establish any type of consistent running game, never allowed Bonacquisti enough time to find an open receiver and get the ball downfield to him. Indeed, the intention of the 6-2 defense was to stop the Oatkan Knight rushing trio of Tracy Pike, Phil Caccamise and Mac Thiele, the runners earlier heralded by LeRoy fans as the best to ever play in Hartwood Park, the grim reapers who would put Cal-Mum in its symbolic front lawn grave. The 6-2 defense hadn't been revealed before either, not at any previous game scouted by LeRoy coaches, nor at the previous week's difficult game in Livonia, when the LeRoy players had gotten such a good laugh watching Cal-Mum from the end zone.

The defensive scheme was brilliant. The execution perfect. At the Moonwinks' and Cozy Kitchen's counters that Saturday morning, heads nodded over eggs and coffee as Cal-Mum's super-fans let the significance of what happened the night before sink in. The Red Raider defense had shutout the number one ranked small school football team in New York State.

Said Chris Wyatt, "If they were the number one team in the state before this game, then we're definitely number one now. I think we've been overlooked all along."

Cal-Mum would end the 1977 season ranked number one among small school football teams in New York State, a pinnacle the team would retain for the next three seasons en route to a Section V record 49 straight victories. Cal-Mum was good, sometimes very good, before October 28, 1977. But after the 19-0 victory over LeRoy, the Caledonia-Mumford Red Raider football team would never be overlooked again.

1977 was not the first time, nor the last, that Cal-Mum players, cheerleaders and fans could sing with perfect accuracy, "For none can rank above thee, Caledonia our dear school."

Chapter Two:
1929

PERHAPS it's all a dream. In our collective memory, for all those years, perhaps we needed these boys to be something greater than men.

I'll explain what I mean with two personal stories.

The first begins when I went to Coach McAlee after a game and asked him if there'd ever been a tight end who blocked like I had that night. It was after the 1985 LeRoy game, which we won 28-14. Roland Poles rushed for 297 yards that game, a few of the big gains on off-tackle plays to my side. My question to Coach McAlee was an arrogant one from an adolescent boy who had discovered arrogance and had duly fallen in love with himself.

But McAlee, always wise, played along. He took a drag from his pipe (smoking in the school was allowed back then, especially in the coach's office at the north end of the building) and he looked me square in the eye. He smiled and said, "Pullyblank, you're the best blocking tight end this team has ever had, at least since the last one."

I pumped my fist in jubilation. I smiled the whole time I showered and got dressed, singing "Broken Wings" by Mr. Mister at almost twice the normal tempo. I repeated McAlee's praise to my teammates and to all who would listen, and to some who wouldn't, later that night as we cranked Ronnie James Dio and drank "pop" at the Cox Road bonfire, as we cheered on the Boop brothers during their attempts to ascend Two-Try Hill.

For weeks I smiled when I recalled McAlee's comment. No—for years. I had done something worthwhile. I had pleased an authority figure whom I admired. I was the best at *something*.

Then, sometime in my twenties, in the process of growing out of my adolescent arrogance, I recalled also that my next older brother was a tight end. And my brother next up from him. And my older cousin. (My oldest brother was a quarterback, an All-American one at that, but as a back he didn't figure into the equation.) And all of us had played under McAlee on run-happy teams. All of us, perhaps, had considered ourselves the best. All of us, perhaps, had been affirmed as the best by McAlee in response to our arrogant questions. What did "since the last one" mean when there were so many of us who played tight end? With at least one Pullyblank playing Cal-Mum football from 1973 to 1985, what value did "since the last one" have in our family's gridiron hand-me-down culture of maroon and white football jackets with the family name emblazoned across the shoulders?

Later, in my thirties, humbled by life's lessons, I thought back to that post-game conversation with Coach McAlee and wondered why I had asked the question in the first place. We had won the game. Roland Poles was unquestionably the best player on our team. He had conquered LeRoy, in magnificent fashion, as his brothers had before him, as my brothers and cousins had before me. But we were all, as a team and as a community, part of the victory, just as Jeff Sweet had explained it after the legendary 1977 triumph.

I didn't necessarily want to be better than my brothers and cousins, or even my father, who played back in the early 1950's. What I wanted was to be remembered. To be part of some larger achievement that no one would forget. Part of what I wanted was to be part of something like a Cal-Mum victory over LeRoy. Like 1977.

But it went even deeper than that, because what I *really* wanted was to be like *him*, or at least like my idealized image of him. What I really wanted, if only just for a moment, was to be like my grandfather, Eugene Pullyblank, who had played on the undefeated team of 1929 that scored 274 points against their opponents and had given up none. What I really wanted, I know now, was to live a dream. And where better for a proud adolescent boy to live that dream than on a football field, where, in Caledonia at least, mere boys were often treated as if they were better than men.

The next story takes me back to my childhood, long before arrogance had set in, when uncertainty and curiosity ruled my heart and when the world seemed, at least to me, a wonderfully exciting and terribly dangerous place.

If one of the benefits of having older brothers was the eventual receipt of a nicely worn-in maroon and white winter coat with the family name emblazoned across the shoulders, another, at least for a kid who saw the world as a wonderfully exciting place, was having access to my older brothers' books. One of my favorites in my strange little world was a paperback owned by my brother Jim—an exhaustive tome on every imaginable detail of the history, potential causes and likely consequences of nuclear warfare.

I read the book from cover to cover. I reread it over and over again. It thrilled me, terrified me. It motivated my waking hours to the point where I would spend hours drawing coastlines of fictitious countries and then literally erasing them from the map. It haunted my sleeping hours as I dreamed of a nuclear holocaust in far greater detail than that which I saw on the "Day After" TV movie. When I went off to college (still arrogant) I could quote payload figures and estimated delivery and detonation times to my classmates and dorm neighbors, some of them cute girls from Long Island who were at least entertained by, but unfortunately not attracted to, the hick from Caledonia with the strange ICBM obsession. It was the threat of nuclear war, more than any mere personal setback, that would present me with the most significant challenge to my faith in God.

Long before that, however, in the years when we still practiced air raid drills in school, and the village tested its new air raid siren on Saturday at noon, I would go out in the backyard with my cork gun, take cover under the picnic table, and fire away at the Soviet MiG's that I imagined were flying overhead.

Sometimes I was Sergeant Rock. Sometimes I was a survivor of Khe Sahn. Sometimes I was Jan Baalsrud, the lead character in one of my favorite childhood novels, *We Die Alone*. This, despite the fact that the historical Baalsrud fought against the Nazis and not the Soviets.

And sometimes as I lay under that picnic table, aiming my cork gun at the Communist contrails that filled the sky above, I would pretend I was Stuart Griffin. Or Mason Ashford. Or Jimmy Jackson. Or Tony Angelo. Or Ed "Banjo" Coots, the last member of the 1929 team to die.

And sometimes I was my grandfather, Eugene Pullyblank, whom I didn't remember because he had died before I was born.

Those boys of 1929 were, in my imagination, boys greater than men, shooting down the enemy from foreign shores that threatened our American way of life. And they were the same thing in the reality of their lives—boys greater than men, succeeding to a level of perfection that few others, in any endeavor, have ever reached.

Perhaps, during the years that followed their accomplishment, during those years of economic collapse and world war, of nuclear threat and societal change, of small town people like us caught up in the enormous, confusing forces of the world that took our loved ones from us and changed them and us forever—perhaps, in all those years that followed what they did, we needed those boys to be something greater than men.

So what do we know about them, these football playing boys from 1929?

The first thing to note about them is that they, too, were part of something bigger. The 1929 team had the stats, but, as Jimmy Breslin tells us, stats are like a lamppost to a drunk—they can provide either support or illumination. To shed light on what the 1929 Caledonia Red Raider football team really meant, we must get a clear picture of the several contexts in which they achieved greatness.

The first context is Caledonia itself. The earliest known settlements were at Canawaugus, in the southeastern corner of the present town. This was Seneca land, the birthplace of Chief Red Jacket, the raider from whom the Cal-Mum sports teams get their nickname. In the 1790's, European settlers from eastern New York found and coveted the area's building stone and gypsum deposits. Lime was quarried in the town. "Caledonia plaster" earned a solid reputation among builders. The land was organized by the New York State government in 1797 and called Southampton. It became Caledonia[*] on April 4, 1806.

The name, of course, is the Latin word for Scotland, and reflects the nationality of the majority of settlers around the Big Springs, called "Gan-e-o-di-ya" by the Iroquois. Today the Big Springs are known as the Caledonia Fish Hatchery, the first of its kind in America, established by Seth Green.

The following colorful description of these Scot-Presbyterian settlers is given in a *History of Livingston County*, published in 1881. "The pioneers of Caledonia brought with them Scotland's vigor, Scotland's customs, and Scotland's names. This region in early days was called New Inverness, for the Inverness left behind in the fatherland, and when that name became obsolete the more national name of Caledonia clung to it like the mists which cling to the highland crags. Those hardy sons of Scotia plied the ax, and from matted forests sprang forth fields of grain, and the wilderness gave place to the broad and cultivated farms that grace that town today." And still do, over a century and a quarter later.

The Scottish settlement of the land has left its mark on Cal-Mum football. The 1929 team had McPhersons, father and son, as head coach and player, a MacDonald, a McWilliams, and a McGinnis. These family names would show up in later years' rosters as well, alongside various McKays, MacLeods, Fitzgeralds, Wallaces, Callans, Cullinans, MacWilliamses, McIlwains and McGintys. Family lore says that my grandfather Eugene Pullyblank converted from his Presbyterian faith, the national religion of Scotland, to the Roman Catholic church in order to marry my Irish grandmother, Anna O'Brien.

The Scottish settlers also had an influence on the early years of the Caledonia school. In 1876, William Hamilton, a local brewer and politician, arranged the making of bricks for an early schoolhouse, which now houses the village police department

---

[*]Several pop songs over the years share the title. My personal favorite, by Louis Jordan, lacks the second vowel and contains the immortal refrain, "Caldonia! Caldonia! What makes your big head so hard?" Very appropriate for a kid who, wearing a 7 ¾ size helmet, had the largest head on the football team.

and the Big Springs Historical Society. Silver John McNaughton, a manufacturer of agricultural equipment, returned from a trip to Scotland with several roots of Inverness ivy, which he replanted around the schoolhouse and which are still there today. Wilson Hamilton, William's son, donated thirteen acres of land for the construction of the current elementary school in 1938. The school opened for students in 1939. Hamilton Field, the home of Raider football, was named after this benefactor and was first used in the late 1940s. Back then it was located where the middle school is today. It was then moved to its current location when the high school, today's middle school, was built in 1964. Finally, in 1926, another Scot, Margaret McCabe, wrote the lyrics to the school *alma mater*, printed on the front pages of this book and known by heart by countless Cal-Mum graduates.

But there was no Cal-Mum in those earliest years of football competition. Centralization of the Caledonia, Mumford and Clifton schools happened in 1950. Before that, the team was the Caledonia Raiders. And another difference—until 1931, the school colors were, first, purple and orange,* and then, blue and gray rather than today's maroon and white.

The earliest records for Raider football date to 1904 and 1905, although there is some evidence that Caledonia played the LeRoy Monarchs three times in 1900, going 2-1, and twice again in 1902, losing both games by the identical score of 11-0. Caledonia also played away games against Sodus and Holley in those early years, begging the question of how the team got there. Regardless of transportation method, the Raiders won both games, 6-0 against Sodus in 1904 and 17-0 over Holley in 1905.

The 1905 "Caledonia High School Catalogue" (they were called "yearbooks" by 1927 and, also by that time, looked more or less as they do today) said this about "Athletics":

> A healthy, strong and vigorous body is necessary for an active, capable and efficient mind. Any form of exercise that trains the body also trains the mind. Athletics form a natural and safe outlet for the surplus energy of youth. The best authorities hold that athletics in our institutions of learning tend to raise the moral tone of the student body. Mind and body should be developed simultaneously in order that one may not strengthen one at the expense of the other. All legitimate athletic sports will be encouraged by the faculty.

---

*I didn't realize the significance of it at the time, but I inadvertently honored these early teams during my senior year by wearing a long sleeve orange sweatshirt and a purple elbow-length shirt under my shoulder pads for all games. Why did I do it? For the simple reasons that orange and purple had always been my favorite colors, and that the combination looked great to my eyes with both our maroon (home) and white (away) jerseys.

Update the language by a few decades and this doesn't sound all that different from one of Coach McAlee's or Coach Monacelli's annual football banquet speeches. Despite the sentiments, scheduling was erratic in those early days, perhaps because of transportation difficulties. From 1900 to 1925, the Raiders played anywhere from two to eight games, when there was any competition scheduled at all. Perhaps students interested in football played intramural games.

CALEDONIA RAIDER FOOTBALL HISTORY starts to emerge from the mists of the distant past in the year 1925, what I, as a kid, always knew as the first year of Caledonia Raider football history. The team went undefeated that year with one tie, and outscored its opponents 83-8. This would be the pattern for the following seven years as well, as the Raiders posted at least a winning record each season and usually outscored their opponents by wide margins, most notably, of course, by a tally of 274-0 in the undefeated 1929 season.

But as I wrote a few pages ago, the 1929 team can be best understood in the context of its times, and the era 1927-1932 was, without a doubt, the first great era of Caledonia Raider football.

It didn't look that way at first. The 1927 yearbook referred to a team with "material practically 'green'," two of the veterans missing all or part of season due to serious injuries. The highlights of the 1927 season were two hard fought games against Greigsville, the first a 12-7 victory and the second a 13-12 defeat, and a 7-6 victory over Avon, a victory that demonstrated a great deal of heart on the part of the Raiders since it followed a 32-0 throttling at the hands of Webster High School the week before. That lopsided loss to a larger urban school wouldn't deter Caledonia's schedule-makers from embracing the same challenge of playing games against stronger opponents in later years. As we'll see, those future games would end in results quite different from the 1927 defeat.

The strength of Caledonia's opponents, in fact, was a worry going into the 1928 season. Caledonia's football Raiders, reported the yearbook, had "a difficult schedule, and everyone wondered if [they] had 'bit off' more than the team could 'chew'." The first two games of the season against Avon and Perry both ended in 6-0 victories for the Raiders. This was not good enough for the yearbook's authors, who wrote that "prospects did not look so bright" and that "the light was very dull." But Caledonia would go on to an undefeated season, highlighted by a 38-0 victory over Batavia and a 37-6 triumph over Attica on Attica's home turf. Overall, the Raiders outscored their opponents 137-18, giving up 6 points on three occasions and shutting out the opponent in the other six games.

Six players from the 1928 Raiders made the All-Livingston County team. Earl Stone, Ronald Wilson and the great James Jackson were accorded first-team honors, while Everett Youngs, Carl Gibson and team captain George McPherson earned second-team honors. The players were feted twice at season's end, once by the community and once by Coach McPherson. The yearbook summarized, "With these delightful festivities the 1928 football season came to a close as one of the most successful in the history of Caledonia High School."

That age-old sports fan mantra can also have a positive spin—if you think this year was good, wait 'til next year!

THE HIGH SCHOOL YEARBOOK says this:

> "The football team of '29 of Caledonia High School" will ever be famous as far as every student in school and everyone in the village is concerned. They have also been the admiration of many citizens of the surrounding towns, as they won the Livingston County Cup. The team was victorious in each of the nine games that were played and the opponents were held scoreless in each case.
>
> Mr. Matthews, the coach, deserves a great deal of credit for the success of the team in that he devoted much of his time in training them—a job that is not to be laughed at.
>
> The big game of the season was with LeRoy High School, which was defeated 6 to 0. There was much excitement in Caledonia following the game. The Honeoye Falls Military Band played not only during the game at Le Roy, but after the victorious team returned home.
>
> The business men of Caledonia very kindly gave the team a fine banquet at the close of the season. The members of the Homemaking Classes also gave the team a banquet.

The game against LeRoy was also by far the lowest scoring victory that year. Caledonia put up 35 points against Attica, 28 against Batavia, 47 against Livonia, 21 against Warsaw, 48 against Dansville, 40 against Greigsville, 21 against Avon and 28 against Geneseo. Take out the game against LeRoy and the Raiders averaged almost 34 points per game.

The 1929 team remains famous to everyone in the village, as the 1929 yearbook correctly predicted. But how impressive a feat was it? Where does the accomplishment stand, not just in Caledonia football history, but also in the context of New York State high school football and, indeed, in the annals of high school football in America?

To begin with, there were only two other undefeated, untied, unscored-upon high school football teams in New York State history, the 1937 Norwich team (today known as the Purple Tornado) and the 1989 Nanuet Golden Knights. Amazingly, Nanuet played no home games in 1989 as the school's new football field was being constructed during the season. Despite this, the Golden Knights won the Section II championship and were voted number one among large schools in New York State.

Nationally, complete statistics are difficult to come by, but a few comparable accomplishments in other states can help put Caledonia's achievement in perspective.

Three Pennsylvania teams—Lower Merion, outside Philadelphia, in 1923; Washington, outside Pittsburgh, also in 1923; and Hurst, in coal country near Reading, in 1927, won all their games and allowed no points in the early heyday of football in the Keystone State. Hurst's offense in 1927 was as remarkable as its defense, scoring 82, 99, 51, 69, 65 and 72 points in six of its eleven games.

Also in 1923, the Waco (Texas) Tigers went undefeated and allowed no points—at least until the December 21 state championship game in Dallas against the Abeline Fighting War Eagles. Waco lost, 3-0, in a wet and muddy affair, clearly demonstrating one of the major drawbacks of playing high school football on the cusp of the winter season. The Tigers were thus unable to replicate their 1921 season, when they did allow no points while going undefeated, a season that included victories of 97-0 and 138-0. Almost as impressive in Texas football lore was the near-perfect season put together by the Daingerfield High School team in 1983. With Dallas Cowboy-like swagger, the Tigers made their claim for the title of greatest high school football team ever by outscoring their opponents 631-8 en route to a state championship.

In 1941, the North Muskegon (Michigan) Norsemen went undefeated, untied and unscored-upon, and went undefeated again in 1942, although the team did give up 6 points. Also in Michigan, the 1958 and 1959 Reese Rockets went undefeated and allowed no points scored. The team's only blemish, if you can even call it that, was a scoreless tie in the first game of the 1959 season. Equally impressive, and also in Michigan, were the Saginaw Arthur Hill Lumberjacks who, in 1973, outscored their opponents 443-0.

In 1977, the Hamilton (Mississippi) Lions also went undefeated, outscoring their opponents 375-0. Ironically in the context of this story, the last win of Hamilton's eighteen game streak came against its first opponent of 1978, Caledonia High.

One of the most impressive gridiron accomplishments of all time belongs to the Pittsfield (Illinois) Saukees, who won 64 straight games in seven consecutive seasons from 1966 to 1972. During that span, the Saukees enjoyed fifteen straight shutouts, including all nine of their games in 1970 for an undefeated season. In all, 46 of the 64 wins were shutouts. On three other occasions the team almost achieved perfection.

In 1967, Pittsfield gave up only one touchdown in a 9-6 victory in the last game of the season. In 1969, Pittsfield gave up an 88-yard interception return for a touchdown for the only points allowed all season. In 1972, as well, only one touchdown was allowed during the undefeated campaign.

None of these achievements, however, compare to what the Shelbyville Bedford County Training School in Tennessee did between the years 1942 and 1949. The all African-American school no longer exists, but the Fighting Tigers went down in history with a record that will probably never be broken: 52 consecutive shutouts spanning seven complete seasons. To put this accomplishment in perspective, the country's next longest streak of shutouts is eighteen.

The Caledonia Raider football teams of the late 1920's and early 1930's belong right up there in this elite company. This claim is born out by the statistics, which I will now use for support as well as for illumination.

The 1929 unscored-upon season was part of a larger thirteen game stretch during which the defense allowed no points. It was also part of a 22 game winning streak from 1927 to 1930. From 1928 through 1932, the Raiders only once allowed more than one touchdown per game, win, lose or tie, and that (of course!) to LeRoy in 1932, when the Raiders gave up 18. In other words, from 1928 through 1932, Caledonia allowed either 0, 6 or 7 points in 42 of 43 games. The combined team record from 1927 through 1932 was 44-6-1. During this era, the Raiders outscored their opponents, 1215-93.

"All politics is local," Tip O'Neill once said, and notwithstanding these impressive numbers that compare well with some of the best high school teams to ever play on an American gridiron, all Caledonia football is local too. What mattered even more than the numbers and the streaks were the games themselves. Several stand out from the perspective of hindsight.

First, of course, there were the games against LeRoy. Caledonia and LeRoy had played intermittently since the two schools met for the first time in 1900. The rivalry resumed for five of seven years between 1926 and 1932. LeRoy was, by far, the Raiders' greatest nemesis in those years, limiting Caledonia to one victory, 6-0 in 1929, and one tie, 6-6 in 1931. LeRoy was victorious in all the other meetings, winning 2-0 (!) in 1926, 6-0 in 1930,* and 18-7 in 1932, which was the worst defeat handed to

---

*Eugene Pullyblank barely escaped death the week before the 1930 LeRoy game. In a nighttime fog, the car he was driving ran into the rear end of a parked, unlit flatbed truck. He was seriously injured in the crash and never played football again, although he was voted honorary captain for the 1931 season and managed the team in 1932. The collision also ended his baseball career, which had, before the crash, held great promise. Just a week before the crash, my grandfather had signed a contract to leave school early and play first base in the St. Louis Cardinals organization.

Caledonia in these five-plus years of excellence. The 1931 tie was played on Halloween, with a similar level of buildup and an equal level of intensity as the 1977 game, as well as so many others.

The games against Avon were also important, primarily because the Braves were the closest Livingston County rival Caledonia had until LeRoy joined the conference in 1965. Some years Caledonia was barely able to defeat Avon, as in the 7-6 win in the final game of 1927 and the 6-0 victory in the opening game of 1928. But most years the Braves were no match for Caledonia's powerhouse teams. From 1929 to 1932, Caledonia defeated Avon by the scores of 21-0, 47-0, 51-0 and 34-0, respectively.

Impressive margins of victory were the rule rather the exception during these years. In 1929 the Raiders won games 47-0 against Livonia and 48-0 against Dansville. In 1930, in addition to the rout against Avon, Caledonia defeated Attica and Geneseo 39-0 and 45-0, respectively. In 1931, the blowout of Avon was bested by a 55-0 rout over Livonia. And the 1932 Raiders amassed a total of 254 points in seven shutouts, the worst of which was a 67-0 demolition of Nunda to close the season. That point total of 67 would remain a Raider record until 1993. Caledonia football fans had quite a lot to cheer about during those early years of the Great Depression, when there was so little else in America to nourish good feelings.

OF ALL THE RAIDERS' VICTORIES during this first era of greatness, no game stands out as much as the Saturday, October 15, 1932, contest against the Aquinas Institute Fighting Irish, a football team of almost sixty players from a Roman Catholic prep school of over one thousand students.

The Rochester *Democrat and Chronicle* told the story.

Jim Jackson Stars as Caledonia Swamps Aquinas
Irish team outclassed in setback

Coach George Reynolds' eleven "Galloping Iron Men" staged one big track meet yesterday afternoon at the Edgerton Park Paddock. A Caledonia halfback, Jimmy Johnson, black streak of greased lightning as far as the Irish were concerned, ran through Johnny Sullivan's Aquinas Institute team. He scored five touchdowns to be a big factor in Caledonia's 43-to-6 victory over the Irish.

The invaders, piling up a big score in their fourth straight win, showed with the exception of their aerial game everything that could be desired as they smothered the Aquinas outfit. The visitors put on a display of deceptive football—flashing reverses, double reverses, wide end runs and slashing off tackle plays which showed all the evidence of Coach Reynolds' Colgate training under Andy Kerr.

With the opening whistle Caledonia let loose an attack which swept the startled Aquinas defense off its feet, rolling across three scores in the opening period. The first score came in the first few minutes when Jackson got away on a reverse which was good for 28 yards. Capt. Bob Freeman then knifed his way to the seven-yard line from where Jackson scored around end. Freeman then kicked the only converted point of the game.

Before Aquinas could recover Freeman smashed off tackle to score from the 12-yard line after King had brought the ball within scoring distance on a 28-yard gain.

The score mounting in the face of a baffled Aquinas eleven rose to 19 to 0, when King, whose ball carrying enabled Freeman and Jackson to score, gained 20 yards on a double reverse placing the leather on the Irish 15-yard line. Freeman plunged four more and the "colored flyer" Jackson went again around end for 12 yards and the third score.

Visitors Run Wild

The victors pushed across two more scores in the second period as the result of another series of marches into Aquinas territory. The fourth touchdown was a result of Freeman's score on a spinner from the 10-yard line. With Jackson and Freeman alternating in the scoring attacks, it was the colored lad's turn and he answered with a slashing off tackle play good for 27 yards and the score.

Before the half ended Aquinas held Caledonia for downs for the first time. In the second half the Irish looked as if they might go somewhere, but with the ball deep in Caledonia territory Jackson intercepted one of Joe Farrell's passes on the six-yard line and raced 94 yards through the entire Aquinas team for his fourth touchdown. The score now stood 37-0 for Caledonia. The big grief to Aquinas repeated his performance with another interception in the final quarter, grabbing the intercepted pass this time on Aquinas' 25-yard stripe…

Jackson Big Noise

> Jim Jackson and Captain Bob (Powerhouse) Freeman were the big guns in the constantly successful Caledonia attack. These boys accounted for the entire winning score with Jackson intercepting two passes, pulling off runs of 94 and 25 yards on both plays for two of his five touchdowns.

Several points from the article deserve further elaboration. First, there's Jimmy Jackson, one of the all-time great players in Red Raider football history. Jackson played on the football team for five years, although he was ineligible for games against Livingston County opponents in his fifth and final season of 1932. Jackson's rushing and defending were major reasons why Caledonia was so good in that five-year span. He was annually among Livingston County's leading scorers, and anecdotal evidence says he could punt the ball sixty yards with consistency. In 1930 he scored two touchdowns on two interceptions to single-handedly beat Perry 12-0. Of all the young men who contributed to the incredible run of Caledonia football in this first blaze of glory, Jackson was the most impressive.

Another Rochester newspaper wrote this about Jimmy Jackson's once-in-a-lifetime game against Aquinas:*

> A loping, swiveling ghost stalked across the white-striped greensward of Edgerton Field paddock yesterday afternoon in the person of James Jackson, sporting the uniform of Caledonia High School which smothered Aquinas Institute by a score of 43 to 6.
>
> This scythe-legged colored boy galloped up and down and all-around the field in streaking to five of his eleven's seven touchdowns and he struck the fastest tempo seen by a scholastic attack in many moons.
>
> Ubiquitous, brisk and alert on every play, blocking effectively, a bear on the defense, he found time to sprint for touchdowns after intercepting passes for two of his scores.
>
> His first of two tallies in the opening quarter came on a reverse play which started on the Aquinas 30-yard line. Masked in deception, the play

---

*There's an interesting historical footnote to these articles. In October 1975, the Rochester *Democrat and Chronicle* contained a reference praising Aquinas' undefeated seasons of 1931 and 1932. Donald Pullyblank, my uncle, caught it and challenged the paper's claim by producing these two articles, which he also had in his collection. Pullyblank, a player on the 1951-1953 teams and a fine local historian, proved once again how important it is to maintain a record of the past.

moved speedily and before the defense was aware, Jackson was swinging around the Irish right flank. He raced the distance scarcely molested…

Again at the fag end of the opening chukker, the ever-brilliant Jackson shook himself loose from several would-be-tacklers and scampered on to score…

The racial references in both articles bring out another point about Jackson—he, and his African-American teammates, were welcome members of a squad that did not discriminate based on race, as did so many other teams on all levels of athletic competition. 1932 was at least two decades before the full racial integration of the National Football League after several fits and starts. African-American football players had some options, attending an all-black college and playing in the Canadian Football League, for example, but overall, the role models available to young African-American footballers in mainstream college and professional football were few and far between.

In Caledonia, however, African-Americans had always had, and would continue to have, a presence, especially on the west end of the village. The number of African-Americans might have been small compared to the European-American (especially Scottish and Irish) populations, but what would Cal-Mum football have been without the Jackson, Day, Robinson, Anderson, Phillips, Poles or Leach families?

The second point to elaborate upon is Caledonia's coaches. The '29, '30 and '31 teams had been coached by J. Allen Matthews, who went 21-3-1 for a winning percentage of .750, outstanding by any measure.

The 1932 season saw the introduction of George F. Reynolds as head football coach and history teacher at Caledonia. Having graduated the year before from Colgate University, Reynolds brought no coaching experience but much football knowledge to his new Red Raider team.[*] He introduced a new play calling scheme consisting of a simple series of signals (AR-25, for example, or AL-29 or ARI-33[**])

---

[*] There are other connections here besides the shared team name. The Colgate Raiders went undefeated, untied and unscored-upon in 1932, matching the 1929 accomplishment of the Caledonia Raiders. Snubbed by the Rose Bowl committee yet declared national champions of college football, the Raiders team was thereafter known as the only team to be "undefeated, untied, unscored-upon, and uninvited." In addition, Colgate played (and plays) its home games in Hamilton, NY, a village that shares the name given to Caledonia's home field. Several Raider alumni went on to play at Colgate, including John Freeman, son of Bob Freeman.

[**] For this and much other information in this chapter, I owe a great debt to Carol Matthews, who passed on to me the notes and collection of her late husband Ed Matthews, who taught me almost as much about football and life as Bill McAlee did. My rekindled friendship with Ed in the last year or so before he died was one of the major factors that led me to write this book. Contained in Ed's collection were several important pages from Eddie Coots' 1932 scrapbook, including these plays and a copy of the Christmas 1932 edition of the student

which resulted in the "display of deceptive football" that the Rochester Democrat and Chronicle remarked upon.

Reynolds had learned this system from the great Andrew Kerr, who had learned it in turn from Glenn "Pop" Warner, the inventor of both the single and double wing formations. Kerr, like Warner before him, was a gridiron genius who loved to pull out all the stops on the plays he designed. Reverses, laterals, fakes—all of these and more became standard weapons in Colgate's arsenal, and were brought from one Raider squad to another by George Reynolds, who found in Jimmy Jackson and in Bob Freeman the perfect players to execute his scheme.

Bob "Powerhouse" or "Bulldog" Freeman is the third and final point of emphasis from the articles describing Caledonia's victory over Aquinas. Also on the 1929 team, Freeman has become, along with Jackson, the personification of early Caledonia football greatness. Born and raised in Mumford, Freeman came to Caledonia with his family in the ninth grade, seeking, as the student newspaper "The Elm" put it, "a higher education." Freeman was a baseball and basketball player as well, but it was in football that he excelled. He was honored as captain of the 1932 team and won, along with Jackson, a place on the Western New York State high school "Mythical" team, as the all-stars were called back then. Unfortunately, Freeman broke his leg in the game against Aquinas, and could only watch the remainder of the 1932 season from the sidelines. No doubt he, and his teammates, wondered whether the 18-7 loss to LeRoy would have been different with Freeman on the field. As we'll see, the monumental victory over Aquinas would not be the final chapter in Robert Freeman's Caledonia Raider football story.

Nor would the success of 1929 be the final chapter of success in Cal-Mum football history. Whether we realized it consciously or not, all of us who played after 1929 fed off their success to nourish our own. Some of us matched what they did, others of us fell somewhat short, but we all tried to emulate them, and in reaching so high we were all able to touch the glory that they lived.

---

newspaper, "The Elm," which offered brief biographical sketches of Jimmy Jackson and Bob Freeman.

Chapter Three:
Football Families

THERE WERE ONLY three undefeated seasons from 1929 to 1973, and never in these years did Caledonia (Cal-Mum after 1950) win more than seven games. Ten times during this span the Red Raiders failed to post winning records at all. Unlike 1927 to 1932, eye-popping blowouts were the exception rather than the rule.

Moreover, from 1933 to 1965, when LeRoy joined the Livingston County League, Cal-Mum and LeRoy played only seven times, all between 1948 and 1954. These seven years were also the best years of Red Raider football during this era. The same correspondence happened in the late 1920s and early 1930s. As we'll see later in this book, gridiron competition between Cal-Mum and LeRoy would often make both teams better.

Yet the forty years from 1933 to 1973 were a significant period in Cal-Mum football history, not so much for what was accomplished on the field as for how the legacy of 1929 was internalized into Cal-Mum football culture. It was during these years that the seed of greatness, planted in 1929, would germinate and grow into the mighty tree that withstood all attempts to knock it down in the later 1970s, and again in the early 1990s.

The forties, fifties and sixties were years when football families established themselves as Cal-Mum gridiron aristocracies. Look at the rosters from these Red Raider teams and you'll find names that are repeated over and over again in future years.*

---

*The following family names were arrived at using the least scientific means possible. I sincerely apologize to any family left out of this list. Please email me, and the omission will be rectified in future editions of this book. The list is composed of families whose boys belonging to one generation played in the 1940s, 1950s and 1960s, and whose boys belonging to the next generation played in the 1970s, 1980s and 1990s. The list is based solely on *paterfamilias*—maternal grandfathers, uncles, etc. are not included. Also not included are families whose boys cannot trace a Red Raider ancestor back to the 1940s, 1950s and 1960s. Thus, the Cicorias, Dearcops, Edwardses, Monacellis, Moyers, etc., are not found here. But these family names will be found later in the story,

Football Families

Ball. Barton. Beach. Bonaquisti. Callan. Cappotelli. Clements. D'Angelo. Day. Donegan. Fisher. Freeman. Geer. Goodburlet. Grant. Grattan. Griffith. Hanna. Harmon. Harrington. Jackson. Keenan. Kingsbury. Krenzer.** Loomis. MacDonald. Martin. Mattice. McKay. McIlwaine. McQuilken. Mooney. Nelson. Nothnagle. Paladino. Pangrazio. Parnell. Poles. Pullyblank. Randall. Rapone. Reid. Robinson. Shaughnessy. Sheffer. Shelton. Sickles. Sisson. Stephany. Vink. Vokes. Wade. Wall. Ward. Waters. Whiteside. Williams. Wood.

Not all of these families produced superstars. Some of them had seats on the bench that served like family heirlooms, passed down through the generations until the second or third string was called into the game with the score well out of hand, hopefully in the Raiders' favor. But all these players were important for the way that they carried on the legacy of Red Raider football. Outside observers often remark that there must be something in Caledonia's water to produce such perennial gridiron powerhouses. But it's deeper than that. Where you'll really find that something is in the blood.

THE 1941 YEARBOOK included the following paragraph in the sports section.

> In the 1940 football season Coach Freeman worked diligently with a small squad of boys. Courage, determination, and fight could not entirely make up for inexperience and lack of size, but the team fought inspiringly against overwhelming odds. As a result, this season turned out to be a great one for the Maroon, as they won four and lost only two contests.

"Courage, determination and fight:" these words also aptly described the effort of the Allied armies against the Axis threat. The Allies were indeed fighting "inspiringly against overwhelming odds" in those dark days of world war. The war effort, which the United States had already joined between the time the football season ended and the yearbook was published, defined much of people's lives for the next three years, even in a small town in western New York.

The most significant consequence of the war on Caledonia football was the loss of several former players. George Ball, who played in 1929 and 1930, Earnest John-

---

and in a prominent way.
**From 1940 to 1969, there were more boys from the Krenzer family who played Red Raider football than from any other family. Overall, there were 25 roster spots taken up by Krenzers in these years. The various branches of the Cappotelli family are second with 21 roster spots. Post-1969, the Cappotelli's ran away with the prize for the most roster spots.

son, who played in 1935, and Milton Swarts, who played in 1943, all gave their lives for the far greater good of victory over the enemy. They were, and are, remembered with love and honor for their service and sacrifice.[*]

The second most significant consequence was the cancellation of the 1942 season due to lack of transportation facilities, as the newly created US Army Transportation Corps mobilized resources to send our soldiers to Europe and the Pacific islands. Buses were requisitioned from high schools across the country for domestic use, and gasoline was funneled into the war effort. No doubt the citizens of Caledonia missed their football, but no doubt too they saw that loss as worthwhile.

The third most significant consequence was a shortage of competition. Caledonia was lucky in being able to field teams throughout the rest of the war years. Other schools were not so fortunate. In 1943, Caledonia played only three other teams, Dansville, Industry and Avon, each team on a home/home basis. The 1943 Red Raiders went 4-2, splitting with Dansville and Avon and shutting out Industry twice by the identical score of 13-0. They lost to Avon in the Livingston County championship game—lost big, in fact, by a score of 34-0. In 1944, Caledonia played three teams, Dansville, Irondequoit and Avon, again on a home/home basis. Caledonia won only two games, both against Dansville, but nevertheless played Avon for the Livingston County championship for the second year in a row. As in 1943, the Raiders lost to the Braves, this time 33-20. 1945 was even worse, with the Raiders going 1-2-2 and finishing last of three teams in the truncated Livingston County League.

The good news was that Coach Robert Freeman returned home safe from his service in the US Army, resuming his career at the helm of a Red Raider team that missed him dearly in his two-year absence. Indeed, this was the same Robert Freeman who was known as "Powerhouse" and "Bulldog" back in the late twenties and early thirties. Back home and with the war won, Coach Freeman was ready to lead the Red Raiders to another era of glory.

PERHAPS it was in the Army that Freeman picked up a new set of motivational skills. Perhaps having lived through the clear and present danger of war, Freeman realized that football could be a way to instruct boys in how to be men without really putting them in harm's way. Perhaps, having gone overseas for a few years, Freeman now knew how special the excellence of the late 1920s and early 1930s had been.

---

[*]Sadly, these would not be the only former Red Raiders killed in action. David Fellows, who played on the 1962 team, would meet his end in the jungles of Vietnam. He, too, is remembered with love and honor by all of us who survive him.

Whatever the reason, Coach Freeman returned to Caledonia and led his Raiders to a new era of superiority, winning four Livingston County championships in a row from 1947 to 1950.

How did he do it? What were his motivational tactics? Freeman saved one of his favorite techniques for big games, usually against Avon or LeRoy. On Monday of game week, he would read to the team a "letter" that he had "received" from the opposing coach. The "letter" would deride the Raider players, point out the team's multiple shortcomings and confidently predict a Raider loss. Then, at practice, Freeman would blow his whistle more than usual and criticize his players' mistakes down to the smallest detail. After an hour or so he'd dismiss the team in a huff, telling the boys to go home and stay there because the were not worthy of wearing the maroon and white. The next day, the team would be there at practice, eager to prove their coach wrong, angry at the opposing coach and his "letter," ready to take out their anger on each other and, especially, on whatever team had the misfortune of lining up against the Raiders come Friday or Saturday.

During the week's practice, Freeman would make his players suffer through one-on-one or one-on-two drills, during which a ball carrier would have to find his way through a defender or defenders, and the defender would have to work his way through a block in order to tackle the ball carrier. If any player showed any lack of effort, he would run. And run. And run. Coach Freeman was notorious among his players for ordering them to run wind sprints, laps around the track, and laps around the school, often while wearing full equipment.

Coach Freeman was at his motivational best come game time. Before the game he would give a speech to the entire team. Then he would give a second speech to the offensive and defensive starters. He would often end these speeches in tears—if they were of the crocodile variety, then they were expertly disguised by this master motivator. On one occasion, playing a game on the road, Freeman got the team so pumped up for the opening kickoff that they ran out of the locker room the wrong way and ended up trapped in a corridor barred by locked doors. This was no obstacle for Freeman—he simply gave his team another speech, led them out the correct way, and watched as his Raiders destroyed another opponent.

Motivation is one thing, gridiron execution is quite another. In this category, too, Freeman was an expert. He used the same system throughout his coaching career at Caledonia and Cal-Mum. He preferred the Notre Dame Box, or the Straight-I with a Notre Dame shift, a precursor to the T formation which was on its way to becoming the dominant style in both college and professional football. Freeman used the Notre Dame Box and its various iterations with great creativity, often calling multiple shifts that left the defense confused. Yet his plays were simple once the shifts had taken place, and were called using an equally simple numeric system. No "pitch to the right halfback into the three hole with a double team," no "power pitch left on 3," just a simple "32" and everyone would (or should, after those practices) know what to do. Coach Freeman also had his linemen usually call the plays. In 1955, the on field calls were made by Bernie Fagan, a tackle. In 1956, they were made by Jim Vokes at center.

What were the results of Freeman's leadership? Although the Raiders under Coach Freeman did not match the incredible record Freeman helped set as a player in the late 1920s and early 1930s, they did enjoy a long stretch of football at or near the top. As mentioned above, the Red Raiders won four consecutive Livingston County championships from 1947 to 1950, a stretch of success that was book-ended by two undefeated seasons.

"The 1947 football campaign proved to be the school boy's dream bursting into reality," said the 1948 yearbook. Two lopsided wins against Industry, two more against Livonia and then Warsaw, and the scene was set for the Avon game, which, said the yearbook, "was witnessed by one of the largest crowds in C.H.S. history." Having not played LeRoy since 1932, Caledonia now looked east for its main gridiron rival. What they saw in those war years was usually not pretty. Caledonia had a 2-5-1 record against the Braves from 1943 through 1946, a stretch of futility which included four Livingston County championship game losses in a row.

1947, however, was different. Tied 7-7 at halftime, Caledonia opened up the scoring floodgates in the second half and ended up winning the game, 34-7. "The second half proved disastrous for Avon," the yearbook editors wrote rather laconically. "Caledonia's condition was superior to Avon's. We scored at will."

Indeed, scoring at will was the theme of the 1947 season, as the Red Raiders produced 239 points to the opponents' total of 33. No doubt about it, Coach Freeman had returned Caledonia football to nearly the level of greatness it had achieved when he, in his younger years, had strapped on the helmet and carried the ball to one victory after another.

1948 and 1949 were similar seasons, approaching but not quite reaching the level of accomplishment of 1947. Nevertheless, the only losses suffered by the Red Raiders in those closing years of a hard decade were in non-league games. Within Livingston County, Caledonia remained undefeated both years, bringing home two more county championship trophies.

The victories in both years were not even close. The losses were suffered to two very good Bath teams and, in 1949, to a LeRoy team in a game that was marred by a steady downpour and thickening, deepening mud. The 1948 game against Bath was a thriller, with the Rams scoring the winning touchdown on a last second flat pass and run that fooled the otherwise stalwart Caledonia defense.

1950 would be remembered as a special season for two very significant developments. First, this was the year that Cal-Mum was born, a child of centralization between the Caledonia and Wheatland school districts.* So many players from Mumford, Riga, Clifton and Garbutt have contributed to the success of the Red Raiders since then. It would be hard to imagine the same level of consistent success over the years following 1950 without them.

Second, 1950 was the first year that lights shined on Hamilton Field. It would be equally hard to imagine all those great Friday night home games, preceded by an Iroquois Hotel fish fry, being played on Saturday afternoon instead. The first night game in Caledonia, in fact, also marked the first memorable moment of the 1950 season.

The Caledonia *Advertiser* put it thus the week before the game:

First Football Game Under New Lights

At last it has been accomplished! The athletic field at Caledonia-Mumford Central School has been put under the lights, or, to be more accurate, lights have been put over the field. For the last three weeks the work has been going on. Eight poles carrying 6 lights each have been put into place, and now 72 thousand watt power will illuminate the field. The job was done by the Embling Electric Company of Batavia, they being the lowest bidder. The cost is $9,950. And now on Saturday, October 21 at 8 P.M. will find the football teams from York and Caledonia meeting again in football competition. New, too, will be the lighted field bringing to Caledonia the same playing conditions under which the Caledonia boys have to play in most of their games.

The Caledonia team has a perfect record to date with wins over Warsaw, Dansville, Perry and Livonia.

Games to play: Caledonia at Avon, Friday, October 27. LeRoy at Caledonia, Saturday, November 11—Night game.

---

*There is some historical discrepancy here. The most common claim was that centralization happened in 1952. The 1950 Caledonia *Advertiser* article about the Hamilton Field lights refers to the "Caledonia-Mumford Central School," and Eddie Coots' scrapbook contains *Advertiser* announcements of bond sales to pay for the costs of centralization. Other community members have told me that centralization happened in the late 1940s. My working hypothesis is that the centralization was gradual, involving sports teams first, then the classrooms and other clubs.

Despite an early threat from the York offense, which took the ball to the Cal-Mum 5-yard line before losing it on downs, the Raiders won the game handily 33-12. The Cal-Mum offensive line of Fagan, Cullinan, Nelson, Wall, Coppini, Geer and D'Angelo continued to show its mastery of the line of scrimmage. Harold Sickles followed his blockers into the end zone for three of the team's five touchdowns.

The 1950 season closed with big wins against both Avon and LeRoy. The Avon game, a 33-0 shutout, was the fifth victory in a row against the Braves. The LeRoy game, the second game ever under the lights at Hamilton Field, also drew the largest crowd to watch a game there to that point. Cal-Mum scored in every quarter and allowed only one late touchdown to the Oatkan Knights. The second string got to play for much of the second half. The final score of 31-7 gave Cal-Mum a 9-8-1 edge in the rivalry, which had begun fifty years before.

But LeRoy got its revenge in 1951, defeating Cal-Mum 25-6 in the opening game of the season. It went like that the rest of the year, as the Raiders also lost to Avon in a 15-13 nail-biter and Dansville in a 20-6 blowout for a final record of 5-3.

That won-lost record would be matched the following year, 1952, as Cal-Mum again lost to LeRoy, and again took an unexpected loss from a team it usually beat, this time Mt. Morris.

1953 saw similar results, as the Raiders complied a 4-2-1 record, losing to Livonia for the second year in a row and tying Avon in the season's final game.

The next two years, 1954 and 1955, would see a return to Livingston County glory for Cal-Mum, as the Raiders went undefeated in 1954 and lost only to Madison, by one point, in 1955. Besides the loss to the larger school from Rochester, the closest game in these two years came against another tough Mt. Morris team in 1954, a 13-6 Raider victory.

The decade finished up on a less than successful note, however, with the Red Raiders never winning more than four games in any one season. There were other endings, too. 1954 was the last year Cal-Mum and LeRoy would play until 1965. More significantly, 1956 would be Coach Freeman's final year at the helm. He left over a decade's worth of football players thankful that they had known him and had learned from him a set of lessons that would serve them well for the rest of their lives.

"CMCS IS PROUD to welcome a new member to its high school faculty," the Caledonia *Advertiser* wrote before the 1959 school year. "He is Ed Matthews, a recent graduate from State Teachers College where he specialized in Junior High Social Studies. However, it is not for this that he is held in such high esteem by the students.

His main claim to fame is that he has taken over as the new football coach for the '59 season."

1959 and the early 1960s poses one of the great unsolved mysteries of Cal-Mum Red Raider football history. How could these teams, coached by Ed Matthews, who later would have such great success for so many years as an assistant coach to Bill McAlee and Mike Monacelli—how could these teams have been so bad? The years 1959-1962 were the worst years ever in the annals of Caledonia football, with the Red Raiders faltering to a total three-year record of 7-17-3. The only comparably bad stretches were Frank Ruane's final two years of 1971 and 1972, when the Raiders went 7-9, and the first two years of Mike Monacelli's head coaching career, when the combined record was 6-10. But Matthews' 1960 team had the ignominious distinction of ending the season with a winless record, eking out only a tie against York. It was only the second winless record in Red Raider football history, the other being back in the "prehistoric" era of 1902.

Players from Matthews' years have offered several explanations. Some say that the teams were too young. Others say that Matthews' offensive scheme was too complicated. Others point to the three down linemen who each played blind in one eye. Still others say that the lack of games against LeRoy left the Red Raiders uninspired.

Matthews himself didn't talk much about those years, preferring instead to reminisce about the good times, about the big games won, about the championships earned, about the collegiality he shared with McAlee and Monacelli, and with Roger House, his fellow assistant coach for many gridiron campaigns.

Perhaps this is as it should be. When I played under him, one life lesson I learned above all others was the importance of resilience, of coming back strong after suffering a defeat, of knowing that any particular failure was not the end of the story. Coach Matthews taught this lesson. Coach Matthews lived this lesson.

The losing ways were short lived, however, as Coach Chuck Holland, with Ed Matthews as his assistant, returned Cal-Mum to the top of Livingston County in 1965. The team went 7-1, losing only to LeRoy in the final week of the season. The defense, led by Bob Krenzer, Mike Cannon and Bundy Price, held the opponents to a total of seven touchdowns, blocked five punts and secured four shutouts. On offense, Gerry Simms gave one of the most impressive rushing performances in Red Raider history against York, carrying the ball 20 times for 172 yards and 3 touchdowns.

1966 BEGAN the Frank Ruane years, which would become the most controversial years of all for those Monday Morning Quarterbacks who loved to analyze their Red Raider football not just on Mondays, but on every other day of the week as well.

A statistical assessment of the Ruane years shows some success. His Cal-Mum football teams went 38-17-1 over seven seasons, giving him a .690 winning percentage. The Raiders lost only one game per season in 1967, 1968 and 1969. Cal-Mum also won three straight shutouts against LeRoy in those same years. Those teams of the last years of the 1960s, in fact, secured a total of 14 shutouts over their opponents, giving up season totals of 32, 61 and 45 points. Defensively, these teams were as good as any other Cal-Mum Red Raider team had been since the greatest glory years of the late 1920s and early 1930s.

And yet, Ruane's final three years at Cal-Mum were an avalanche of ever-growing disasters. It isn't so much the season records that people remember—a still-respectable 5-2-1 in 1970, 4-4 in 1971, and 3-5 in 1972. It isn't so much the breakdowns in trust and communication between the coach and his players that resulted in several penalty-plagued games like the 1970 20-0 loss to Avon.

What really mattered in those years was Ruane's inability to win the big games—indeed, his inability to avoid embarrassing losses in those big games. There was the aforementioned 1970 penalty- and fumble-fest against Avon. There was the 0-0 tie against LeRoy that same year. There was the 19-18 disappointment against Avon in 1971 and the 14-0 drubbing at the hands of the Braves in 1972. Then there were those last two LeRoy games. 32-0 to end the 1971 season. 48-0 to bring the 1972 campaign, and Coach Ruane's Cal-Mum career, to a close.

How did it happen? How did success so quickly and irreversibly sink into failure? Much of the answer lies in Frank Ruane's coaching style, a style that, paradoxically, contributed to both the success the team enjoyed and to the failures it endured.

Ruane taught his players that discipline was the key to success. The defenders were to huddle in the same formation before every play. Only the captain talked. Once the captain called the formation, usually a basic 4-4, he would holler "Break!" and his teammates would respond "Hit!" Moving to the line of scrimmage, defenders were expected to set themselves up in a standard stance, either 3-point or 4-point depending upon the position, with no individual variations allowed. Upon the snap, players were supposed to perform their tasks as instructed in practice, striking a blow, protecting their area, finding the ball, pursuing the ball and tackling the carrier. Pass rushers and defenders alike were taught specific ways of delivering a forearm blow or a forearm lift. Tackling was to be accomplished quickly and efficiently. Allowing the ball carrier to carry a defender as well was not acceptable.

Ruane's offensive scheme was also strictly taught. The offensive huddle and signal calling was even more regimented than they were for the defense. Ruane would sometimes stop practice in order to ensure that his offensive players were exactly eight yards back from the line of scrimmage, that the backs and ends had their hands on their thighs and the linemen had their hands to the sides, that the quarterback stood to the side until the rest of the offensive group was properly in order and then stood two feet away from the group while calling the play, and that the team ran, not walked or jogged, up to the line of scrimmage. Once at the ball, players were taught to line up with the proper split between positions, 12-36 inches between tackle and guard, 6-24 inches between the guards and the center, depending on where exactly the defensive linemen positioned themselves. The offensive plays, most of which were run from a simple I formation, had to be run with perfect precision in order to succeed. The blocking scheme had to be followed exactly. The runner had to move at a certain speed to a certain hole. Any derivation from the system would put the play in danger of failure. The offense, even more than the defense, was composed of pieces on Coach Ruane's chessboard. His coaching, using his system, would lead the Red Raiders to success.

Coach Ruane was also committed to taking the boys who played under him and molding them into men. The game of football was to be the gauntlet through which each boy must pass if he is to come out a man on the other side. Ruane was fond of quoting Charles Loftus' essay, "What Is a Football Player?" which he found in the introduction to James Gibson Holgate's 1958 book, *Fundamental Football*.

Here is Loftus' text, quoted in full.

> Between the innocence of boyhood and the dignity of man, we find a sturdy creature called a football player. Football players come in assorted weights, heights, jersey colors and numbers, but all football players have the same creed: to play every second of every minute of every period of every game to the best of their ability.
>
> Football players are found everywhere underneath, on top of, running around, jumping over, passing by, twisting from or diving through the enemy. Teammates rib them, officials penalize them, students cheer them, kid brothers idolize them, coaches criticize them, college girls adore them, alumni tolerate them and mothers worry about them. A football player is Courage in cleats, Hope in a helmet, Pride in pads and the best of Young Manhood in moleskins.
>
> When your team is behind, a football player is incompetent, careless, indecisive, lazy, uncoordinated and stupid. Just when your team threatens to turn the tide of battle, he misses a block, fumbles the ball, drops a pass, jumps offside, falls down, runs the wrong way or completely forgets his assignment.

A football player is a composite. He eats like Texas, sleeps like Notre Dame, but, more often than not, plays like Grand Canyon High. To an opponent publicity man, he has the speed of a gazelle, the strength of an ox, the size of an elephant, the cunningness of a fox, the agility of an adagio dancer, the quickness of a cat and the ability of Red Grange, Glen Davis, Otto Graham and Doak Walker combined.

To an alumnus a football player is someone who will never kick well, run as far, block as viciously, tackle as hard, fight as fiercely, give as little ground, score as many points or generate nearly the same amount of spirit as did those particular players of his own yesteryear.

A football player likes game films, trips away from home, practice sessions without pads, hot showers, long runs, whirlpool baths, recovered fumbles, points after touchdowns and the quiet satisfaction which comes from being part of a perfectly executed play. He is not much for wind sprints, sitting on the bench, rainy days, after-game compliments, ankle wraps, scouting reports or calisthenics.

No one else looks forward so much to September or so little to December. Nobody gets so much pleasure out of knocking down, hauling out or just plain bringing down the enemy. Nobody else can cram into one mind assignments for an end run, an off-tackle slant, a jump pass, a quarterback sneak, a dive play, punt protection, kick-off returns, a buck lateral, goal line stands or a pitch out designed to result in a touchdown every time it is tried.

A football player is a wonderful creature—you can criticize him, but you can't discourage him. You can defeat his team, but you can't make him quit. You can get him out of a game, but you can't get him out of football. Might as well admit it, be you alumnus, coach or fan, he is your personal representative on the field, your symbol of fair and hard play. He may not be an All-American, but he is an example of the American way. He is judged, not for his race, not for his religion, not for his social standing or not for his finances, but by the democratic yardstick of how well he blocks, tackles and sacrifices individual glory for the over-all success of his team.

He is a hard working, untiring, determined kid doing the very best he can for his school or college. And when you come out of a stadium, grousing and feeling upset that your team has lost, he can make you feel mighty ashamed with just two sincerely spoken words, "We tried!"

Coach Ruane required his players to attach Loftus' essay to the front cover of their football playbook. No doubt he quoted often from this puzzling source during team meetings.

One of the marks of manhood is taking responsibility for one's own success or failures, and this lesson, too, was one that Frank Ruane tried to impart. "This is your team <u>win</u> or <u>lose</u>," Ruane wrote to his players with the added emphasis included. "It takes hard work to become a champion and only individual drive, determination and effort can make a <u>true</u> <u>champion</u>. We [coaches] furnish everything that will help you be a good player except <u>desire</u> and <u>effort</u> on your part. Do your very best at all times. Go all out on every play—be it in practice or on a Friday night or Saturday afternoon. We can have a <u>championship</u> season if each and every player gives his <u>all</u>."

There was another ingredient in Ruane's recipe for success: strict obedience and respect from his players at all times. Smoking, drinking, breaking the 10 PM curfew or "any conduct deemed disrespectful to your family, school or team" was punishable by immediate "expulsion" from the team. Red Raider football players were expected to wear no "unusual or gaudy clothes."[*] On game days and coming to and from all games, home and away, players were required to wear clean suits or coats and ties. "No unusual, long or bushy haircuts, sideburns, beards or mustaches" were allowed. Hair was to be cut short, above the neckline, and sideburns were regulated to be "short, above the middle lobe of the ear." Ruane informed his team in writing, underlined and in caps in his instructions, that "you step out on the football field to play football, not to model clothes or hair styles."

"Pupil-teacher disagreements" were punishable by harsh rebuke and then expulsion from the team. Classroom expulsion would be followed by expulsion from the team. Any type of vulgarity would be met with expulsion from the team, as would fighting. Quitting for any reason, including "a) it is too tough, b) not playing enough or c) lack of fun" was not tolerated. "Any boy who, after making a squad, leaves the squad without first informing the coach in a personal interview and turning in his equipment, will not be allowed to participate in any other interscholastic sport for the remainder of that year."

Regimented systems, moral goals, clear rules and Draconian punishments: this was Frank Ruane's style as coach of the Caledonia-Mumford Red Raiders. Whether you loved Coach Ruane or hated him, or felt something in between, whether you remember more the good years or the bad years, there's no denying that he knew what he was doing and was committed to doing it his way.

Yet the culture of our nation had changed dramatically in the six years from when Frank Ruane first stepped onto Hamilton Field at game time in September 1966 to

---

[*]Reading these old notebooks, I shudder to think what Coach Ruane would have thought about the orange and purple shirts I wore beneath my shoulder pads, especially my senior year in our road whites, my gaudy undergarments quite visible as I blocked LeRoy's linebackers and defensive ends, springing Roland Poles for several long gains.

the last time he walked off it as Cal-Mum's coach in November 1972. Those cultural changes had seeped into Caledonia and Mumford's culture by then as well.

A new direction was called for. A new man was needed to lead Cal-Mum football in that new direction. As Red Raider football families would soon find out, that man, William McAlee, turned out to be as different from Coach Frank Ruane as another man can get.

Chapter Four:
The Big Mac Attack

THE STORY of the Ruane-to-McAlee transition is told most compellingly in the high school yearbooks, the *Ainodelac*, where the pictures speak at least thousand words.

In both the 1972 and 1973 editions, which show the team pictures from 1971 and 1972, the football players are seen properly groomed, with hair that might be a little thick on top but nevertheless well above the neckline in back. The managers wear coats and ties. There are few smiles. This is Coach Ruane's army of boys, not quite happy with being pushed into manhood, at least not along the way he wanted them to go.

But the 1974 *Ainodelac* shows a 1973 team with hair a little scragglier, cheeks a little bristlier, sideburns a little longer, smiles a little wider. A year later, the hair of most Cal-Mum players is thick on top, long in the back, and threatening to cover the eyes if a stiff breeze kicks up and sweeps the boys' long bangs down. The sideburns are definitely below the middle ear lobe. Fake tough-guy looks, the emblem of an adolescent boy having fun, can be seen on many faces. All this despite the warnings they received against such posturing just a few years before, warning that were issued in bold, in caps, and underlined.

Look, too, at the words. The 1972 write-up covering the 1971 season is vague and without feeling. It reads like a forced confession, begrudgingly given.

> Just before school begins every year a group of young men begin a vigorous workout. Their objective is to play the best game of football they can. Win or lose they must keep trying. Each individual works hard to develop the team spirit. Whether or not he and the team succeeds depends on how you measure success. We measure it by effort.

Tellingly, there is no 1972 season summary at all in the 1973 yearbook. Coach Ruane's 1972 football banquet comments were terse, a mere list of the people he wanted to thank.

Like the pictures, the words spoken during and following the 1973 and 1974 seasons were different. In those first years of the McAlee regime, Cal-Mum players, coaches, cheerleaders and fans expressed themselves with the same type of glee that the Munchkins displayed when they realized that the Wicked Witch of the East was indeed really most sincerely dead.

Becky McAlee captured the enthusiasm and confidence in her 1975 yearbook review.

A Second Perfect Season

> The Red Raiders compiled a 16-0 record in two years. Throughout this time much honor and praise has been given to this well-deserved team.
>
> In 1973 Coach Bill McAlee was named "Greater Rochester Coach of the Year." Also, in that same year several of his players were named to All-County and Greater Rochester teams.
>
> Because of the team's unfaltering endeavors throughout the '73 and '74 seasons, the Red Raiders team has acquired a status well-respected in the Rochester area.
>
> By their accomplishments, this…Cal-Mum football team has shown their success and also have proven the right to be called number "1."

The enthusiasm began, of course, at the top. "We're a fun-loving organization," Coach Bill McAlee told Tom Fitzgerald of the Rochester *Democrat and Chronicle* before the 1974 LeRoy game. When asked about how many people he expected to come see the game, and if a large number of fans would make him nervous, McAlee just joked. "I was reading where Webster Thomas had a couple thousand for a game," he said. "We get that many when it rains. I don't know where we're going to put them all." Even more emphatic were McAlee's post-game exclamations, like his "What a feeling!" shout after the 1974 season-ending victory over LeRoy.

McAlee's enthusiasm and good-cheer were contagious. "When we were sophomores everybody was fighting with each other," said tight end Chris Batzing with a brutal honesty that's born out by those yearbook photos. "Then Coach McAlee came and he made it fun for everybody. He united the team." Long-haired center Randy Grattan echoed Batzing's words. "He ignited the team. We're working hard and enjoying it."

The Big Mac Attack

HARD WORK and enjoyment were the twin pillars of Bill McAlee's football philosophy. The hard work came in the standard football practice form of wind sprints, blocking drills, gauntlets and rolls, which strengthened the players' muscle memory and ensured that they remained in peak physical condition throughout the season. But McAlee focused even more attention on scrimmages, in which he and his coaches would teach and his players would repeat his relatively simple system of defensive lineups and offensive plays.

Of course, McAlee, like any successful coach, demanded one-hundred percent effort from his players, both physically and mentally. What was lacking in McAlee's practices was the strict regimentation that the players struggled through in the Ruane years. Within McAlee's system was a wide degree of latitude for individual nuances, as long as each individual contributed to the success of the whole team. Also, there was plenty of room for the development of individual responsibility.

Rick Woodson of the Rochester Times Union put it this way: "Cal-Mum may have the only football team around that doesn't spend August two-a-days on conditioning. McAlee expects his players to get in shape on their own, but he doesn't hide in the bushes to see if they are doing it."*

The fun side of McAlee's coaching philosophy was just as important. "Football is fun," he would say over and over again, to newspaper reporters, to television interviewers, and to boys he recruited to join the team.

Fun in football was a product of an early coaching experience. "I had one losing season in my life," McAlee said much later, just before his retirement. "I was 2-7 in St. Mary's. I had a good football team but we couldn't win. We played a murderous schedule. We couldn't win. I made a decision at the end of the year that I either had to get out of football or I had to adjust my philosophy to the game. I took away the business part of it and made it more fun."

The joy McAlee found in the game was an essential component of his life philosophy, which placed a premium on the relationships that were truly important. "The most important things in the world to me are my family…my teaching and my coaching—and in that order. I think anything you do, you should do to the fullest. Competitiveness is important. There has to be merit in competitiveness, but I think a lot of people take life too seriously."

To repeat another part of McAlee's philosophy that I quoted in the opening chapter, when he answered the question of what he would say to one of his players if

---

*Nor did he check up on his players in a roundabout way. He and his wife, Eileen, were good friends with my parents, but when they got together for dinner and drinks they always had other—and better—things to talk about than whether the Pullyblank boys were doing their off-season training.

the opponent scored a winning touchdown on that player's fumble: "Maybe we expect too much of our children because we think they are ready for something they're not ready for. A 17-year old is a 17-year old. If a kid fumbles and it costs you the game—the kid doesn't WANT to fumble. Life is too complicated for him to have to carry that fumble around with him."

From that core philosophy of life, McAlee approached his coaching with an infectious exuberance. He would often join in the play during practice, blocking, running and kicking field goals alongside boys more than half his age. I can personally attest that even at fifty years old, the man could still deliver a hit.*

And then there was "hat day" on the Thursdays before games. Players were encouraged to wear hats of all shapes and sizes onto Hamilton Field. Green ones, red ones, Dr. Seuss ones. Hats with ear-flaps and propeller beanies. Cowboy hats, Indian headdresses. McAlee would wear his fedora, and would comment on some of the more outlandish ones, including an orange knit cap with little mirrors hanging off it that one of my brothers and I both wore. Red Raider players would walk through the game plan on hat day, taking the final steps of preparation for the upcoming game, to be sure, but loosening up with a laugh or several as well. Practice was over when the 5:30 church bell rang. McAlee wanted to go home to his family, and he wanted his players to do the same.

McALEE CAME to Cal-Mum from Elk County Christian High School, a private institution in the western Pennsylvania town of St. Mary's, where he had coached and taught history for eight years. Before that, he had played and coached at Alfred State in southern New York, where he had first met his fellow Saxon, Ed Matthews. McAlee had been to Caledonia a couple times before to visit Ed and his wife, Carol.

On August 16, 1973, McAlee saw an advertisement in the New York *Times* for the Caledonia-Mumford jobs—teaching and coaching—and made a verbal agreement later that afternoon to take the job. McAlee, with his wife Eileen and their five chil-

---

*McAlee talked me into joining the wrestling team the winter of my junior year, promising me that wrestling would keep me in excellent football shape during the off-season. It did, but the on-mat results were less than impressive as I went winless for the season. But it was fun, thanks in large part to McAlee himself. Seeing him at practice in his shiny silver sweat suit was priceless. Facing him in the circle, and being encouraged to really wrestle him, was invigorating. Being told that I was a much better football player than wrestler was somehow encouraging. My senior year, following in my father's footsteps, I agreed to MC the matches rather than wrestle in them. It was some of the most fun I ever had in high school. McAlee kindly expressed his appreciation for that contribution, too.

dren, moved to their Belcoda Road home in Mumford on August 20. Football practice began on August 22.

"I came in and told [the team] we were changing everything offensively and defensively," McAlee told the *Democrat and Chronicle's* Bob Matthews. "Our first practice was the first time I set sight on ninety percent of the players, and there I was, telling them we were starting over. I didn't even watch any films of [1972's] games. I wanted to start fresh." According to Bob Matthews, "Cal-Mum's old I-formation offense was spread out to become a split-T. The former 6-2 defense was switched to a 4-4. Line coach Roger House and offensive coach Ed Matthews helped McAlee remold thirty-four teenagers into a new football team."

Among those teenagers in 1973, McAlee, House and Matthews had plenty of talent to work with. Mike Tucci scored 78 points that season, Don Carpenter 72. Tucci and quarterback Bob Chiverton, who went 30-48 for 638 yards passing, were honored with selection to the All-Greater Rochester team. The offensive linemen who blocked for them, led by Randy Grattan, Ed Peet, Tim Harrington and Tim Nothnagle were ferocious, barreling down opposing defensive linemen and linebackers, leaving the smaller boys in the defensive backfield in the unenviable position of having to make the tackles.

Playing against such a powerhouse was not pleasant. "Our biggest problem is fear," Avon coach Dick Fagan said before his team's game against the Raiders. "Cal-Mum has been destroying opponents. They've been eating people up on the scoreboard and statistically." Cal-Mum ate up the Braves, too, although the 34 points scored to Avon's 19 was merely a snack compared to the feasts the Raiders enjoyed against most of their other opponents.

Geneseo's Mike Pilznicnski spoke from on-field experience when, following his team's 43-0 defeat, he described one particularly punishing Red Raider off-tackle run. "First they ran over our defensive end's face," Pilznicnski said, "then they ran over my face, then [safety Scott] Hicks made the tackle." Fear, indeed, both acknowledged by an opposing coach and visible between the lines in the statements of an opposing player.

The 1973 Red Raider offense racked up 2,828 total yards and scored 389 points, an average of just under 49 points per game. Some of the per game point totals are jaw-dropping. The Raider eleven scored 55 against Dansville, 66 against York, 62 against Livonia and 53 against Canisteo.

In 1973 and in other years McAlee was accused of running up the score against his outmatched, overwhelmed opponents. McAlee dismissed the criticism as unjustified. "We definitely didn't run up the score," he explained after the York game. "I couldn't tell the subs not to score." In the 34-0 victory over Mt. Morris, McAlee played the second and third string offense for most of the game, dissatisfied as he was with the poor mental and physical performance of his starters. Most of the team got to play in every other game as well. Several times throughout the season, McAlee worried that this strategy would backfire by not allowing his starters to accumulate enough game-time. By the end of the season, he could rest comfortably with the fact that the strategy didn't backfire at all.*

The 1973 Red Raider defense, led by Tucci, Tim Harrington, Rich Brown, Gary Mattice, Chuck Van Gorder, Chris Batzing and Randy Grattan, gave up only 67 points. But Coach McAlee wasn't optimistic about the defense as the season began. Switching back and forth from a 4-4 to a 5-3, he couldn't seem to find an alignment that suited him. Personnel is what mattered most, however, and after shutting out three of the first four opponents, McAlee was starting to feel better about the defense's prospects. He needn't have worried. Cal-Mum's closest game of the year was the 34-19 victory over Avon, a game which Cal-Mum led at one point 34-7. It was in large part because of the defense that the Red Raiders would end the season ranked eighth in New York State among small schools.

The big game, of course, came against LeRoy on October 26 at Hartwood Park. With the cheerleaders and fans chanting "Remember! Remember!" and with the same word taped to the players' helmets, the Chiverton and Tucci-led Raiders demolished LeRoy 42-16. Chiverton, Tucci and Don Carpenter rushed for an eye-opening 230 yards in the third quarter alone.

"This was the greatest team performance I've had," McAlee enthused when it was all over. "Those kids went out and really put it to them."

Looking back on his magical first season, McAlee said that the 1973 team "put Section V football on the map of New York State. I have coached some good teams, but by far, [the 1973 team was] the best."

Mike Monacelli, who would later coach some pretty good Red Raider teams of his own, called the 1973 team "the measuring stick" against which all other great Cal-Mum teams are evaluated.

Bob Pullyblank, the "Voice of the Raiders" who began announcing Cal-Mum football games that year, said the 1973 team taught people that "there are many who

---

*The same accusation dogged McAlee during the years that he and his Red Raiders were competing for the top spot in New York State's small school football rankings, long before the playoff system was adopted. One of the most important criteria in deciding who's number one was total points scored, leaving coaches competing for the top spot with the dilemma of either scoring as many points as they can or scoring enough to win and thus compromising their team's chances of being voted into the top spot. Fortunately for McAlee, Cal-Mum had enough good players on the second and even third strings that he could play it both ways.

wish they could have worn the Raiders colors, but few have been honored and privileged to."

In their reminiscences, the Red Raider players themselves would recall the combined voices of cheerleaders and fans, chanting the refrain, "We're from Caledonia and no one could be prouder! And if you don't believe us, we'll yell a little louder!" Cheerleaders, players and fans had plenty to yell about after that magical season of dreams fulfilled and destinies altered.

The 1973 team intimidated other schools far and wide. In trying to plan the 1974 schedule, Coach McAlee was unable to find a ninth, non-league opponent. McAlee claimed that several athletic directors told him they didn't want their schools to be embarrassed by having their football teams blown out by a small school like Cal-Mum. Whether or not those timid athletic directors even knew about the historical precedent of the 1932 Aquinas game, their reluctance was justified by the results of the 1973 season.

BIG MAC and his Cal-Mum Raiders continued to attack opponents with a relentless efficiency that was nearly unbeatable. The 1974 team scored 308 total points for an average of 38.5 points per game. This was significantly lower than the record-setting 48.6 points per game the 1973 team racked up, but it was still excellent by any measure.

Defensively, the Red Raiders were even better than they had been the previous year, giving up only 30 points, almost half of them in a 22-14 victory over LeRoy to end the season.

Mike Tucci and Don Carpenter were back for the 1974 season, as were the previous year's standouts Rich Brown, Gary Mattice, Tim Harrington and Randy Grattan. But Bob Chiverton was gone at quarterback, replaced by junior Mike Pullyblank, who had acquired some important real-game experience in several of the 1973 blowouts.

New to the team was Duane Priestley, who started at quarterback for Pine Forest High in Fayetteville, North Carolina the year before. Priestley had spent his 1974 summer vacation in Caledonia. He liked the players and coaches he met so much that he decided to move in with his grandfather and play football in Cal-Mum his senior year. When Pullyblank went down with an ankle injury before the Livonia game, Priestly filled in admirably, leading Cal-Mum to a 40-8 victory.* Priestley also started in the defensive backfield, from where he tackled well, covered tightly and even inter-

---

*Spectators couldn't tell the score by looking at the scoreboard, however, as a lightning strike had knocked out its power early on in the game.

cepted a few passes that would lead to Red Raider scores. Priestly also took over quarterbacking duties when Pullyblank re-injured the ankle against Perry. The game began as a close battle, with the Raiders being shut out in the first quarter for the first time since 1972, but it ended with the usual result, a 42-0 victory for Cal-Mum.

As usual, the big game was against LeRoy, at home on All Saint's Day, November 1, 1974. Both teams came into the game undefeated. Tom Fitzgerald of the Rochester *Democrat and Chronicle* labeled the Oatkan Knights the "unbeaten underdog" for the way that Don Santini's team, ranked eighteenth in New York State, had defeated its previous opponents by convincing margins but were still overshadowed by Cal-Mum's steamroller of a team.

With over 6,000 spectators from all over the Rochester area watching, LeRoy initially made good on Santini's claim that "we don't fear any team." The Oatkan Knights scored first on the game's opening kickoff, and the red and black defense held the Red Raiders to a mere 6 first half points, scored on a 36-yard touchdown pass from Pullyblank to Chris Batzing.

But the second half was a different story, as Donnie Carpenter ran for a total of 81 yards and scored two rushing touchdowns of 4 and 8 yards. Richie Brown overshadowed both Carpenter and Mike Tucci, however, carrying the ball 13 times for 106 yards.

What changed in the second half? Coach McAlee explained what had gone wrong and what now went right. "We tried a new blocking scheme in the first half," he said. "We were criss-crossing and we just weren't doing it. We were confused. So in the second half we went back to one on one blocking where you pick one man and just take him out." Flexibility, McAlee and his Red Raiders knew, is what often wins games.

The Oatkan Knights made the game interesting in the fourth quarter, scoring a late touchdown to bring them within 8 points. But the Raiders held on, and the offensive line took out enough defenders to move the ball forward twice to first downs, bringing the game to an end.

"On your feet Raider fans!" said Bob Pullyblank as the clock wound down, rousing the Cal-Mum faithful to a cheer that could be heard all the way up and down Routes Five and Twenty.

"What a feeling!" yelled Bill McAlee as he ran off the field with his team.

McAlee was now 16-0 after two years as coach of the Red Raiders. Not since the greatest glory years of 1928 and 1929 had the hometown football fans enjoyed this much success.

The Big Mac Attack

THE NEXT TWO YEARS would see similar success, blemished only by losses to Livonia in 1975 and to LeRoy in 1976—the latter defeat on the night the lights went out at Hamilton Field. Cal-Mum, Livonia and Le Roy—these three teams would reign as the triumvirate of Livingston County football for the next several years.

Some attention should be given here to the Cal-Mum/Livonia rivalry that developed in the mid-1970s. Coach Mike Haugh, "the quiet-lipped Tom Landry of high school football," according to one sportswriter, led his Bulldogs teams to impressive records of 8-0 in 1975, 7-1 in 1976 and 7-1 in 1977.

As for the rivalry, 1975 was the big game, the one that put Livonia on the Livingston County football map and the one that left Bill McAlee with his first loss in his Cal-Mum coaching career. Both teams came into the game undefeated. McAlee's Red Raiders had rolled over everybody up to that point, scoring 40, 32, 39, 33 and 43 points in five games and giving up a total of 42. Jim Freeman and Chris Wyatt led the running attack. At quarterback, Mike Pullyblank was both an additional running threat and a fine passer. The offensive line was anchored by Paul Brandes, Jim Goodburlet, Kevin Geer, Mike Mooney, Kenny Troyer, Steve Krenzer and Mike Kelley. The defense, as usual featuring several two-way players, was as stout as it had been during the previous two years. Caledonia had routed Livonia in both 1973 and 1974. But the Bulldogs were a much better team in 1975, as the October showdown against Cal-Mum would prove.

It was a cold, rainy Saturday afternoon at Saunders Field in Livonia. The night before, in LeRoy, coaches McAlee and Haugh rued the fact that cold, wet weather would continue to hang over Livingston County for the next day's game. "We agreed that it was too bad the field was going to be wet because there was so much talent on both teams," Haugh later said.

The first quarter might have mollified the coaches' fears. Livonia fullback Scott Yarnes scored the first touchdown of the game on a 30-yard run. Cal-Mum's offense, led by quarterback Mike Pullyblank and running back Jim Freeman, marched the ball 88 yards on 18 plays and scored on Pullyblank's 1-yard run into the end zone. But the rain continued to fall in large, heavy drops. The sod quickly collapsed. Quarterbacks and runners could no longer hold onto the ball. Boys on both sides of the line of scrimmage could only wallow in the thickening mire.

Somehow, the Schuster brothers, Bob and Bill, were able to connect on a few passes. One of these was for a 4-yard touchdown play that was set up by a coaching mistake. With a fourth and 3 on the Red Raider 24-yard line, McAlee decided to go for it rather than punt. The Bulldogs stuffed Jim Freeman for no gain, and Livonia cashed in with seven points to take a 14-6 lead. That lead would hold, despite three

Bulldog fumbles. The Red Raiders as well could simply do nothing with the ball.*

For the first time "since coming to Caledonia," McAlee wrote in his Caledonia *Advertiser* recap, "it now becomes necessary to describe a losing football game." In his usual way of putting life lessons ahead of football, McAlee continued, "but did those cold, wet, tired young men really lose? They gave all they had on the field, and I, as their coach, could not have asked for more. To win 21 in a row and then have the bubble break can effect different folks in different ways. These men can walk the streets of Caledonia and Mumford with their heads held high."

McAlee's positive attitude was once again his most successful motivational tool. The Red Raiders returned to form, defeating Letchworth 38-8 and LeRoy 22-6. The LeRoy game, played at Hartwood Park, was especially interesting for two reasons. First, the game was played on Friday, October 31, 1975. The game attracted 5,000 paid fans, which might seem odd given that so many parents and their children would have normally been trick-or-treating on Halloween. But both villages had declared Wednesday, October 29 the official trick-or-treat day, thereby avoiding any bothersome scheduling conflicts for both the junior varsity game on Thursday and the varsity game on Friday.

The second interesting fact about the 1975 Cal-Mum/LeRoy game was the presence of Frank Ruane as the new head football coach of the LeRoy Oatkan Knights. The drama of Ruane coaching Cal-Mum's most bitter rival three years after his ignominious departure from Red Raider country was obvious. Did he seek revenge? Did he feel that he'd been wronged by Cal-Mum in the way his tenure there ended? Were there bad feelings on Ruane's part? No, no and no, a diplomatic Ruane clearly explained. The 1971 and 1972 losses to LeRoy "did not cost me my job [at Cal-Mum]. It wasn't because of that at all. That's been reported in the past and it's totally inaccurate. That had nothing to do with my firing." Instead, Ruane claimed that it was "three or four people" and "people on the school board" that had wanted him gone. As for the rivalry itself, now that Ruane was on the other side, "I seek no revenge against Cal-Mum," he said. "I had some good kids play for me there and I appreciated that." For the next ten years, Ruane would stand tall as the proud and honorable face of LeRoy Oatkan Knight football. His presence made the rivalry even better.

The rivalry against Livonia remained an intense one. By the end of September 1976, Livonia had won thirteen in a row. But then, on October 2, they traveled to Hamilton Field. Senior Jim Freeman and Junior Jeff Sweet each ran for 100 yards and two touchdowns as the Red Raiders defeated the Bulldogs 28-18.

---

*A video clip form this game, and from several other Livonia football games, is on You Tube, uploaded there by Livonia alumnus eagleteam1.

LeRoy had already defeated Cal-Mum the week before, Livonia would defeat LeRoy the week after, and all three teams would end up tied 4-1 atop their Livingston County division.

The 1976 Livonia game also saw the coming out party for Robert Poles, Junior, known as "Junior" to friends and family. He was a sophomore that year, settling into his 6'6" 270 pound body just as he was settling into his role as Cal-Mum's prime defensive tackle and, more and more frequently, as Cal-Mum's deadliest blocking fullback.

Most of the drama of 1976 was contained in those early rivalry games—they were followed by four blowout victories against Letchworth, York, Dansville and Honeoye Falls-Lima. The season ended with a close 13-12 victory over Avon.

The Livonia game was also the closest game in 1977, won by Cal-Mum 21-13 on Livonia's home turf. This was the game that was laughed at by the contingent of LeRoy players watching from the end zone. The Red Raiders, most likely looking forward to the following week's "war," were clearly not into the game. They missed blocking assignments and ran to the wrong holes on offense. They arm-tackled or were pushed out of the play on defense. They got too many penalties on both sides of the ball. At halftime and after game, Coach McAlee hurled his clipboard down to the locker room floor and yelled at his players like he never did before. But even his tirades were teaching tools, looking forward to the next challenge. He was sincerely angry at his team's poor performance that day, yes, but he also wanted his players to know that a performance this bad, next week, would end in embarrassment in LeRoy's Hartwood Park.

Which, of course, it didn't. Cal-Mum won "the war" 19-0 in 1977. Cal-Mum won every game that year by an average score of 29-6. These weren't 1929 or 1973 numbers by any means, but they were enough to propel the Caledonia-Mumford Red Raiders to the team's first ever New York State championship.

That number one ranking was not just the accomplishment of the 1977 team, as good as that team was. It was, rather, the culmination of five years of effort on the parts of coaches Bill McAlee, Roger House, Ed Matthews and Mike Monacelli, the culmination of five years of commitment from all the older and younger brothers who followed in their fathers' and grandfathers' Red Raider footsteps, the culmination of five years of support from a community that breathed and bled maroon and white.

Chapter Five:
Monumental Meetings, 1978-1981

OFFICIALLY CALLED the "Soldiers' Monument," the structure at the center of the village of Caledonia was built by J.M. Hamilton and Son for a cost of just over $2,000.[*] It rises 33'4" in height and weighs 37 tons, five times higher and over 400 times heavier than your average Red Raider. It can be seen from quite a distance when approaching the village, especially from the east.

On closer inspection, made easier today by the new traffic pattern which guides cars into a circle eight feet out from the monument's center, the observer can read the inscriptions on each face: "In Memory of the Men Who Served In Defense of Our Country" on the western side, "1900" on the eastern side, "Erected By The Citizens of the Town of Caledonia" on the northern side and "1861-65" on the southern side. Above these inscriptions, spread out across all four sides, are listed the names of the men from Caledonia who died in the American Revolution, the War of 1812 and the Civil War.

The Soldiers' Monument was unveiled on June 13, 1900. The ceremony included a large parade from the Erie Station to the monument, then east on East Avenue to Jersey Street to Church to North, Main and Leicester, and then back to the monument. Over six thousand people attended the day's festivities. The most distinguished guest was New York's governor, Theodore Roosevelt, who gave an inspiring speech in homage to Caledonia's Civil War heroes. Then, as now, the monument served as the spiritual center of the village.

---

[*]This was the same Hamilton family that played such a significant role in the early years of Caledonia, as described in chapter two. It was also the same Hamilton family for whom Hamilton Field is named, making the Soldiers' Monument a particularly appropriate gathering place to celebrate victories (and at least one defeat) that happened somewhere other than on Hamilton Field.

There was no better place than the monument to meet the Red Raider football team when they returned home from an important game on the road. Doing so became a time-honored tradition of the McAlee years and beyond.

BY THE START of the 1978 season, the Cal-Mum Red Raiders had established themselves as the best small school football program in New York State, a level of superiority they would maintain for the next three and a half years. The team went undefeated in 1978, 1979 and 1980, winning the Livingston County Championship and the newly-created Section V championship game all three years. Also, Cal-Mum was ranked the number one small school football team in New York State each of those three years, as it had been in 1977. These years were also the core of the 49 game winning streak, the "Great Streak," the longest winning streak in Section V history, the second longest winning streak in New York State high school football history, and, for a time, the longest active winning streak in the nation.

The Soldiers' Monument might have been the most recognizable landmark in town, but it was the football team that put Caledonia-Mumford on the map. As "Voice of the Red Raiders" Bob Pullyblank put it, "Everywhere I go when someone asks me where I'm from and I tell them Caledonia-Mumford, they always, and I mean always, say, 'You got some great football there.' People from all over associate Cal-Mum with their football program. I'm very proud to be a part of it. The community of Caledonia-Mumford supports their football program one hundred-fifty percent. It is all about pride and joy."

Rather than examine the years 1978-1981 on a game-by-game basis, in this chapter I will offer snapshots of four important games, one each from these four years of football, placing each game in the context of its overall season. These were all games away from Hamilton Field, monumental games in the history of Cal-Mum football that deserved monumental meetings.

Cal-Mum Red Raiders 42, Lyons Lions 0

Saturday, November 18, 1978

"ALL WE'RE PLAYING FOR, I guess, is Caledonia pride," said Coach McAlee before the game. His Red Raiders were already ranked number one in New York State. The team already had a 22 game winning streak. What was different for Cal-Mum in 1978 was the new Class B Section V championship game, played at Fauver Stadium on the University of Rochester campus. The opponent: the Lyons Lions from the Finger Lakes West conference, a team that had gone 8-1 in a season that was supposed to be a rebuilding year.

Coach Dave Alena was not shy in expressing his anxiety over the Saturday afternoon contest. "That team looks like the Green Bay Packers," he said. "It's got to be the biggest team we'll ever play against."

He was primarily referring to Junior Poles, the 6'6", 275 pound offensive and defensive tackle, the player who had defined Cal-Mum football for the past three seasons. Junior's grandfather and father had both played Red Raider football. Now Junior himself was the first of three Poles brothers to don the maroon and white. He would go on to become a three-time member of the All-Greater Rochester team and a two-time All-State selection.[*] After the 1978 season, he would also be honored as the New York State Small School Player of the Year.

But none of these accomplishments inflated Junior's ego. "In all my time here, I've never heard a bad word said about Junior," said a local gas station attendant. Junior would never "walk the halls of school wearing a sign saying 'I'm player of the year,'" said teammate Bill Dollard. "He's the same Junior I met in the seventh grade. He looks out for you. He's just a fun-loving guy who doesn't put up a front."

Poles shared the awareness of others, and spoke about it openly. "I don't want to get big-headed," he said. "That's how you lose friends. Friends mean a lot to me. Getting along with people means a lot to me."

Coach McAlee tells a great Junior Poles story, from when Poles was a freshman on the varsity squad. "Our JVs were going to play Avon and somehow the rumor got started that Junior was going to play for the JVs. Why, do you know the school attorney at Avon called the superintendent? Parents weren't going to let their kids play because Junior was so big."

And fast. And strong. On defense Poles could fight off just about any double team and get to the runner before the ball got back to the line of scrimmage. Try going outside, and Poles would slide off his block and run laterally to the ball, meeting the runner with an impenetrable obstacle that no one could get through and few could get around. On offense, Poles would open up holes large enough for two or

---

[*] In 1977, Junior Poles earned first team All-State honors. But he was not selected to the All-Livingston County team, a snub that happened frequently during the McAlee era. Was it envy on the part of the county's other coaches? Whatever the reason, players like Mike Tucci, Don Carpenter, Mike Pullyblank, Chris Wyatt, Jeff Sweet and, especially, Junior Poles, were the ones who suffered from the poor choices of Livingston County's coaches.

three backs to run through, carrying his block well downfield. Also on offense, Poles would sometimes line up in the backfield, allowing him to get a running start and roll over the opposing defensive linemen two or three at a time. McAlee used Poles in this particular scheme, as the coach put it, "when things got down to the nitty-gritty."

The Red Raiders were not a one man show, however. On defense, Poles was joined by 6'2", 220 pound Dave Trojanski, who was just as strong and even faster than Poles. Also on the defensive side was Bob Cesare and Dale Wynne, who would often join Poles, Trojanski or both on vicious gang tackles of opposing runners, and ends Paul Toland and Tim Grant, who would often get plenty of play-making opportunities as opposing runners attempted to avoid the big guys in the middle by springing their runs to the outside.

On offense, Poles, Trojanski an their teammates opened holes for the fine trio of running backs composed of John Freeman, Ron Poles and Larry Anderson. Mark McGrath was the team's very capable quarterback. Sometimes Poles and Trojanski opened holes from the fullback position. In 1978 against Dansville, for example, Junior Poles and Dave Trojanski alternated playing fullback on ten straight plays during the winning scoring drive. McAlee called it his power backfield. "We just use those two big guys out of the power-I and hug a back right behind them," he said. The power-I would appear again, delighting Raider fans every time they saw it.

"We're hoping we can offset all that size with quickness and finesse," said Dave Alena before the game. "Our line, as small as it is, gets off the ball pretty well, but I don't know if we can keep [Cal-Mum] honest inside. You can't try a lot of reverses and junk plays against a team like Caledonia, either. You just have to avoid mistakes and play great defense."

UNFORTUNATELY for the Lions, none of Alena's hopes came to fruition. Cal-Mum ran roughshod over Lyons, gaining a total of 375 yards rushing and thirteen first downs. After a scoreless first quarter, the Red Raiders drove 91 yards for the first touchdown of the game, a 15-yard run by Freeman. Ron Poles took the ball in from the 8-yard line just before halftime, scoring his first of three touchdowns. Ron, the middle Poles brother, would also end the game with 128 yards and an outstanding offensive player of the game trophy. Junior Poles and Dave Trojanski got into the blocking act on Ron's touchdown, working from the power-I and opening the hole that put the Raiders up 14-0 at halftime.

But the real offensive star of this show was Larry "Super-flea" Anderson, who ran up, down and all around the Lyons defense for a total of 150 yards. He also put the game out of reach on an 68-yard scamper at the beginning of the second half. It would go down in history as one of the most memorable of all the long touchdowns that the Raiders ever scored. "I love running the ball," said Anderson, who usually played only defense. "I like those TDs."

McAlee was impressed by his team's offensive performance, much more than he had been for the final two games of the regular season, a 13-10 win over Dansville and a 13-3 victory over LeRoy. "We had something to prove," the coach said. "We've been down offensively. The kids just came in and did the job."

They did the job defensively as well. Lyons took the ball all the way to the Cal-Mum 13-yard line in the first drive of the game, but Junior Poles stopped Lyons' Bill Keifer at the 9-yard line on a fourth down play to force the loss on downs. Ron Poles scored one of his three touchdowns on a 37-yard interception return to put Cal-Mum up 35-0. Overall, the Red Raiders held the Lions to a mere 51 yards, well short of their regular season average of 257 yards per game.

"We've got to stay number one [in the state]," McAlee said after the final whistle had sounded. "Let's face it. There may be teams better in some areas than us," he said referring to the excellent Olean team from Section VI. "But we worked hard for this. We deserve it." They did deserve it, and they got it. In the final poll of the year, Cal-Mum was unanimously voted the number one small school football team in New York State for the second straight year.

Cal-Mum Red Raiders 26, Clyde-Savannah Golden Eagles 20, OT

Saturday, November 17, 1979

JUST ABOUT THE ONLY SIMILARITIES between this game and the previous year's Section V Class B championship game was that Clyde-Savannah, like Lyons, came from the Finger Lakes Conference and that Cal-Mum, as in 1978, came into the game undefeated and ranked number one among small schools in New York State.

Cal-Mum's undefeated season in 1979 was as impressive as any that came before it in the McAlee era. They averaged almost 36 points per game and gave up an average of 6. As in 1978 the defense allowed double figures only twice, to Livonia and, as usual, to LeRoy in a close game that Cal-Mum came back to win from a 14-0 deficit.

McAlee was as confident before the championship game as he was before the beginning of the season. When asked about the graduation of both Junior Poles and Dave Trojanski, he said that Cal-Mum doesn't rebuild, it just fills in the slots. McAlee didn't have much to worry about with Ron Poles on his team. And Poles was a bit more brazen that his older brother, explaining towards the end of the season how the Red Raiders simply caused other teams to fold when the maroon and white came out strong in the first half.

They had certainly done that the year before against Lyons. Would the pattern hold against the Clyde-Savannah Golden Eagles?

It seemed it would after each team finished its first possession on that cold, drizzly afternoon in Brockport. Cal-Mum took the opening kickoff at its own 20. Eight plays later, Bill Dollard caught a Mark McGrath pass for a 15-yard touchdown. John Freeman kicked the extra point, and Cal-Mum had a 7-0 lead. Then the defense, led by end Tim Grant, who would earn the defensive most valuable player award, stopped Clyde-Savannah's offense in its own territory. When McGrath returned under center with Freeman, Poles and Anderson behind him, it looked like the same old path to victory was wide open for the Red Raiders to roll on down. Poles, licking his chops, was ready to make the Golden Eagles fold. But the Clyde-Savannah defense held with patience and some fine tackling. They returned the ball to the offense, which took it 81 yards in ten plays for a touchdown.

McGrath threw to Dollard for another touchdown in the second quarter. When John Freeman ran the ball into the end zone from the 12-yard line early in the third, it again seemed like the Red Raiders, now up 20-6, were on the verge of putting the game away.

But again Clyde-Savannah showed its resilience. Jesse Maestre scored on a 4-yard run, the offense made the two-point conversion, and the Golden Eagles were down by only a touchdown. The fourth quarter was tense as the chill in the air deepened. Cheerleaders and fans on both sides of the field alternately blew into their hands to keep warm and clapped them to encourage their team. As the three minute mark approached, it looked like the Red Raider defense would hold, as it had so many times before that year and the year before.

Then something unexpected happened, unexpected at least to most of the fans on both sides of the field, and to the entire Cal-Mum defense.

Bill McAlee knew Clyde-Savannah coach Nick DerCola would attempt something wild at some point in the game. "There was no doubt in my mind that Nick would have something special for us," he said after the game.

The question is, did McAlee know that the "something special" would be a perfectly executed flea-flicker in the most significant do-or-die moment of the game? Did McAlee crack a told-you-so smile when Golden Eagle quarterback Tim Montemorano pitched the ball to Jesse Maestre, who then handed the ball to Steve Johnson, who then tossed it back to Montemorano? If so, the smile would have quickly faded as a wide-open Rick Riviello caught the ball for a 27-yard touchdown. While not shocked, McAlee was certainly surprised. But his defensive players were indeed shocked as they watched the ball sail into Riviello's arms—they had paid no attention to a player they thought was a mere decoy on a pitch left.

The score was now tied 20-20 with time quickly running out, the first time all season the Red Raiders had found themselves in such a desperate situation. But they, too, regrouped. The Raiders stopped Clyde-Savannah for the two-point conversion. If Nick DerCola had had a kicker, the Golden Eagles would have most likely taken a 21-20 lead, forcing Cal-Mum to score at least a field goal to win the game. The Red Raiders ran out the clock, however, and both teams prepared for a sudden death overtime tie-breaker.

The tie-breaker system called for each offense to take the ball at the 10-yard line, where it would have four downs to get the ball into the end zone with either a field goal or a touchdown. Each team would get an equal number of chances to score on four downs, and the game would be over when one team held the lead.

Clyde-Savannah won the coin toss and lined up at the Cal-Mum 10. The Red Raider defense was pumped up, and stopped the Golden Eagles cold, pushing them back to the 15-yard line. The large contingent of Raider fans ignored the chill now. Gloves off, they clapped and yelled wildly, led by the cheerleading crew that always got Raider fans on their feet. Clyde-Savannah missed a field goal, and Cal-Mum lined up at the Clyde-Savannah 10 to take its turn.

All three Red Raider running backs ran the ball. Larry Anderson took it to the right on the pitch. John Freeman ran it right up the gut. Then Ron Poles dove over left tackle from the one-yard line for the touchdown. Game over! Cal-Mum's fans and cheerleaders were ecstatic after watching the closest, most thrilling victory the team had yet won in the McAlee era.

The players on both teams were exhausted. Several Clyde-Savannah players, including game MVP Steve Johnson, broke down crying. The Cal-Mum players congratulated the Golden Eagles, wished them well, then headed off to the team bus, which would take them back to route 19 south and through LeRoy, and then onto Routes Five and Twenty to Caledonia, to the Soldiers' Monument, where, once again, the fans would be waiting.

Cal-Mum Red Raiders 26, LeRoy Oatkan Knights 20

Friday, November 14, 1980

CAL-MUM WENT into the 1980 Section V championship game with all cylinders firing. It had been a "Tale of Two Seasons" type year, with the worst of times coming early in close games against Albion, Avon and Livonia, and the best of times happening late in blowouts against Honeoye Falls-Lima, Notre Dame of Batavia and Lyons.

Ron Poles ran the ball 24 times for 228 yards in a 14-6 win over Section VI champion Albion to open the season. The Red Raiders' lead was endangered by a bad decision on Coach McAlee's part when he called for Poles to run a dive play on fourth-and-two at midfield with three minutes left in the game. "It was a coaching mistake," McAlee admitted after the game. "I thought it was third down." The Purple Eagles stopped Poles for no gain. Albion's offense took the ball almost all the way to the goal line. Cal-Mum was saved from a possible tie by the clock's triple zeros when Adam Wightman and Tim MacDonald stopped quarterback Jim Holt at the six-inch line.

Cal-Mum was down 13-0 to Avon in the second game of the season, but two touchdowns and one 75-yard interception return, all by Ron Poles, gave the Raiders the victory. Some old-timers whispered that Poles might have been channelling the ghost of Jimmy Jackson that game.

The Raiders faced the same deficit against Livonia in the fifth game of the season. They won that game with two Kevin Zimmer touchdown passes, one to Brian Bowers and one to Mike Grattan. That game, played in soggy conditions that reminded Coach McAlee of the 1975 loss to the Bulldogs, was the closest Cal-Mum had come to defeat since the winning streak began in 1976. It wasn't the last time in 1980 that defeat was not only knocking at the door, but had its hand on the handle.

The six other regular season games were quite different. Cal-Mum blew out Dansville with its most varied offensive attack of the season, scoring on two Zimmer touchdown passes to Bowers and Grattan, two touchdown runs by Dan Parnell, and even a blocked punt recovery in the end zone by Tom Pearse.

Ron Poles again lit up the scoreboard against LeRoy, scoring three touchdowns on 226 yards in a 47-12 victory.

Against Wellsville, running backs Eric Sheffer, Dan Parnell and Barry Robinson all joined in on the running fun. Down 7-0 after the first quarter, the Raiders scored 20 points in the second quarter alone to put the game away.

None of the next three opponents, Honeoye Falls-Lima, Notre Dame of Batavia or Lyons, could do any better. Poles, Parnell, Sheffer, Robinson—all four of Cal-Mum's horsemen ran wild in these games, let loose by the ferocious blocking of All-Greater Rochester guard Bill Bernard and his offensive linemates. Bernard also led the defense to two shutouts in the final three games, allowing only one touchdown to Notre Dame, and that with the game well in hand.

The victory against Honeoye Falls-Lima was number 39 in a row, which broke the Section V unbeaten streak record previously held by Bolivar in the late 1940s and 1950. Now, McAlee's Red Raiders had their sights set on Massena's New York State record of 55 wins in a row.

To take one more step closer towards that record, they would have to get through LeRoy again. No one believed for a moment that the second round against the Oatkan Knights would be as easy as the first.

LeRoy had its own share of come-from-behind thrillers in 1980. The Oatkan Knights beat Wellsville 13-12 and Avon 22-21, and fought off a tough Attica team 16-12. Both Bill McAlee and Frank Ruane insisted that won/loss records should be thrown out the window when these two teams meet during the regular season. How much more intense, then, would the Class B Section V championship game be? Not only were records irrelevant that year, so were past performances.

"We've improved a lot" since the 47-12 mauling the Red Raiders put on the Oatkan Knights back in September, Coach Ruane claimed.

"I'm afraid," McAlee said candidly. "I'm scared to death. I'm afraid that we aren't going to play the kind of ball that we're capable of playing."

McAlee's fears were justified. LeRoy began the game on a tear, scoring twice in under three minutes to take a 14-0 lead. The first touchdown came as a result of Cal-Mum punter's Tim MacDonald's kick that went straight up in the air and back down for a total of -1 yards. It was a trick we all practiced in our backyards as kids—this was just the wrong time and the wrong place for it to happen.[*] LeRoy scored the touchdown on a fake field goal pass completion from holder Dan Wright to Jim Mathews, who was wide open in the end zone. The second LeRoy touchdown came after a Dan Parnell fumble at the Cal-Mum 24. Wright ran the ball in from the 10 on the fourth play of the drive. Those two plays contributed to Wright's well-deserved offensive player of the game award.

Football is a game of redemption, and both MacDonald and Parnell had opportunities to make up for the mistakes that put the Raiders in their worst hole of the

---

[*] I was on the sidelines keeping defensive stats for the game. I distinctly remember someone on the bench yelling something to the effect of "this isn't the backyard!" after MacDonald's kick.

season. First, MacDonald caught the kickoff that followed the second LeRoy touchdown and ran the ball 85 yards down the middle of the field for a score. After halftime, Parnell made a great cut through the LeRoy linebackers on an off-tackle run that resulted in a 35-yard gain for Cal-Mum's second touchdown.

The Red Raiders were moving now, and stopping LeRoy as well. After Bernard, Sinclair and Company forced the Knights to punt from their own 10-yard line, Zimmer hit Chris O'Dell for a 35-yard gain and Eric Sheffer scored on a 7-yard run to give the Raiders a 20-14 lead.

The game became a stalemate for the rest of the third quarter and well into the fourth. Each defense, it seemed, somehow moved quicker and tackled harder. The teams traded several punts, but LeRoy slowly took the upper hand in the battle for field position. Cal-Mum had the ball deep in its own territory and was able to do nothing. Fourth down came and with it a punt. Perhaps it was the quicker-off-the-ball and harder-hitting Oatkan Knight defense that caused the Cal-Mum center to snap the ball a bit to softly and too low for second-string punter Chris O'Dell to handle. O'Dell fell to a knee to catch the low snap, and the officials called the play dead and gave the ball to LeRoy on the 1-yard line. With just under seven minutes to go, the Knights scored the touchdown and extra point to take a 21-20 lead.

LeRoy's defense continued to hold. The Red Raiders kept the ball moving, but barely, and found themselves faced with a third-and-four on its own 38-yard line. There was just over a minute left in the game. Kevin Zimmer took the snap and moved back to pass. Cal-Mum's speedsters ran down the field on fly and post patterns, trying desperately to get open. Ron Poles stayed in the backfield, turning left and then right, protecting his quarterback, giving Zimmer as much time as he could to find that open receiver and get that receiver the ball.

Then suddenly, almost slyly, Zimmer tucked the ball into Ronnie Poles' gut. "We only ran [the play] one time in practice and it was open then," Poles said after the game. "I said if it was open like that again, I'd be gone."

"We thought for sure they were going to pass," said LeRoy's outstanding defensive player of the game John Piazza. "Everyone got sucked back."

It was, therefore, "open like that again" for Poles. Holding the ball tight, he ran it through the hole that must have been ten yards wide, down the sideline and into the end zone for the winning score.

"You're brought up in Caledonia to know that the game's not over 'til the clock says zero, zero, zero," Poles said after he'd received the game's most valuable player award for his 131 yards rushing that day, but really for that one dramatic touchdown, the last of his very successful high school career.

Cal-Mum's coaches, players, cheerleaders, managers and fans were more ecstatic after this victory than after any that had come before or would come after. We streamed onto the field, cheering wildly, hugging Zimmer and Poles and Parnell and whoever else we could get our arms around. We drove back to Caledonia in a caravan, honking horns and yelling out the windows all the way, the cheerleaders holding their pom-poms out the windows of their bus in a wild display of exuberance. And when we turned onto Union Street we met up with a multi-car police escort that led us through Mumford, right past the school and all the way down North Street to the monument, where the Voice of the Raiders could be heard above all other voices chanting "We're number one! We're number one!" There were police and fire truck sirens sounding between the chants. The party took place below a giant "number one" finger, made by Sam DiLiberto's Pardi Foam Products, which town highway superintendent George Kelly had placed on the monument over the Civil War hero's head, 33 feet and 4 inches above the ground.

The Cal-Mum Red Raiders were again voted the number one small school football team in New York State. Ron Poles was named New York State Small School Player of the Year. Bill McAlee was honored as the New York State High School Football Coach of the Year. These were, indeed, the best of times.*

Cal-Mum Red Raiders 0, Notre Dame of Batavia Little Irish 16

November 7, 1981

THE IDEA WAS CONCEIVED by someone in the visitor's bleachers towards the end of the third quarter. First it came out as a question. "If they lose, should we do it?"

Then, as the impending loss became more and more certain, it became a suggestion. "Maybe we should do it."

Finally, by the halfway mark of the fourth quarter, it was a certain proposition. "We meet at the monument, win or lose."

---

*On March 2, 1981, the New York State Assembly passed "Legislative Resolution Assembly No. 244…congratulating and commending the Caledonia-Mumford Red Raider football team of Caledonia-Mumford Central School on their outstanding record over the past four years." Two other legislative resolutions followed during the Monacelli years.

The message was passed from fan to fan, across the bleachers and along the fence. As the final seconds of the game ticked away, tears streaked down the faces of the Raider faithful, smeared the makeup of the cheerleaders' faces. When their boys walked back to the end zone after congratulating the victorious Little Irish, the Raider fans stood and cheered.

They cheered again when their boys walked off the bus at the Soldiers' Monument in the middle of the village. Someone started to chant, and by the time the last player had disembarked, the whole crowd had joined in. "Thank you, Raiders!" we repeated as players, cheerleaders and parents cried and hugged. "Thank you, Raiders!"

BACK DURING THE GAME at Van Detta Stadium, as the question was turning to suggestion and then to certainty, Coach Bill McAlee knew it was over.

"We had decided to go back to some basic stuff at halftime," McAlee explained after the game. "But we just didn't do anything. Right then and there, I knew we were in trouble. We tried everything in our playbook. I even tried taking some stuff out of the Sears-Roebuck catalog. But they didn't give way."

Accordingly, when it became crystal clear that the Little Irish were not going to give way, McAlee did two things. First, he turned to his coaches and shook their hands. He especially thanked Coaches Roger House and Ed Matthews, both of whom had been there with him from the beginning, and also Mike Monacelli and Gary Fredericks, the junior varsity coaches who had groomed their young players towards excellence and had been just as important to The Great Streak as anyone.

"We've got nothing to hang our heads about," he said to his staff with a smile. "We've had a hell of a run. If we had a play on Broadway for 49 weeks, we'd be rich today."

Then, with under a minute left to play and with his offense stuck at the Cal-Mum 30-yard line, McAlee called a timeout and asked his players to huddle up around him. He took off his fedora and ran his hand over his bristles.

"Well, I guess we're in a real bind," he said with a straight face and a shake of his head. "Any suggestions?"

Several of the players looked up and caught the gleam in McAlee's eye. They giggled, then, one by one, laughed outright.

"We couldn't help ourselves but to laugh," Senior fullback Rich Goodburlet said after the game. "If we look back at it all, we've done everything else but lose. Now we've lost. So now we've done everything."

You might wonder why I picked "The Loss" as the fourth and final example of monumental meetings during the second act of the McAlee-era drama. This is the one most of us would rather forget rather than relive. This is the one that hurts the most. But there was a meeting at the monument after this game, too, and of all the meetings this one was perhaps the most profound, precisely because it demonstrated McAlee's insistent claim that a football player's effort, and a community's giving thanks for that effort, are more important than the wins themselves.

Besides, The Great Streak almost ended at least four other times in the course of the 1981 season.
     Almost.
     The first time victory was snatched from the jaws of defeat was in the opening game against Albion. This time Cal-Mum had the big lead, 19-0 thanks to two touchdowns by halfback Jerome Phillips, one a run and one a pass from Kevin Zimmer. MC Bob Pullyblank had the Raider faithful, and several hundred others in the crowd that topped four thousand, in a frenzy. But then Albion came back on two big touchdown runs by Ken McNeil. When Albion recovered a Cal-Mum fumble at its own 32-yard line, Pullyblank implored the crowd to pump up the defense with cheers. The fans responded, but to no avail as Albion ran and passed, on first down and fourth, all the way down the field. Ken McNeil took the ball at the 1-yard line on a sweep left, but linebacker Scott Moran grabbed him from behind by the heel for no gain. With Pullyblank roaring into the microphone—"GET ON YOUR *FEET*, RAIDER FANS!"—the Cal-Mum defense prepared itself to save the unbeaten streak. The Purple Eagle's quarterback, Ken Burke, couldn't handle the snap from center. Mike Grattan came around the end and hit Burke just as he was reaching for the ball. Bob Clements, a linebacker, came up the middle and recovered the fumble at the five. Game over. Streak preserved.
     The next close call came against LeRoy in a game at Hartwood Park that matched —some say exceeded—the drama of the 1980 sectional contest. LeRoy opened up an early 13-0 lead, but Cal-Mum, as usual, came back strong. The teams went into halftime tied at 13, thanks to two touchdown runs by Barry Robinson behind some inspired blocking. LeRoy scored near the end of the third quarter to take a 20-13 lead. It seemed it would hold when they forced Cal-Mum to punt with just over a minute to play. But LeRoy was penalized 15 yards for roughing the kicker, and Cal-Mum was given a new set of downs. The LeRoy defense held for three plays, and Cal-Mum faced another fourth down on the LeRoy 23 with less than a minute to play. McAlee called a flood right special, a seldom used play given the priority of the run in Red

Raider football. Kevin Zimmer rolled right, checked down his receivers, and threw the ball to split end Brian Bowers, who was running a fly down the sideline. He was well-defended by two Oatkan Knights, one of whom tipped the ball. But the Oatkan Knight defender tipped the ball close enough to Bowers' hands for him to reach out and grab it.

Cal-Mum had narrowed the score to 20-19. McAlee now faced a decision. It was a quick and easy one, since, as McAlee wrote in his weekly summary for the Caledonia *Advertiser*, "as the coach I had decided we would go for the win and not for the tie." His players, expecting no less from their coach, wholeheartedly agreed. LeRoy, it seemed, knew this, even though the Red Raiders lined up for the kick. They had the play well-covered as Zimmer, the holder, took the snap, stood up, rolled right again and flipped the ball into the end zone. Fullback Rich Goodburlet had gotten open, but barely, and had to slide in order to catch the ball. 21-20. Game over. Streak once again preserved.

Cal-Mum Red Raider players, fans and coaches once again celebrated at the monument.

THE FOLLOWING WEEK'S GAME against Livonia was another nail-biter, witnessed by another huge Hamilton Field crowd of over five thousand spectators. The Bob Pullyblank-led crowd, welcomed to "number one country" as they always were by the MC, had its impact on this game, too. The fans cheered so loudly that the Livonia offense was penalized for either offsides or illegal motion four straight times to open the game.

"It was no mistake on our part," coach Mike Haugh legitimately explained after the game. How could a visiting team's offense function with that much noise, that much pressure?

But the Bulldogs, true to their mascot's name, regrouped after Cal-Mum took a 6-0 lead. Led by split end Kevin Schuster, whose older brothers Bob and Bill had led the team in the mid-seventies, Livonia came back strong to take a 14-9 lead into halftime.

"We couldn't stop Schuster," McAlee said, referring to the Raiders' special 6-3-1 defense, with the eleventh man covering Schuster one-on-one wherever he went. Nor could Livonia stop Barry Robinson, the Cal-Mum running back who had yet to break out this season, but who did so in a big way right when he needed to on this night. With the ball on the Cal-Mum 35-yard line early in the fourth quarter, Robinson took a handoff from Kevin Zimmer, ran right, avoided two tacklers with some fancy dancing down the sideline, and scored. It was an electrifying run that made the crowd go wild with excitement. The upfront blocking of Jim Pullyblank, Joe Gustainis, Francis Krenzer, Don McQuilken, Jim Laubach, Dave Betz and Brian Bowers had done it again. The cheering had hardly subsided when Robinson caught a lateral from Zimmer, took one step forward and then passed the ball to a wide open Chris Cappotelli for the two-point conversion. The defense held and Livonia turned the ball over on downs. Game over. Streak yet again preserved.

But there were ill-omens in the air. One was an overabundance of media coverage. A Rochester television station featured the school and the team on it's "Live at 5:30" program the week before the LeRoy game. The week after that, a reporter from the Rochester *Democrat and Chronicle* spent hours around town—in the diners, in the school, at practice, in my family's living room. The resulting article, " 'It's the only show in town,' " appeared on the front page of the *Democrat and Chronicle's* sports page on Friday, October 16. Despite the good reporting and the enthusiastic reception the article received, it was not exactly the type of distraction the team needed on the day of the Livonia game.

Interviews with Coach McAlee inevitably turned to the topic of The Great Streak, more specifically, to the topic of the undefeated streak coming to an end. "The idea of losing doesn't bother me," McAlee insisted. "There's nothing wrong with losing if you get beat by a better team. The sad thing about losing is when you beat yourself because you don't want to win badly enough."

When asked how he wants the streak to end, McAlee responds that he hopes his Raiders "get blown out" rather than lose because of one player's mistake. "That's what I worry about, that some kid gets blamed for the mistake that broke the streak. The loss wouldn't bother me, but what it could do to the boy or the boys, that has me worried."

Cal-Mum's players, however, simply didn't want to lose. "All I'm hoping," Jim Pullyblank said, "is that I'm not on that team that loses and ends the streak. They'll remember that a long time around here." Barry Robinson admitted after the Livonia game that "the close [games] are tiring us out. It puts more pressure on us."

The pressure even got to McAlee by the middle of the following week. With 48 hours remaining until his Red Raiders faced a tough Wellsville team on the road, McAlee admitted to Gary Maloney of the Olean *Times Herald* that "I wish the streak would end so things would get back to normal around here. The kids…make a little mistake and everyone's on their back. Consequently the coaching staff gets on them trying to get them to do something different so we're not on their backs. Everyone's getting a little edgy around here… If we get beat Friday night, I hope it's by 40-0. Then I can sit back and say I did a 'bleep-poor' job of coaching."

Cal-Mum didn't lose against Wellsville. The Red Raiders got ahead 28-13 at the half and held on for a 34-27 victory, clinched when Cal-Mum recovered Wellsville's on-side kick with under a minute to play. However, Wellsville had scored two long touchdowns in the fourth quarter, one a 75-yard pass play and another an 80-yard kickoff return. As Gary Maloney put it in his Saturday morning write-up, "Wellsville showed what Albion, LeRoy and Livonia already had shown this year—the clock is quickly ticking on 'The Great Streak.' "

NOTRE DAME COACH Bill Sutherland was gracious both before the game and after. "It's an honor to play them," he said a couple days before the game. "We wanted to play them. The worst we can do is lose. We're looking forward to it. They're number one in the state and this gives us a yardstick to measure our football team by."

Sutherland coached a brilliant game on that cold, wet November night at Van Detta Stadium. The Little Irish controlled the ball on offense with runs and short passes, staying one step ahead of the Red Raider defense at all times. On defense, Notre Dame used a nine-man front to stop the Cal-Mum running game cold. On passing downs they put just enough pressure on Zimmer to make him uncomfortable. Their man-to-man coverage scheme worked brilliantly on Bowers and any back that Zimmer tried to connect with out of the backfield. When the final gun sounded, McAlee had gotten his wish—The Cal-Mum Red Raiders football team had lost for the first time since 1976 not on a close play or because of one player's mistake. They had been soundly beaten in all phases of the game.

"The streak is an unbelievable accomplishment," Bill Sutherland said after the game. "When you think of all the things that can go against you, a bad break, a bad call… I've been scouting them for years and I've almost become a fan of theirs. Their kids were real good after the loss. They're a class operation, from McAlee on down. People are still going to talk about how great they are. But at least now we'll be mentioned in the second sentence."

Coach McAlee had this to say in his Caledonia *Advertiser* recap, which many citizens of Caledonia and Mumford, myself included, read with tears welling up in the eyes.

> It took six years, but the day finally came. The Raiders lost a football game. I know towns and players that losing is part of living, not so with

my Raiders. It is not a part of living but rather a part of life that meets us on the way through this world.

What was wrong with 49-0? If you had a hit show that ran that long on Broadway, you would have made a bundle. I am sitting by a fire place looking out at a beautiful fall day. Remember, I always said the sun would shine, well it is and the Caledonia-Mumford School District is still on task.

I look up at the wall in my den and see the plaques presented to me over the years and I think of the young boys who became men on the athletic fields of upstate New York. Each of you that ever wore the maroon and white of Caledonia lived a period of history that may never come again. Enjoy your memories, but live for the future. Remember the past, both good and bad, but strive to achieve just as you achieved on the field of athletic competition…

To the many people that met us at the center of town, thank you. You proved you are the greatest, your team is just as proud of you as you are of them. Walk with your heads high.

At the Cozy Kitchen or Moonwinks on the morning after the game, one of the Monday Morning Quarterbacks walks in, sits down and orders his coffee and eggs. The waitress, a cheerleader back in her high school days, asks him how he's doing. He had been at the monument the night before, and then at the Iroquois trying to figure it all out. He shakes his head, sighs and smiles. He takes a first sip of coffee. "At least it wasn't LeRoy," he says.[*]

---

[*]The end of the 1981 season is also the end of my brother Jim's Cal-Mum football scrapbook, which he kept from 1973 to the end of his final game as a Red Raider, the 35-14 loss to Livonia. I practically memorized the scrapbook as a kid and inherited it when he forgot to take it from my parents' Jane Street house when they made all of us kids clear out the attic. Over the years I'd look through it every now and again, thinking that I might use the articles and notes my brother had collected as the basis for a book on Cal-Mum Red Raider football history. Well, Jim, here it is—I couldn't have written it without your fine work as a research assistant!

Chapter Six:
Under Pressure

BILL MCALEE COACHED for six more years after The Great Streak ended against Notre Dame and the season ended against Livonia the following week in the Section V Class B semifinal. The burden of history was heavy on those of us who played during those years and those of us who could claim older brothers and fathers and grandfathers who had been champions before us. There were two ways to deal with that burden—either lighten the load with solid effort and good humor or crack under the weight of it. Most of us, at one time or another, did both.

In the good humor department is a personal story from the 1985 game against LeRoy. Early in the week before the game, Matt Taylor, our quarterback, and I took a nickel from 1932, the year LeRoy beat Caledonia 18-7, and hid it behind a rock at Hartwood Park. All that week we would randomly shout out, "The Nickel!" when we saw each other in the hallway, or punch our fists into a teammates' shoulders and yell, "Do it for the nickel! Yeah!" By the time the game rolled around, we had several of the more animated players on the team shouting nickel-esque slogans along with us. A few of them had no idea what they were yelling about. I even used the cheer several times during the game, clearly befuddling the LeRoy defenders who thought it was some kind of formation call or blocking scheme. On our way back to the bus Matt and I peeked behind the rock and there it was! Who knows, it might still be there today, a monument to how two rather kooky kids successfully dealt with the stress of big-game week.

Maybe that particular week was so stressful because the previous year's game against LeRoy did not go so well. The Oatkan Knights had one tough team in 1984, crushing all opponents en route to a Section V Class B championship. One of the opponents LeRoy especially crushed was Cal-Mum, by a 33-6 score. Worse, the game was at Hamilton Field, and by time the final whistle sounded the home team sideline was littered with injured players, myself included. Separated shoulders, sprained ankles, bruised knees, concussions—in all my years watching and playing Red Raiders football I had never seen such carnage in one game.

One injury was even frightening. Scott McClenny, playing defensive back, was laid out on a hard, legal downfield block by Oatkan Knight runner John Bundy, a block that left McClenny literally convulsing with pain near the home sideline. I can't recall who was sent in to take McClenny's place, but I do recall that he wasn't too enthusiastic about entering the game. As LeRoy pounded the ball down our throats at will and stymied any momentum we tried to create with well-timed and usually vicious defensive hits, I saw the clear look of fear on more than one face.

The malaise continued the following week, as we were blown out by Red Jacket 27-7 on their home turf. We were never in that game either—never in it in terms of the score or in terms of our mental attitude, perhaps because we could guess that if we won, we'd have to play LeRoy again in the Section V championship game. That year, we failed where so many previous Red Raider teams had succeeded. No wonder Matt Taylor and I covered our anxiety with humor in 1985.

Pressure came from, or perhaps resulted in, losses, which Cal-Mum players and fans were not used to during the incredible 1973-1981 run of 73 victories and four defeats. But the Red Raiders lost a total of 10 games in McAlee's final six seasons, winning 44 and tying two. While this record would have been more than respectable to many other teams and communities, it was not up to Cal-Mum's standards. Success had spoiled us.

THE COMPETITION was more challenging in those years, as it had been, increasingly so, since the institution of the sectional playoff system in 1978. In Livingston County, there were the three usual teams to challenge Cal-Mum. Livonia was perennially tough, although the Bulldogs had lost Coach Mike Haugh to the school administration. Haugh had certainly gone out a winner, defeating Cal-Mum 35-14 and Clyde-Savannah 25-8 to win the 1981 Section V Class B championship. Avon was also a difficult team to beat each year, especially from 1983 through 1986. And then there was LeRoy. The Oatkan Knights continued their stand as Cal-Mum's nemesis, not just in that 1984 disaster but every other year as well.

Coach McAlee summed up the difficulty of competing against these, and other Livingston County teams. "We've won so many games in nine years, there are a lot of teams in our league who have never beaten Caledonia. The big streak isn't there to be knocked off, but the 'maybe this year we can beat Caledonia' will still be there."

Good Livingston County teams joined good Finger Lakes teams and even a few good Monroe County teams as Cal-Mum's sectional playoff opponents in these years.

Avon, Livonia and LeRoy were often there in either the semifinals or finals. The Red Jacket Indians, from Shortsville in Ontario County, proved to be a difficult adversary in McAlee's late years, defeating the Red Raiders twice in a row in 1984 and 1985. Success against the Indians came only in the Monacelli era, with big wins for Cal-Mum in consecutive years in 1994 and 1995.

One team that provided no competition for Cal-Mum, perhaps because they'd already beaten the Red Raiders in the game that counted most, was Notre Dame of Batavia. The Raiders blew out the Little Irish by scores of 35-0 in 1982, 40-0 in 1983 and 19-0 in 1984, and won a deceptively one-sided game 20-14 in 1985. The two teams would play occasionally in the Monacelli era, but even then the games weren't anywhere near competitive, with Cal-Mum winning all three games by a cumulative point total of 122-24.

Did it all amount to sufficient revenge? The 1982 victory did, at least as starting quarterback Tom Ball saw it. "I've been thinking about this game since June," he said after the victory. "I've never seen enthusiasm on a team like there is on this one. This was unbelievable."

WHAT MADE the 1982 schedule so interesting was that LeRoy was so good. Imagine how much more interesting 1982 would have been had the following alternate history come to pass.

Cal-Mum defeats Notre Dame at Van Detta Stadium in November 1981, then continues its winning ways through the sectional tournament. The 1982 LeRoy game is scheduled third. In our alternate reality, Cal-Mum enters that game with 53 wins in a row, two shy of the all-time New York State record. LeRoy is a Livingston County powerhouse in 1982, clearly Frank Ruane's best team in years. Imagine how much more pumped up the Oatkan Knights are coming onto Hamilton Field with the opportunity to end The Great Streak at 53.

Would LeRoy win 34-14, as it did in reality that third game of the year?* Would the Oatkan Knights triumph 29-6 as they did in the sectional semifinal game? Or would the game have been even more of a blowout with LeRoy having so much more incentive? Finally, imagine the angst of those Monday Morning Quarterbacks at the Moonwinks and Cozy Kitchen with the streak now ended—and ended by them!

---

*The day after the game, about 60 people showed up at the Caledonia monument, not to cheer on the football team but rather to watch Dennis Cohen of Caledonia push Marlene Perkins of LeRoy around the monument in a wheelbarrow. Cohen had lost his bet on the previous night's game to Perkins, and had to pay up with the wheelbarrow ride. He wisely obeyed all traffic regulations as he gave Perkins her "victory lap."

One pleasant surprise in 1982, and again in 1983, was Cal-Mum's passing attack, usually a non-factor in previous years under McAlee. The new found aerial success was primarily a result of quarterback Tom Ball's talents. "When you've got a kid who can pitch the ball like Tommy Ball, I guess you've got to adjust your thinking," McAlee said with a laugh after his quarterback completed 13 passes for 149 yards and two touchdowns against Notre Dame in the 1982 season opener. In 1983, Ball threw for a Red Raider record 14 touchdown passes, an accomplishment that would have been unheard of during the smash-mouth years of the previous decade.*

Just as important were the receivers. They were tall, fast boys who, again, were not of the same mold as Raider players from previous years. The leader of the pack was Don Wade, an All-Greater Rochester selection in 1983. Wade caught a total of 27 passes for 468 yards and 10 touchdowns that year. Ball and Wade led Cal-Mum to a very impressive 16-3 combined record in 1982 and 1983. In 1983, the Raiders scored a total of 271 points, the most since the final streak year of 1980 and the most until the sectional championship year of 1987. Unfortunately, the sectional runs of 1982 and 1983 fell short, first to LeRoy and then to Avon.

CAL-MUM RETURNED to its traditional run-first attack in 1984, not so much due to a talent shortage at quarterback and end as due to the presence of another Poles, this time Roland, the youngest of the three brothers to don the maroon and white.

Roland was already a force to be reckoned with in 1983, his sophomore year, contributing the necessary yin to the passing attack's yang. He could score from the one- or two-yard line by going hard up the middle or even over the top. He could turn the corner and outrun the entire defense for a 50-yard touchdown. He could block a rushing linebacker, thereby supplying Ball, and later Russ Loughry, necessary protection to find the open receiver. He could catch the ball out of the backfield, too, on a quick out or while squeezing through the middle. However you got him the ball, you could guarantee that it would usually take more than one defender to bring him down. On more than one occasion Roland Poles carried the ball for several more yards after first contact, sometimes with a struggling defender holding onto his ankle or clinging to his shoulder pad. In 1983, as a sophomore, Poles ran for 153 yards

---

*One day in the summer of 1982, I was riding my bike around the school property when Tom Ball called me over to play catch. For the rest of that summer and the next I would join him on Hamilton Field, running routes and trying to catch his blistering ten-yard outs and fifty-yard bombs. All this off-season work was an investment with diminishing returns—I had the only catch of my Red Raider career against Honeoye Falls-Lima in 1985 for a two-point conversion. Still, I will never forget the thrill of being an eighth- and ninth-grader playing catch with one of Cal-Mum's best.

against Notre Dame of Batavia, 94 against LeRoy, 164 against Honeoye Falls-Lima and 97 against Avon.

How did Roland stack up to his brothers? Said McAlee, "the baby brother takes the brunt of the pressure from older brothers, the father and the uncles who were all good players. Roland gets pressure, but he does a great job handling it."

"They have given me incentive," Roland himself said about his brothers. "Ever since I was small I have had speed…because Ronnie would chase me around the yard."

McAlee continues his comparison: "Junior was a peach of a kid. He was just a super person. And Ron was a producer. When he knew he had to do something he did it. I think Roland is a mixture of the two."

Roland heard the comparisons all through high school. "You're not quite as good as your brother," people around town would tell him, most often referring to the other runner in the family, Ronnie. "But then sometimes Ronnie says, 'you look like me.'" Roland admitted. "That means a lot to me."

All the pressure, all the comparisons, all the hype—Roland was able to channel the good and the bad to become the clear leader of the 1985 team that I also played on. "He's the leader," McAlee affirmed. "He's the first Poles who had to assume that leadership role. The other two were good kids, but they never assumed that role. Roland took it. We're only going to be as good as he's going to be."

If family was the first key to Roland's success, faith was a close second. "People said I wouldn't graduate," Roland said, referring to a reading handicap that he struggled with during all his years of school, "but I kept my eye on the Lord and here I am, graduating!"[*] His faith taught him humility, a difficult lesson perhaps for someone with so much strength, so many skills. "If it wasn't for the Lord, I'd have a big head and do stupid things." His faith also taught him the way of peace, which, as his older brothers also discovered, sometimes comes in conflict with what's demanded of a football player while on the field. "During the game I get very emotional. But after the game I'm best friends with everybody. I want to be remembered as a nice, peaceful person who liked everybody."

Roland's faith also taught him perhaps the most important lesson of all, to treat others as you would have others treat you. "People ask me, 'how can you like that person? He's low class.' I tell them, 'that's the way the Lord made me.'" And I can

---

[*] I played a small auxiliary role in this particular accomplishment. During our senior year, twice a week, I would tutor Roland in reading and in math. In all my years as a student and a teacher, I've seen few people work harder or commit themselves more than Roland did in his effort to graduate that year.

see in my mind's eye Roland's ear-to-ear smile as he shares his life philosophy, a way of life that we would all do well to emulate.

One major difference between Roland and his older brothers—a difference that I and several other teammates shared—was that he won neither a sectional championship nor a state title. This shortcoming was no fault of Roland's. As Coach McAlee said about the 1985 team, "we're only going to be as good as he's going to be." Few us even approached Roland's skill level. His running and linebacking mate Chris Falgenhauer came closest to Roland in the talent department. Ken Moyer, our 5'10", 210 pound center, came closest in size to Roland's 6'2", 220 pound frame. Despite his teammates' shortcomings, Roland still had some tremendous games during his three years in the Red Raider spotlight. His most memorable games were also Cal-Mum's most memorable games during those years. It should come as no surprise that they were against Avon and LeRoy.

The first came in Avon in 1983. Poles scored the first touchdown of the game from the two-yard line, but Avon came storming back to hold a 19-7 lead with six minutes to go in the fourth quarter. On fourth down at the Avon 11, Tom Ball threw a touchdown pass to Don Wade. A successful conversion made the score 19-14. Cal-Mum got the ball back on a fumble at the Avon 30. On another fourth down at the Avon 11, Tom Ball threw another touchdown pass, this time to Poles, who had run a delayed pattern out of the backfield. He got the first down with the catch, but had to bull his way into the end zone over two Avon defenders for the score. "I wasn't taking any chances," Poles said. "I wanted to win that game." Poles also recognized kicker Paul Hanna, whose three extra points were the difference in the two-point victory. In all, Poles ran the ball 21 times for 97 yards, caught two passes for 14 yards and scored two touchdowns. The Braves got their revenge a month later, however, by defeating Cal-Mum 27-0 at Fauver Stadium for the Section V Class B title.

The 1984 game against Avon is known in the annals of both teams' histories as the "fog game." Avon led 6-0 at halftime, when the fog started to descend upon Hamilton Field. By the time the fourth quarter started, the players on the field were practically invisible to the fans, and to the coaches, players and cheerleaders on the sidelines. Even the officiating crew had trouble keeping track of such basic plays as offsides and pass interference. Poles had a good game on the ground, rushing for 81 yards on 17 carries. He also contributed to the late touchdown drive that gave Cal-Mum the win. And on the winning touchdown, Poles went right, following his linemen, but quarterback Russ Loughry threw left to a wide open Andy Wilcox, the only player on either team on that side of the field. As McAlee wrote in his Caledonia *Advertiser* weekly summary, "If you stayed home you missed a great game between two fine high school football teams. If you left early you failed to see a well-organized

74-yard TD march for the game winner. If you stayed you may not have seen the game winner anyway."

The 1985 season witnessed three classic Poles games. He rushed for 139 yards on 31 carries in the first game against Avon that year. On one of those runs, it took four Avon defenders to push Poles out of bounds—and right into Coach McAlee. "That's the first time that's happened to me in 26 years of football," McAlee said after the game. He ended up with a bruised shoulder and broken glasses, but also with a 7-0 victory after Tony Cicoria took the ball in for a score on a one-yard run. That was a bruising game, with Cal-Mum gaining 272 total yards on the ground and Avon only 70.[*]

For Poles, however, the next game against Avon in the sectional playoffs was even more memorable, although for a totally unexpected reason. He ran the ball 24 times for 84 yards, but did not score a touchdown. Nor did he even factor into any scoring drives: Cal-Mum got its touchdown on the opening kickoff when Ray Dearcop ran the ball 95 yards for the only score of the game. Where Poles excelled against Avon this time was on defense. He played linebacker, and twice he literally denied the Braves touchdowns. The first time was with 30 seconds left in the first half. Avon had the ball on the one-yard line on a fourth-and-goal. They ran the ball up the middle, but Poles was there, hitting the runner, knocking the ball free, and falling on it to protect the Red Raider lead. Amazingly, he did the same exact thing in the third quarter, also at the one-yard line, also on fourth-and-goal. Cal-Mum held on to win 6-0.[**] Poles' defensive performance was phenomenal that night. Few Raider fans had ever seen anything like it.

The other big game for Poles that year, for all of us, was the LeRoy game. I and several other players taped, "REMEMBER 33-6" on our helmets, referring to the 1984 drubbing the Oatkan Knights dished out and echoing the great battle cry of the 1973 team. I already related the story of the 1932 nickel. We were pumped up for this game, but by Wednesday of that week we were also having a lot of fun, in large part

---

[*] I got beat up pretty badly in that game. Although I didn't realize it at the time, I probably had a concussion, which would explain why I was seeing double the next morning. A concussion would also explain why I ran my father's 1978 Mercury Cougar, with it's powerful 358 Windsor engine, into the garage while trying to back it out of the driveway. Neither players nor coaches knew nearly as much about concussions then as they do today. Coach Mike Monacelli is even something of an expert on the topic, and was invited to testify on concussion management for student athletes before the United States House of Representatives Committee on Education and Labor in May 2010.

[**] An argument against McAlee running up the score comes from this game. Cal-Mum marched down the field after Poles' second great defensive play, and had the ball first-and-goal on the one-yard line with the clock running out. Instead of calling time and trying one more play—Poles up the middle perhaps—McAlee let the clock run out.

thanks to Roland's upbeat and supremely confident attitude. We were, in a word, ready.

I still have the game on video. Watching it, I'm astounded at how small the rest of us, on both sides of the ball, seem compared to Roland. I'm impressed by how quickly he was able to burst through the line of scrimmage, or able to round the corner and outrun opposing defenders and his teammates alike. Roland scored touchdowns of 70, 16 and 69* yards. He ran for a total of 297 yards on 24 carries. He almost reached the Section V single game rushing record of 312 yards, at that time held by Wayne McMillan of Corning East. More importantly for Roland, he performed at the peak of his abilities before his entire family, who was there at Hartwood Park to support him against Cal-Mum's perennial gridiron enemy. So many Red Raider players have said about so many other games the same thing I'll write about this one—the victory over LeRoy was the most fulfilling athletic experience I've had in my life.

Unfortunately, we lost 6-0 to Red Jacket in the Section V Class B championship game at Fauver Stadium that year. Why? The Indians simply stopped Roland Poles. They stopped him from breaking through the line of scrimmage all game. They stopped him on fourth down at the Red Jacket 5-yard line with under a minute to play. They didn't have to stop the rest of us—they only had to stop Roland, something no other team had been able to do all year. But the rest of us knew we'd achieved something great just by getting to that championship game. It was with this deep sense of accomplishment and pride that we broke out in song as the bus pulled out of the University of Rochester campus. We sang, "Caledonia, hear us praise thee, all hail to thy dear name…"

THERE WAS ONE other great success that year along with the victories over Avon and LeRoy. On Friday, October 18, 1985, at Hamilton Field against Dansville, Coach Bill McAlee won his one-hundredth game as coach of the Red Raiders. I wrote the following poem to honor Coach McAlee, which I read at the pep rally the afternoon before the game and which McAlee included in his post-game Caledonia *Advertiser* recap:

---

*After this touchdown, and with my orange sweatshirt clearly visible, I came sliding into the end zone on both knees, Pete Townshend-like, then sprung up off the ground and gave Roland a big hug. I vaguely remembered doing this until I watched the game video while writing this book. My wife was completely embarrassed to see such behavior (she and Frank Ruane would've gotten along well!) and my son, then nine years old, was quite awestruck until I explained that no, I could absolutely not do that slide again, right now, out on the front lawn.

> It was in 1973 when it all began
> the Raiders needed a coach and Mac was their man.
> He came along with high hopes of winning
> And Dansville was the team he first sent spinning.
> Week after week the Raiders put on a show
> To finish with a record of 8-0.
> Season after season the scene was repeated
> It was a rare occasion when Cal-Mum was defeated.
> The cheerleaders and fans supported us great
> with their help we won 49 straight.
> During this time four state titles were won.
> The victories were many and the losses were none.
> After the Streak Cal-Mum was still tough.
> We played some great games, but few had enough.
> Number one hundred will not be the last.
> A Section V title is coming up fast.
> So thanks so much Mac We owe you some more
> You're the best damn coach a team could ask for.

Cal-Mum won the game 26-0, with Poles and Chris Felgenhauer each scoring two touchdowns.*

After the game, we celebrated the triumph as a team, but the real celebration came the following week at halftime against Marshall. McAlee received numerous gifts, including a letter from Governor Mario Cuomo, a 100-victory sign made by Pardi Foam Products, various plaques and scrolls from the school and other local organizations, and 100 silver dollars donated by Chase Lincoln First Bank. A total of 26 representatives from McAlee's previous teams were there, and joined the entire 1985 team to shake Coach McAlee's hand and offer him our congratulations. It was a momentous occasion celebrating not just a man but an entire community's accomplishments over the years.

---

*My mother, Betty Jane Pullyblank, was thrilled by all the attention Cal-Mum got during the week before the game. The team, she wrote in a letter to the Caledonia *Advertiser*, "was chosen by WOKR, Channel 13 to be the 'team of the week.' What excitement!! The students' had one of the best pep rally's ever held at the school; everyone was looking for something maroon and white to wear to school on Thursday. The coverage by the news media was great… To Coach McAlee, Coach Matthews, their families and to all the young men of our community who played a part in attaining this great accomplishment of 100 wins since 1973, congratulations!! Caledonia can be very proud."

But McAlee was focused. What was the gift he really wanted, he asked the team in the end zone when all the festivities had come to an end? A victory that night over Marshall, which the Red Raiders duly provided, 21-8. What was the gift he really, really wanted, he asked us again in the locker room after the game? A victory over LeRoy next Friday night. We listened, and we obliged.

I HAD MENTIONED in my poem that "a Section V title is coming up fast." It didn't come in 1985, nor in 1986. It did happen in 1987, however, which was, appropriately and by his own design, McAlee's last year as coach. Also appropriately, the road to the Section V championship went through Cal-Mum's usual rivals, the Braves of Avon* and the Oatkan Knights of LeRoy. Cal-Mum won both regular season battles, 19-0 against Avon and 20-14 against LeRoy. Running backs Tony Cicoria and Stuart Edwards starred for the Raiders on offense, while linebacker Mike Edwards, Stuart's older brother and an All-Greater Rochester selection, anchored the tough defense. In the sectionals, Cal-Mum again beat LeRoy, this time by a 28-7 score. Stuart Edwards scored three touchdowns in that game, and Cicoria ran for a total of 149 yards. The victory was McAlee's last game on Hamilton Field. Next up for the Red Raiders was Avon.

For once, McAlee was not ready. "It was tough today," he said. "It was a terrible day because I wasn't in control of myself. I was thinking back to all the things—the good things—that had happened over the years." McAlee had delegated some of the emotional responsibility for the game onto his players. "I told them that last week [against LeRoy] was my game and this one was theirs," he said.

The team was there for him when he needed them. "Everyone said there was no way we wanted to lose that last one," Tony Cicoria said. "There would be no way we could come back and enjoy ourselves every year if he had lost that last one."

They played well for McAlee. Trent Morris ran back an interception 37 yards for a touchdown in the first quarter, and Todd Marble hit Stuart Edwards for a 27-yard score to put the Raiders up 14-0 at the half. Avon came back to make the game 14-11, but Cal-Mum was in control and was not about to let go. Cicoria scored his eighteenth touchdown of the season to give the Raiders a 21-11 lead. The score would

---

*The three games against Avon in 1986 were three of the strangest games in Cal-Mum football history. The first game was won by the Braves 10-0. The second, a sectional playoff game, ended in a 0-0 tie. The third, the Section V Class B championship game, was also won by Avon, 7-0. Thus, Cal-Mum was 0-2-1 against Avon that year, with 0 points scored and 17 points scored against.

hold until the clock ran down to triple zeros. Cicoria was named Most Valuable Player for the game, and immediately handed the trophy to McAlee.

"Coach has been a friend for me," Cicoria said after the game and after the awards had been presented. "It meant a lot playing for him for four years."

Cicoria's sentiments were shared by dozens of us who wore the maroon and white during the McAlee era, dozens of us whose lives were made better by having him as our coach.

1) The 1928 undefeated, untied team is often lost in the shadow cast by the legendary 1929 team. The 1928 Red Raiders were certainly part of something great: the 22-game winning had started with the last game of 1927 and continued all through 1928, and the 13-game shutout streak started with the last game of the 1928 season. The 1928 defense allowed only three touchdowns all year. Row one, L to R: Chet Hardman, Jimmy Jackson, Eddie Davis, Pete MacPherson, Roy MacDonald, Charles Carson, John Harvey. Row Two, L to R: Coach MacPherson, Ronnie Wilson, Everett Youngs, Carl Gibson, Bob Johnson, Gene Pullyblank, Earl Stone, Prof. Vanzile.

2) The 1929 team, undefeated, untied, and unscored-upon, set the standard of excellence for Red Raiders football for years to come. The perfection they achieved in every category of gridiron accomplishment makes them, in our collective memory, boys who were something greater than men. They alone made wearing the maroon and white a privilege for all of us boys who followed them. Row one, L to R: Ed Coots, Arlie Burkhart, Earl Stone, Jim Jackson, Ed Davis, Bob Johnson, Bill Miller, Tony Angelo. Row two, L to R: Coach Matthews, Pete MacPherson, Charles Carson, Ronnie Wilson, Gene Pullyblank, Felix Balonek, Dunc Cameron, Roy MacDonald, Preston Sinsanick, Mason Ashford, Prof. Vanzile, George Ball. Row three, L to R: Stuart Griffin, Chet Hardman, Bill Jackson, Bob Freeman, Jack Skivington, Stuart Grant.

3) The 1932 offense scored a remarkable 43 points against a larger, stronger Aquinas Institute Little Irish team. Jim Jackson (right) was the star of the game with 5 touchdowns, but was ineligible for Caledonia's Livingston County contests because he had already played 4 years of football. No matter—his performance against Aquinas on that October afternoon is still talked about eighty years later. RE: Kenny Alexander, RT: Tony Angelo, RG: Dalton Vokes, G: Felix Balonek, C: Stuart Grant, LG: Ram Cameron, LE: Arthur George, RHB: Eugene Kingsbury, LHB: Stan King, QB: Eddie Coots, FB: Bob Freeman.

4) "Bulldog" Bob Freeman scores a touchdown against Aquinas in 1932. Freeman broke his leg later in the game and missed the remainder of his senior season. Freeman would return to coach the Red Raiders from 1939-1941 and then, after serving in World War II, from 1945-1956.

5) Stan King scores a touchdown against Aquinas in the 1932 43-6 Red Raider victory. In 1933, Caledonia and Aquinas would tie, 7-7. The teams never played again, but later often traveled the same road through the Section V and New York State playoffs and onto the Carrier Dome for the State championship game.

6) In 1932, LeRoy handed Caledonia its only loss of the season, 18-7. It was the last time the teams would play until 1948. It was hardly the last time that one team would deal the other its only loss of the season. Now that's the stuff great rivalries are made of.

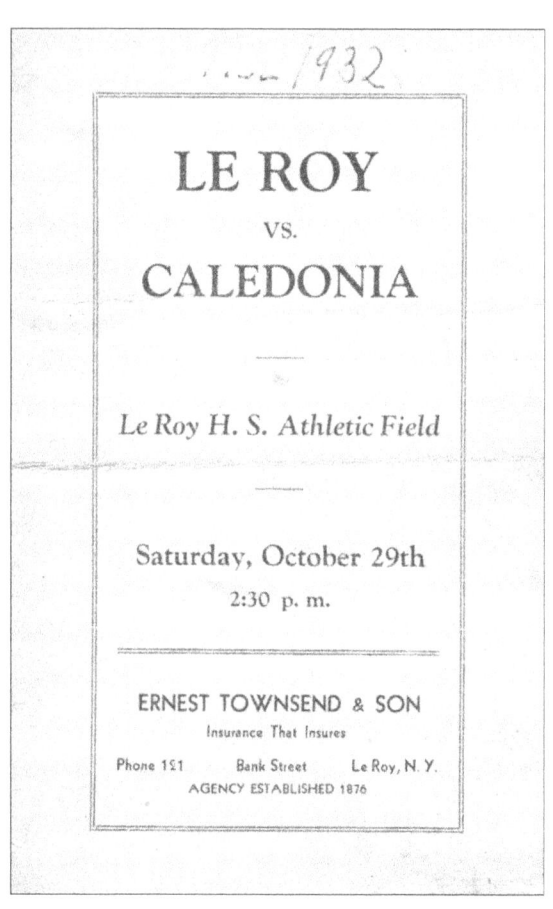

7) The 1947 undefeated, untied team under Coach Freeman's leadership scored an impressive 239 points. The defense allowed only 33 points, and never more than a touchdown per game. James R. Smith (Captain), Robert Washburn, William Donegan, Tony Bartalo, Laverne Thompson, Robert Steedman, James Hank, Leslie Callan, Stewart Campbell, Charles Waters, Richard McKay, Edward Keenan, William Goodburlet, Murray Cohen, Robert Sickles, Ronald Greene, Joe Fagan, Gerald Callan, Gene Mooney, Howard Nelson, Dean Fisher, Manager Buster Brown, Mr. Freeman, Head Coach; Mr. Eaton, Assistant; Harrison Brown, Manager; Robert McKay, Assistant Manager (note: roster incomplete, list of names does not correspond to team photo).

8) The 1950 undefeated, untied team, known for the first time as the Caledonia-Mumford Red Raiders, was the first to play under the lights at Hamilton Field. The big game was a 31-6 thrashing of LeRoy to close the season. Row one, L to R: George Henry, Richard Wall, John Vink, Robert Darling, Gary Hone, Anthony Coppini, Tom Shaughnessy, Richard Cullinan, Philip D'Angelo, Gerald Swanger. Row two, L to R: Robert Minster, Anthony Merola, Loren Geer, Ralph King, Harold Sickles, Peter Coppini (Captain), Howard Nelson, Dean Fisher, Ira Geer, Richard Sisson. Row three, L to R: Mr. Martin, Assistant Coach; Mr. Vail, Assistant Coach; James Walker, Donald Smith, Donald Pullyblank, Truman Clements, Robert Sheffer, Thomas Robinson, Lawrence Bonacquisti, Robert Beyer, John Ball, Mr. Freeman, Coach. Row four, L to R: James Wall, John Poles, Robert Pullyblank, Everett Vail, Melvin Nelson, Joseph Tallo, Victor Cappotelli, Francis Fisher, David Cargill, Richard Fagan, Clement King.

9) A program from the first night game with lights at Hamilton Field. The Caledonia *Advertiser* explained that "eight poles carrying 6 lights each have been put into place, and now 72-thousand watt power will illuminate the field. The job was done by the Embling Electric Company of Batavia, they being the lowest bidder. The cost is $9,950."

10) A ticket for the 1950 season finale against LeRoy. Cal-Mum won the game 31-6. to end the season undefeated and untied. As you can see, the Red Raiders had already clinched the Livingston County Championship, the team's fourth in a row.

11) The undefeated, untied team from 1954. Once again, the Red Raiders allowed no more than one touchdown per game. Once again, the Red Raiders ended the season with a victory over LeRoy. Row one, L to R: Robert Hanna, Lawrence Loomis, Richard Mack, William McQuilken, Richard Fisher, Michael MacDonald, Stanley Latko, Allan Sickles, Assistant Manager William McKernan. Row two, L to R: Manager Donald Hobbs, Peter Coureen, John Keenan, Mark Robinson, Archie Cappotelli, Roger Hill, Harold Connor, Charles Daniels, James Vokes, David McKay, Robert Loomis, Gordon Henry, David Connor (Captain). Row three, L to R: Assistant Coach Collins, Mr. Eaton, Trainer, Frank Ianiro, Joseph Latko, Richard Feeley, Jon King, Bernard Babcock, Paul Janowski, Maurice Hill, Gerald Majors. Row four, L to R: Albert Blaker, James Jackson, Donald Robertson, Albert Poles, Louis Ward, Richard Wilkins, Arthur Kretschmer, Bernard Fagan, Thomas Brew, Washington Williams, Coach Freeman.

12) The 1971 team, complete with appropriate haircuts and (mostly) good posture. Coach Ruane's sometimes severe discipline attempted to mold these boys into men at a time when the winds of change were blowing in the opposite direction. The results were predictable: a 4-4 record and an embarrassing 32-0 end-of-season loss to LeRoy, which was followed by an even more embarrassing 48-0 loss to LeRoy in the final game of the 1972 season. Ruane, who claimed that he left Cal-Mum with no hard feelings on either side, began coaching LeRoy in 1975. For a quick lesson on how quickly and dramatically a team's mood can change, compare this team picture with those of 1973 and 1974.

13) The 1973 undefeated, untied team, Coach McAlee's first, is acknowledged by many as the greatest Red Raider football team ever. Outscoring its opponents 389-67, it was the rod against which all later Cal-Mum teams are measured. Row one, L to R: Manager Donald Cameron, James Harrington, Charles O'Donnell, Robert Perhamus, Richard Brown, Joseph Rapone, Thomas Lauffer, Michael Pullyblank, Steve Kissell, Manager Paul Mooney. Row two, L to R: Robert Poles, Ronald Beach, Timothy Harrington, Randy Grattan, Gary Mattice, Thomas Sullivan, Timothy Nothnagle, Robert Freeman, Paul Day, Manager Steve Pullyblank. Row three, L to R: Coach Edward Matthews, Timothy Lauffer, Edward Peet, Robert Chiverton (Captain), Donald Carpenter, Mark Reid (Captain), Michael Tucci, Thomas Cook, Charles VanGorder, Jonathan Barnes, Coach William McAlee. Row four, L to R: Coach Ted Tackaberry, James Craw, Timothy Balonek, David Mancuso, Clifford Anderson, Christopher Batzing, Steve Cameron, Scott Weitzel, Kevin Geer, Donald MacIntyre, Coach Roger House.

14) The 1974 undefeated, untied team continued right where the 1973 team left off, shellacking its first 7 opponents by an average score of 39-2. The highlight of the season, however, was the 22-14 victory over LeRoy, the "undefeated underdog," at Hamilton Field to end the season. The win would remain one of the most memorable victories in Cal-Mum football history. Row one, L to R: Chris Wyatt, Ron Grant, Joe Rapone, Tom Shaughnessy, Jim Freeman, T.R. Harmon, Terry Nothnagle, Jim Sackett, Tom Lauffer. Row two, L to R: Don Carpenter (Captain), Frank Saeva, Mike Tucci (Captain), Rich Brown, Don MacIntyre, Steve Kissel, Ron Beach, Ron Grattan (Captain), Gary Mattice, Tom Cook, Steve Cameron. Row three, L to R: Jim Craw, Kevin Geer, Mike Kelley, Dave Mancuso, Chris Batzing, Scott Weitzel, Ken Troyer, Duaine Priestly, Toby Weitzel. Row four, L to R: Mike Pullyblank, Steve Krenzer, Jim Harrington, John Garnes, Jim Goodburlet, Mark Seefried, Mark Rothrock, Don Miller, Mike Mooney, Chip Day, Rob Perhamus.

15) Coach McAlee was always teaching, both on the field and off. Here he is giving instructions to his quarterbacks, Mike Pullyblank in 1974 and Chris Wyatt in 1977. But it could have just as easily been Mark McGrath in 1978, Kevin Zimmer in 1980, Tom Ball in 1983, or Matt Taylor and Tim Henry in 1985. McAlee understood football as an extension of the classroom of life. His philosophy that winning wasn't everything made winning easier, and made playing the game that much more fun.

Coach McAlee also loved to play football. Those of us who had the good fortune of taking the field with him knew he could split the uprights from 35 yards and could pass block with the best of them.

16) The undefeated, untied 1977 team was the first to be voted the #1 small school football team in New York State. En route to earning that honor, the 1977 Red Raiders defeated LeRoy 19-0 in a battle of the unbeatens on Friday, October 28 at Hartwood Park. LeRoy was the #1 small school football team in New York State going into the game. It would remain Coach McAlee's most memorable victory. Row one, L to R: Chris Ennis, Paul Toland, Justin Randall, Paul Mooney, Larry Anderson, Scott Fisher, John Freeman, Bill Clements, Frank Fisher, Jeff D'Angelo, Pat Randall. Row two, L to R: Mark Meyer, Tom Warters, Mark Seefried, Steve Pullyblank, Chris Wyatt (Captain), Jeff Sweet (Captain), Bill Donegan, Pat Harrigan, Steve Burger, Jim Wood, Dave Krenzer, Bob Loomis, Terry Donegan. Row three, L to R: Dan Keenan, James Pullyblank, Steve Sickles, Bob Cesare, Dick Thomas, Tom Matthews, Mark Callan, Dale Wyone, Junior Poles, Steve Balonek, Dave Trojanski, Mark Pullyblank, Rick Riggi, Kevin O'Dell, Doug Nothnagle, Dave Nailos, Dave Reeves.

17) The undefeated, untied 1978 team was the first Red Raider team to win an on-the-field Section V championship game, beating Lyons 42-0 at Fauver Stadium on the University of Rochester campus. That victory was the last game in a Red Raider uniform for Robert "Junior" Poles, who played varsity from his freshman year in 1975. Recruited heavily by several major college programs, Poles chose to play for the Boston College Golden Eagles on a full athletic scholarship. He was then drafted by the Seattle Seahawks in 1983. Many fans consider Junior the greatest player to ever wear the maroon and white. Row one, L to R: Terry Donegan, Tom Ball, Paul Toland, Justin Randall, Billy Clements, Frank Fisher, Jeff D'Angelo, Chris Ennis, Paul Mooney, Pat Randall, Mark Callan, Steve Riggi, Jimmy Grant, Danny Keenan. Row two, L to R: Billy Dollard, Steve Balonek, Robert Poles, Jr. David Trojanski (Captain), Doug Nothnagle, Dave Nailos, Bob Cesare, Richard Thomas, Dale Wynne, Rick Riggi, Pat Shaughnessy, Kevin O'Dell. Row three, L to R: Mark Stella, Doug Clements, Tim Grant, Bob SinClair, Ron Poles, Mark McGrath, Bill Bernard, Chris O'Dell, Charlie Sisson. Row four, L to R: Roger House assistant coach, Jim Pike, Dan Romano, John Freeman, Brian Robinson, Adam Wightman, Richard Shelton, Larry Anderson, Richard Bierbrauer, Ed Matthews assistant coach, Bill McAlee head coach.

18) Ed "Banjo" Coots was for years the living embodiment of Cal-Mum Red Raiders football. The last living member of the legendary 1929 team, Coots worked the sideline chains at Hamilton Field and for other important Red Raider games, including the 1978 Section V Class B championship game. The chain gang badge was a mere formality, because we all knew who he was and would welcome him onto the field at any time. Banjo left us for that great gridiron in the sky in May 1999.

19) The official program from the 1978 Section V Class B championship game, which Cal-Mum won 42-0. This was the first playoff game ever in Cal-Mum Red Raiders football history. It was certainly not the last.

20) The undefeated, untied 1979 team barely squeaked by Clyde-Savannah in overtime to win Cal-Mum's second Section V championship in a row. 1979 was the heyday of The Great Streak, when nothing, it seemed, could go wrong for the Red Raiders. Row one, L to R: Steve Grant, Roger House, Mark Sickles, Mickey Cappotelli, Steve Carpino, Michael Keenan, Leonard Hall, Daniel Parnell, Gregory D'Amico, Jim Grant. Row two, L to R: Charles Sisson, Douglas Clements, Mark Stella, Richard Shelton, Larry Anderson, John Freeman (Captain), Mark McGrath (Captain), Dan Romano, Terry McGinnis, Richard Bierbrauer, Brian Robinson, Steve Riggi. Row three, L to R: Tom Ball, Mike Grattan, Chris O'Dell, Scott Saunders, Brian Phillips, Tim Grant, Mike Connelie, Bill Bernard, Bob Sinclair, Joe Gustainis, Larry Riggi. Row four, L to R: Jim Laubach, Tom Pierce, Dwayne Wynne, Adam Wightman, Eric Sheffer, Scott Favreau, Tim MacDonald.

21) The 1980 team was the first Cal-Mum Red Raider squad to win 10 games and the last undefeated, untied team of the McAlee era. The 1980 team gave its fans plenty of thrilling moments, including a defensive goal line stand to win the opening game of the year against Albion and a last minute touchdown run by Ron Poles to win the Section V Class B championship game against LeRoy at Holledar Stadium in Rochester. Row one, L to R: Gary Heuer, Scott Saunders, Mike Keenan, Tim MacDonald, Ron Poles (Captain), Steve Carpino, Adam Wightman, Bob Sinclair, Bill Bernard (Captain), Brian Phillips, Mark Sickles, Craig Chadderdon, Steve Grant. Row two, L to R: Mike Gratten, Bill Day, Jim Pullyblank, Kevin Zimmer, Joe Gustainis, Richard Goodburlet, Jim Laudbach, Eric Sheffer, Greg D'Amico, Len Hall, Roger House, Francis Krenzer, Doug Grant. Row three, L to R: Larry Riggi, Colin MacKay, David Reeves, Andy Hodge, John Limner, Dwayne Wynne, Tom Pearse, Bob Clements, Brian Bowers, Dan Parnell, Scott Moran, Jerome Phillips, Barry Robinson.

22) Roger House (left) and Ed Matthews (right) were just as responsible for Cal-Mum's success during The Great Streak as Bill McAlee (center) was. Together, the three coaches taught all of us who played under them as much about life as about football.

23) (opposite page) A collection of scenes from the Soldiers' Monument, taken on Friday, November 14, 1980, after Cal-Mum defeated LeRoy 26-21 to win the Section V Class B championship at Holledar Stadium in Rochester. Post-game meetings at the monument became a Red Raider tradition in the early 1970s. None was as raucous as this one. Top left: The monument with a number one finger made by Sam DiLaberto's Pardi Foam Products and put in place by town highway superintendent George Kelly. Top right: Bob "Voice of the Raiders" Pullyblank and Hooks Robertson watch the team arrive. The bus was given an escort by Wheatland town and Caledonia village police cars and fire trucks. Bottom right: Bob Pullyblank and Jake Davis welcome the manager's bus. In the window are Tom Pullyblank, Scott McAlee and Doug Grant. Bottom left: Ed Coots and Bob Pullyblank bought a thank you ad in the following week's Caledonia Advertiser. "Welcome to Number One Country!" was Pullyblank's signature line as he opened each game as Hamilton Field's public address announcer.

24) From 1973-1985, Betty Jane Pullyblank made dozens of cookies like these, which she delivered to the school a few hours before each game. Great coaching, strong tradition, tough farm boys, the fluoride in the water—you can add my mother's cookies to the list of reasons why Cal-Mum football was so successful during the McAlee years.

To: All of Cal-Mum Raider Football Fans
Thanks to all who made Friday night one we will never forget.
Your kind words and generosity are greatly appreciated.
It's great to be a part of No. 1 COUNTRY!

ED COOTS   BOB PULLYBLANK

Annual Dinner

Honoring

Caledonia-Mumford Central School

FOOTBALL SQUAD

1954 LIV. COUNTY CHAMPIONS

Sponsored by

CALEDONIA HOOK & LADDER CO.

Monday, Nov. 15, 1954

★ ★

Caledonia	26	York	6
Caledonia	13	Mt. Morris	6
Caledonia	26	Geneseo	7
Caledonia	22	Dansville	7
Caledonia	21	Livonia	6
Caledonia	27	Avon	6
Caledonia	20	Le Roy	0
Totals	155		38

42nd ANNUAL

FOOTBALL BANQUET

SATURDAY, NOVEMBER 21, 1987
7:00 p.m.

"THE END OF AN ERA"

"THE McALEE REGIME"

"Thanks For The Memories"

25) A selection of programs and tickets from the annual football banquet, sponsored by the fire department. The 66th annual dinner was held in 2011. Since 1985, new inductees to the Cal-Mum Red Raiders football Hall of Fame are also announced at the banquet. A complete list of inductees can be found in Appendix F. 1987 was Coach McAlee's last year as coach of the Red Raiders. Fittingly, he went out in style, winning the Section V Class B championship.

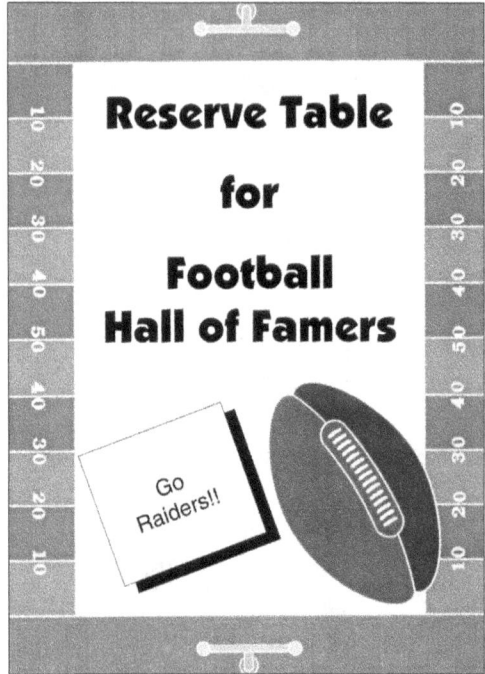

50th ANNUAL DINNER

HONORING

CALEDONIA-MUMFORD CENTRAL SCHOOL

FOOTBALL SQUAD &

Former Red Raider Captains

SPONSORED BY
CALEDONIA HOOK & LADDER, BIG SPRINGS PUMPER CO.,
& LADIES AUXILIARY OF CALEDONIA FIRE DEPT., INC.

SUNDAY, DECEMBER 3, 1995
2:00 P.M.
J.W. JONES HALL

VARSITY

CAL-MUM	45	ELBA	19
CAL-MUM	30	DANSVILLE	0
CAL-MUM	20	LEROY	6
CAL-MUM	43	NOTRE DAME	6
CAL-MUM	29	ATTICA	0
CAL-MUM	49	HF-L	7
CAL-MUM	51	LIVONIA	8

SECTIONALS CLASS DD

CAL-MUM	27	YORK	6
CAL-MUM	50	CLYDE	0
CAL-MUM	33	RED JACKET	6

STATE PLAYOFFS CLASS D

CAL-MUM	18	PINE VALLEY	3
CAL-MUM	27	DEPOSIT	6
CAL-MUM	41	RENSSELAER	0

JUNIOR VARSITY

CAL-MUM	0	YORK	0
CAL-MUM	43	DANSVILLE	0
CAL-MUM	22	LIVONIA	0
CAL-MUM	0	LEROY	22
CAL-MUM	6	HF-L	7
CAL-MUM	20	LIVONIA	8
CAL-MUM	25	DANSVILLE	12
CAL-MUM	14	BOLIVER-RICHBURG	0
CAL-MUM	12	LEROY	0

26) The 1992 team was the first undefeated, untied champions of the Monacelli era and the first undefeated team since 1980. These boys, several of them in the special needs program throughout their school years, still have a special place in Coach Monacelli's heart. Their closest game and most dramatic victory was a 16-8 slugfest against Windsor in the New York State Western Regional. They ended the year ranked #1 among small schools in the state. Row one, L to R: Brain Schneider, Brian Kissel, Adam Paladino (Captain), Josh Randall (Captain), Tom Martin, Bill McNelis, Tom Whiteside. Row two, L to R: Gary Hartford (Captain), Robert Drummond, Carlton Covey, Pat Ball, Eric Thurley, Jamie Vokes, Todd Smith, Dave Day. Row three, L to R: Pete Moyer, Paul Curts, Matt Grattan, David Steele, Aaron Cappotelli, Wade Rowcliffe, Josh Cummings, Jason Brooks.

27) Never much of a talker himself, Coach Monacelli would rather have his players do their work quietly and efficiently on the field. Right: with Tom Martin and Adam Paladino in 1992.

28) Wade Rowcliffe turns the corner against Windsor in the 1993 Class C State semifinals. Rowcliffe excelled behind the ferocious blocking of "The Beef," and the Raiders won 34-0 en route to their third straight state title. Rowcliffe was one in a long line of great Red Raider runners.

29) The offensive line gets ready to spring Rowcliffe for another big gain in the 1994 29-0 victory over LeRoy. Throughout it's history, the Red Raiders football team excelled because of its front seven. Most of the offensive linemen who wore the maroon and white were country boys who played with just as much desire as talent.

30) The 1994 undefeated, untied team won Cal-Mum's second straight on-the-field state championship, it's third state title in a row overall. They won by 16 points in each game of the state playoffs. Before that, their average margin of victory was 35 points. Row one, L to R: Jerrod Dunlap, Tony Monacelli (Captain), Aaron Edwards, Josh Bienko, Stash Merritt, Kevin Kissel, Eric Williams (Captain), Matt Emens, Matt Cappotelli. Row two, L to R: Coach Monacelli, Bob Middleton, Don Peet, Dave Holler, Tim Davis, Mike Leach, Louie Kingsbury, Tim Keeley. Brian Gilman, Mike Hallett, Pat Hammond, Coach Staley. Row three, L to R: Kris Pangrazio, Tim Seifert, Dominic Monacelli, Jamie Vokes, Wade Rowcliffe, Ron Stephany (Captain), Jeremy Peet (Captain), Kevin Donaghue, Brendan Donlon, Coach Fredericks.

31) The 1995 Red Raiders, undefeated and untied, is the only one that can be realistically compared to the 1929 and 1973 juggernauts. They outscored their opponents by a ridiculous 463-67 margin. As in 1994, they won every game by at least two touchdowns. They and the 1994 team were the core of the 35 game winning streak, bookended by the dramatic 1993 loss to Livonia and the shocking 1996 loss to Honeoye Falls Lima. In the years 1994 and 1995, however, no one came close to beating Cal-Mum. Row one, L to R: J.D. Baldeck, Rich Simeone, Kris Mitchell, Matt Cappotelli, Joe Kingsbury, Brad McCreedy, Stash Merritt, Bryan Grattan, Phelps Beardsley, Paul Swartzmeyer. Row two, L to R: Josh Bienko, Joe Hughes, John Beaumont, Jerrod Dunlap, Don Peet, Aaron Edwards (Captain), Mike Leach, Kevin Donoghue (Captain), Jamie Vokes (Captain), Mike Combo. Row three, L to R: Coach Fredericks, Coach Staley, Matt Loomis, Jeremy Dietchler, Tim Seifert (Captain), Dom Monacelli (Captain), Tim Keeley, Louie Kingsbury (Captain), Coach Monacelli

32) Coach Gary Fredericks, "Coach Fred" to most of us, worked with many running backs during his years as offensive coordinator under Mike Monacelli. Here he is with Kevin Donaghue, Mike Leach and Aaron Edwards after the 1995 New York State championship game.

33) At the Syracuse Carrier Dome, the 1995 Raiders celebrate a fourth straight New York State title after defeating Rensellaer 41-0.

34) Matt Cappotelli played in some of the most dramatic games in Cal-Mum football history, including and especially the 1997 Section V Class C championship game against LeRoy, which Cal-Mum won 20-15 on this last second touchdown. Cappotelli's #34 can be seen on the far left of this photo.

35) The 2003 Red Raiders were perhaps the most surprising of all the undefeated, untied teams. But coming off a heartbreaking 12-8 loss to LeRoy in the 2002 Section V Class C championship game, the 2003 Raiders transmuted revenge into excellence, outscoring their opponents 467-65 and capturing the New York State championship in a thrilling 30-26 victory against Hoosick Falls. The 2003 players knew their history, too, proudly proclaiming, but still not quite believing, that they were indeed forever in the company of the great Cal-Mum Red Raider teams of the past. Row one, L to R: Jeff Grattan, Jeff Williams, Chris Paladino, Zack Nothnagle, Tim Chriscaden, John Truscott, Tom Shepard, Chad Pierri, Chris Parker, Tim Gorton, Mike Atwell. Row two, L to R: Mitch Atwell, Evan Scheidel, Jeff Boop, Tom Lauffer, Bob Toland, Joe Darron, Kyle Mynter (Captain), Jamie Fitch (Captain). Row three, L to R: Chris Tomasso, Paul Keeley (Captain), Nathan Rogers, Justin Walsh, Rick Riggi, Ryan Sherman (Captain), Chris Harmon, Jeremy Darron.

36) The 2003 team celebrates their history-making New York State championship victory against Hoosick Falls. 2003 was the fifteenth undefeated, untied season for the Raiders, one of the all-time greatest accomplishments in American high school football.

Chapter Seven:
Monacelli Moments

THERE WAS NO QUESTION that Mike Monacelli, coach of the junior varsity football team for sixteen years, would be McAlee's successor.

"Pressure? There was no pressure," Monacelli joked when asked by Livingston County *News* reporter Chris Metcalf about what it meant to follow in McAlee's footsteps. "[McAlee] went 9-1 with a sectional title, and I proceeded to go 2-6 the next year. I could smell the tar barrels heating up and the chickens being plucked." He knew where he stood from an historical perspective. "There is a burden that you bear. You don't want to be the coach that they pin the label on that says, 'The tradition stopped with him.'"

Monacelli also knew that he could draw from Cal-Mum's football history to handle that pressure. "The community knew that the talent [in 1988 and 1989] was not the same. Our kids worked hard and our staff worked hard—and we learned from that experience. They say you can learn more by a loss than by a win… It made me work harder as a coach but also made me very aware of the history of Cal-Mum football and I was not afraid to tap into that history by getting advice from those who had played in the previous years. It is truly a wonderful sight to see at our football games so many local seniors that played in the forties and fifties especially who still come to the games and offer encouragement to our players."

After two tough seasons of transition, the most disappointing campaigns since the end of the Ruane years, Monacelli got his Red Raiders back into a winning groove in 1990 and back in contention in Livingston County.

It wasn't easy. Some teams the Raiders played were new and difficult. Elba, Oakfield-Alabama and Pembroke gave Cal-Mum a tough time in these early years of the Monacelli regime. LeRoy and Avon were, as usual, forces to be reckoned with. And in 1988, Dansville bested Cal-Mum for the first time in almost twenty years. Overall, Livingston County football was more competitive than it had been in years. Because of southward demographic shifts from the Rochester area to the rural suburbs, the Livonia, Dansville, Attica and Honeoye Falls-Lima school districts had grown significantly in the late 1980s. LeRoy was still a powerhouse.

Several years into Cal-Mum's renewed success, Monacelli gave appropriate credit to the Raiders' perennial in-county opponents. "I think our football in Caledonia is pretty darn good," he told Jack Haley from the Livingston County *News*, "but number one I go back to Livingston County football, where week in and week out you go play the teams of Livingston County and you have to prepare week in and week out for each team and play well. I tell you what, you have to go far and wide to find a league as tough all around as Livingston County."

There was pressure in following McAlee, to be sure. There was no doubt that Cal-Mum played tough opponents week in and week out. Monacelli was up to the task, however. With his long-time assistant Gary Fredericks, he had nurtured Cal-Mum's best talent through the junior varsity and into McAlee's care for a decade and a half. He was just as much a part of Cal-Mum's success as anyone. And quality talent was certainly on his rosters in players who hailed from new football families named Moyer, Hartford, Edwards, Donaghue, Monacelli, Rowcliffe and Cicoria, among others. It was a new era, and, fittingly, Monacelli's Cal-Mum Red Raiders completed their ascent to greatness as a new decade was about to dawn.

MONACELLI'S FIRST BIG WIN came against LeRoy in the 1990 opener. Playing in a driving rain, the Red Raiders scored on touchdowns by Dave Donaghue and Dave Parnell. Donaghue's first score came on the opening kickoff, which he returned 90 yards to give the Raiders a 6-0 lead. Except for the rain, the game progressed much as the 1977 contest had, with the Raider's defense making big play after big play to stymie the Oatkan Knight offense. The final score was the same as in 1977, too, 19-0 when the whistle sounded. Monacelli celebrated his coming-out party with joy, and with more than a little relief.

The Raiders continued their victorious ways throughout the season, winning tough games against Oakfield-Alabama (22-20) and Elba (22-18). The only regular season loss came against a very good York team, which would win the Section V Class D championship later that fall.

Cal-Mum returned to the sectionals that year, defeating Oakfield-Alabama 36-20 behind Dave Parnell's remarkable first-half performance of eight carries for 202 yards. Parnell was on his way to the Section V single-game playoff rushing record, but Coach Monacelli wasn't concerned about that. "We're not into records," Monacelli clearly explained. Nor did Parnell mind overmuch, as he got to watch for most of the second half and rest himself for the Raider's next opponent.

Cal-Mum found out later that afternoon who the next opponent would be—the Clyde-Savannah Golden Eagles, currently the best small school team in Section V and, perennially, one of the top four or five small school football teams in New York State. Under Coaches Nick DerCola (1950-1984—yes, 34 years) and Ron Vitticore, the Golden Eagles had compiled a cumulative record of 257-64-16. The team had won an astounding seven Section V titles in a row in the DerCola/Vitticore years. By way of comparison, Cal-Mum had a cumulative record of 237-82-7 under eight coaches in that span. The Red Raiders had won a total of four sectional titles by that time, none since 1981. One of Cal-Mum's sectional titles, of course, came against DerCola's 1979 Clyde-Savannah team. Red Raider fans with any sense of history—most of them, that is—would have recalled that game as the 1990 contest got under way. The big opening day win over LeRoy wouldn't be the only "flashback" type game that year.

Cal-Mum scored first on the Fauver Stadium field, quickly moving the ball into the end zone on a Dave Donaghue touchdown after a botched punt gave the Raiders the ball on the Clyde-Savannah 31-yard line. Clyde-Savannah came back on a short drive of their own after recovering a Donaghue fumble on the Cal-Mum 41-yard line. A big punt return put the Golden Eagles in business again towards the end of the first half. Wes Smith caught a Derrick Carnevale pass for 10 yards and a touchdown.

The situation looked bleak for the Red Raiders as the second half opened, with Clyde-Savannah executing a good 14 play drive. Then Cal-Mum recovered a fumble at its own 6-yard line. The Red Raiders marched the ball 94 yards to the end zone for the tying score. The drive was highlighted by R.J. Hildebrandt's runs, Matt Moyer's fourth down fumble recovery and run for a first down, and Dave Donaghue's 6-yard carry for a score. Donaghue's two point conversion attempt was stopped a mere inch from the goal line. Cal-Mum's bid for a victory in regulation was again stopped when, with only 20 seconds left to play, Eric Stauffer's 21-yard field goal attempt was blocked. All those historically aware Red Raider fans were certainly thinking about 1979 at this point—it was a blocked extra point that prevented Clyde-Savannah from winning that game in regulation and gave Cal-Mum a new lease on life. Now, in 1990, Clyde-Savannah had a new lease on life as this game, too, entered a sudden-death overtime with the same possession rules as eleven years before.

Cal-Mum had the ball first. The Raiders, as expected in Monacelli's no-frills offense, ran the ball straight ahead. Dave Donaghue almost got the touchdown amidst a fourth down pile-up right past the line of scrimmage—Monacelli thought he did get the touchdown—but the officials called the ball down at the six-inch line, granting

Clyde-Savannah a chance for overtime victory and continued Section V dominance. The Golden Eagles quickly took advantage of the officials' call, and scored the winning touchdown on first down via another Carnevale-to-Smith 10-yard pass.

Two great teams with two impressive gridiron traditions fought against each other in as close of a football game as you'll ever see that day. Someone had to win—literally, it was a sectional championship game—and Clyde Savannah walked away with the 20-14 victory and yet another Section V title, just as Cal-Mum had done in 1979.

THE LEVEL OF ANTICIPATION for the 1991 campaign was high. It was Mike Monacelli's twentieth season as Cal-Mum football coach. Dave Donaghue and Dave Parnell—the "Bruise Brothers"—were back for their final season in maroon and white. Joining them in the backfield was fullback R.J. Hildebrant. Together, the three promised to deliver Livingston County's—and perhaps Section V's—most devastating running game. If Cal-Mum could win the Section V title, the team would go to Rich Stadium in Orchard Park, NY, to play the top team of it's size from Section VI in the inaugural Class C Western Regional. First, however, Monacelli, the Bruise Brothers and their 28 teammates would have to survive its grueling Livingston-Genesee County League schedule. Enrollment numbers in the Cal-Mum school district had been falling and continued to fall—the Red Raiders would have to win with fewer players than they were used to having.

Donaghue and Parnell came through in a big way, as did the supporting cast of Hildebrant and the Harmon brothers, Dan and Tom. Cal-Mum squeaked by Attica 14-13 when Parnell disrupted a fake kick with under two minutes to play. The Raiders demolished Warsaw and Letchworth by scores of 40-0 and 57-0. They snuck by a very good Perry Yellowjackets team, 24-21, then dispatched Honeoye Falls-Lima and York before the game that everyone had circled on their calendar, the annual war against LeRoy.

Cal-Mum won the game 22-18 thanks to the stalwart defensive play of Donaghue, Parnell, Shannon Johnson, Pete Moyer, and Jason Reid. Twice in the fourth quarter the Red Raider defense stopped LeRoy at the goal line to preserve the win. "There was fire in their eyes," Monacelli said in reference to a time-out visit he made to the defensive huddle during one of these goal line stands. "Their back was to the wall. Like an old junkyard dog, they were going to put up a fight when it came down to it and that's what they did."

An easy victory against Pembroke gave Cal-Mum a Livingston County Division I championship. Another blowout against Lyons and yet another against East Rochester set the Raiders up for the Class C Western Regional against Silver Lake.

By this time, Cal-Mum's football team was once again capturing the attention of pigskin fans region wide. In the Rochester *Democrat and Chronicle*, morning coverage of important games returned to the front page, side-by-side again with stories about Aquinas, Canandaigua, Fairport, Greece-Athena, Irondequoit, LeRoy and Rush-Henrietta. Although the Rochester *Times Union* was still around until 1997, it shared a staff with the *D and C* after 1992—both papers were owned by Gannett—and most of the sports reporting was handled by the morning paper.

The *D and C* also offered several human interest stories about Caledonia's football and community traditions, something familiar to Red Raider fans from the seventies and early eighties. The first such profile in half a decade was about the "Bruise Brothers," Dave Donaghue and Dave Parnell. "You want tough? You got it," wrote Allen Wilson. The Bruise Brothers "are big, strong and according to East Rochester coach Ron Rucker, 'really a handful.'" Donaghue and Parnell were the first Cal-Mum players since Roland Poles to be worth all the attention. Both players excelled on defense, earning first team All-Greater Rochester honors for their work on that side of the line of scrimmage.

They were more famous for their offensive talents. Donaghue, a six-year varsity player, had rushed for 1,400 yards and 17 touchdowns through 10 games in 1991. His best friend Parnell had gained 749 yards and scored 12 touchdowns. Donaghue was big and quick, just as willing to juke an opposing linebacker as run over him. Parnell, a 230 pound bruiser who could bench press 340 pounds and squat over 600, had a more direct approach—run over everybody until there were no defenders left to challenge. Either way Monacelli went in his play calling, the Bruise Brothers certainly were newsworthy.

The most thorough coverage of Red Raider football and the most poignant insights into its meaning came not from the big city to the north, but rather from Jack Haley and his staff at the Livingston County *News* in Geneseo. Anyone who wanted to keep their pulse on gridiron happenings in Cal-Mum, LeRoy, Avon, Livonia, or any of the other Livingston County teams had only to turn to Haley's weekly editorial, which perfectly complemented the detailed game recaps to be found in each week's paper. In fact, Haley's reporting and commentary were, in hindsight, the golden era of sports reporting in Livingston County football history and therefore in Cal-Mum football history as well.

Here is Haley's straightforward and very readable account of Cal-Mum's 27-9 demolition of East Rochester in the 1991 Section V Class C championship game.

> Plain and simple, that's the Caledonia-Mumford Red Raiders football team.

> They do not do anything fancy. They do not try to outwit their opponents.
>
> Plain and simple, the Red Raiders run the football, and that's what they did last Friday night…
>
> "We kept it simple, we did the things we were confident in doing, and we executed those things," said Red Raiders coach Mike Monacelli. "The key tonight was continuing to execute the things we've done well so far this season and we really didn't make any mistakes."
>
> What the Red Raiders have done well all season to attain a 10-0 record is run the football. Last Friday they did run the football, in fact they ran into the record books by gaining 405 yards on the ground.
>
> The old record was 396 yards which the Red Raiders set in 1978.

Haley appreciated Cal-Mum's on-field accomplishments as much as any homegrown fan. Even more importantly, he recognized from the very beginning that there was something deeper going on here than only football, something that a young staff reporter coming into town from a Rochester city paper to cover a game or do the usual community and tradition profile could never understand.

A case in point was Haley's column that followed the 1991 loss to Silver Creek.

> They played hard and they played well.
>
> They represented Section V, the Livingston/Genesee Region Football League and the town of Caledonia like champions.
>
> Last Saturday night when the Section V Class C champion Caledonia-Mumford Red Raiders played the Section VI champs, Silver Creek in Rich Stadium, it would be a game that few would forget.
>
> The Red Raiders at 10-0 against the Black Knights at 9-1 on the turf that houses the Buffalo Bills promised to be an exciting match up for the First Annual Western Regional Football Championship.
>
> The series of games that were played on Saturday is the first step for an eventual state championship tournament which will hopefully take place in 1993.
>
> Silver Creek won the match up but an asterisk has to be put at the end of it.
>
> During such an historical game the out come of the game should not be determined by anyone but the athletes and the coaches on the field.
>
> Silver Creek blocked a punt late in the second quarter and took over at the one-yard line. Trailing 8-7 it took the Black Knights just one play to

score and take the lead which would stand when the final seconds ticked off the clock.

But what cost the Red Raiders the game occurred 51 seconds before the blocked punt.

The Red Raiders had the ball first and ten on their own 25 with 1:17 left in the half. Quarterback Gary Hartford dropped back to pass and threw the ball towards Brad Vilcheck. The ball fell helplessly to the turf incomplete because Silver Creek's Jason Sack was all over Vilcheck.

Everyone in the stadium was expecting a pass interference call, but no flag. The foul took place right in front of the Red Raiders bench and the team and coaching staff could not believe that there was no call.

Had the foul been called, Cal-Mum's close to midfield with a first down. Instead the Red Raiders are unable to pick up a first down and forced to punt.

Dave Donaghue, with the end zone to his back had his punt blocked by Matt Taylor. Instead of going into the intermission leading by at least one point, the Red Raiders are trailing by five.

Not one penalty all night was called on the Cal-Mum side of the field. All the flags came out on the Silver Creek side.

A game of this magnitude must have perfection by the officials. It's too crucial of a game to have it settled by a mistake from them.

Despite this final loss the accomplishments that the Red Raiders have worked for cannot be taken away.

They finished as the Division II champions and the Section V Class C champions along with a high ranking in the state poll.

They proved what hard work results in and when the final seconds ticked off at Rich Stadium they finished the season with pride and sportsmanship.

They truly are champions.

Reading the *Democrat and Chronicle's* recap of the game, you would not have known that the play with under a minute left in the first half had even happened. You would not have gotten the deeper understanding of the character that lay at the foundation of Cal-Mum football. Jack Haley was, and would continue to be, the best source for Cal-Mum football information and insights for years to come.

THE RED RAIDERS entered the 1992 season undaunted by the loss that ended the 1991 campaign. There were certainly challenges. The Bruise Brothers were gone, R.J. Hildebrant was gone, the Harmon brothers were gone. Quarterback Gary Hartford returned for his senior season, but his teammates were, to repeat the words from the 1927 yearbook, "material almost green." Underclassmen Matt Grattan, Pete Moyer, Dave Steele and Jamie Vokes would see extensive playing time as linemen on both sides of the ball. Josh Randall, Wade Rowcliffe and Tom Martin would be joining Hartford in the backfield. With a roster of only 22 to 25 boys, depending on injuries, the question wasn't whether Cal-Mum would be good enough—it was, simply, would they have enough players.

The worries proved groundless. The only close game the Red Raiders played all season was against Dansville, in which Cal-Mum entered halftime down 20-18. As Jack Haley put it, "You could sense the feeling on the Red Raiders bench when they came out for the second half, the atmosphere among the players was like a volcano ready to erupt. And that's just what they did." Tom Martin scored two of his four touchdowns, Josh Randall added another, and Cal-Mum walked off the field 38-20 winners.

The fires kept burning as Cal-Mum torched Barker 55-8, Honeoye Falls-Lima 51-0, Perry 63-0 and LeRoy 42-14. Hartford, Martin, Randall and sophomore Wade Rowcliffe did the damage on offense. Using the wishbone formation almost exclusively, the offense racked up 343, 390, 432 and 361 yards in those games. The defense, led by Hartford, Randall, Pete Moyer and Dave Steele, was equally impressive, yielding few yards while making big play after big play to put the offense in position to score. The defense allowed only 60 points the entire regular season.

Worries loomed during the sectional playoffs, however. Tom Martin and Josh Randall both got injured, putting pressure on even more inexperienced players in even bigger games. Coach Monacelli believed in them, though. He didn't bring the freshmen and sophomores up "so they could sit on the bench," he said. "They're up because they have the ability to play."

And play they did, defeating East Rochester 28-0 and Avon 32-0 to win Cal-Mum's second Section V championship in a row. Both games were played in the Fauver Stadium snow, and both games were utter blowouts, with neither opponent able to stop Cal-Mum's running attack or move the pigskin at all against the ferocious Red Raider defense. The new question was—could Cal-Mum keep the momentum going into another regional playoff game, this time against Section III's Windsor?

With both Martin and Randall out of the game, Coach Monacelli decided to rely on his defense. "We wanted to force them to have to do something on offense," Monacelli said. "We wanted to play field position. We wanted to play smash-face football," Monacelli continued, expanding the smashing above the mouth. "Our kids can do that with anybody. They're used to that, and they like it."

The Red Raiders ended up with only 159 total yards while holding Windsor to 149. They relied on a unique strategy to win the game—a quick kick on third down, anticipating a big defensive stop. They got it when Dave Steele hammered Windsor running back Chris Snover, causing a fumble that was recovered by Matt Grattan. Gary Hartford ran for the touchdown and for the two point conversion, giving Cal-Mum a 16-8 lead that the defense would preserve. Hartford, who scored all of Cal-Mum's points, was named the game MVP for his outstanding play on both sides of the ball.

Later that week, sportswriters voted the Cal-Mum Red Raiders the number one small school football team in New York State for the first time since October 1981. Gary Hartford and Pete Moyer were chosen first team All-Greater Rochester. Mike Monacelli was selected the Rochester area's coach of the year. Hartford was also honored as a first team All-New York State selection as a linebacker.

Long-time Red Raider fan Jeff Mallaber shared the following appreciation with the 1992 team once all the champions had been crowned and awards had been won.

Dear Raiders,

There isn't much left to be said about the season you put together. Your accomplishments speak for themselves.

Undefeated and untied. Livingston County Division I Champions. Section V Class C Champions. New York State Small School Champions.

Your effort and your pride have brought this community together again to celebrate something special about Caledonia-Mumford. In that sense, you have created a triumph for our entire community. For that, and for all the hard work and sacrifice that it took to get there, we thank you.

In a larger sense, though, this victory is yours and yours alone. Each of you has paid the price that it takes to become a champion. You have set yourselves apart from the crowd.

You will always remember what it feels like to be on top. Make sure that you also remember what it took to get there. Let this be the beginning, rather than the end. Take the principles of dedication and discipline that brought you this success, and apply them to the rest of your life.

Personally, I'd like to thank all of you for letting me be involved in some small way in the effort. I consider it a privilege to have been associated with such a class outfit.

> To the seniors, congratulations. You set some extremely high goals for yourselves and you surpassed all of them. To the rest of you, see you next year. Let's do it all again.
>
> Fudge

As Jim Kelly and the Buffalo Bills were also fond of saying that year, "We're baaaack!"

ONE POTENTIAL DRAWBACK of using all those underclassmen was pre-game anxiety over their ability to perform in big games. The benefit was the experience that came from playing big games and the confidence that came from winning them. As the 1993 season opened it was clear to Monacelli, Fredericks and their players that the benefits far outweighed the drawbacks. Experience and confidence, in fact, were the two characteristics that would carry the Cal-Mum football team to new heights of accomplishment in the next several years, heights of accomplishment above even those reached by the great Red Raider teams of the past.

Or were they? Ask any ten random Red Raider fans and you'll get at least five different answers to the question of which Cal-Mum team was the best.[*] For those who value their history above all else, the 1929 undefeated, untied, unscored-upon team takes the prize. Those who delve deep in Raider lore might also choose from Robert Freeman's 1947, 1950 or 1954 teams. Others would say the 1973 team, McAlee's first, because they turned the whole program around after the embarrassing failures of '71 and '72. Still others would answer the 1978 or 1979 team, the ones led by Junior Poles and Dave Trojanski, the ones that played at the height of The Great Streak. The 1980 team was the favorite of more than a few Raider fans simply because the legacy of The Great Streak was such a heavy burden for them to carry, and they carried it with class and with success. The 1980 team was also the first Red Raider team in history to win 10 games in one season.

Where, then, do the 1992-1995 teams rank? As with the 1929 team's accomplishment, these teams' feats need to be understood in several different contexts.

First, the competition was much different in the mid-nineties. Some would say that the road through the season was more difficult because of the sectional and state playoff systems. This was certainly true when Cal-Mum got to the sectional champi-

---

[*]See Appendix D for the rosters of fourteen undefeated teams in Caledonia-Mumford Red Raider football history.

onship game and beyond. Can the same be said for the first and second rounds of sectional play, however? The Barker team that Cal-Mum trounced 60-0 in the first round of the 1993 playoffs ended its season 4-4-1. The Avon team that Cal-Mum was scheduled to play in the 1994 playoffs was 0-7 coming into the game and forfeited rather than be embarrassed by the inevitable lopsided loss. The 1995 York team over which Cal-Mum steamrolled in the first round ended its season 2-6.

Fans and coaches had several criticisms of the Section V playoff system. Eight teams per class were too many. There was no way a winless Avon team or a two-win York squad should have been in the playoffs. The problem was section wide—in 1994, 17 out of 48 teams in the six sectional classes had losing records. Critics compared the situation to the NBA or NHL playoffs. Or they shook their heads and argued that high school playoff football should not be like those elementary school soccer tournaments where every participant is a champion.

Some critics said there were also too many classes, with too much movement up and down between them depending upon the school district's enrollment. Cal-Mum went from Class C in 1993 to Class DD in 1994 to Class D in 1996 and back up to Class C in 1997. In all there were eight classes in Section V, a situation that would have more negative than positive consequences.

But by far the biggest criticism of the Section V playoff system was the method used for seeding teams in the playoffs and for deciding which team from DD and D would play in the Class D state tournament, which from CC and C would play in the Class C state tournament, etc., etc.

Cal-Mum faced this problem directly in 1993, when Canisteo axed its football program and thus cancelled its opening weekend game against the Red Raiders. Monacelli called and called and called around, but no one was willing to play Cal-Mum.

"Why the problem?" Jack Haley asked. "Why doesn't anyone want to match up with the Red Raiders?" His answer: "Easy, it's sectional points. No one wants to take the chance of playing a good team and risk losing. The loss to Cal-Mum, a Class C school, is devastating point-wise to a team in a high sectional classification."

When combined with the overabundance of class divisions, the modified Harbin point system, as it was called, eliminated the possibility for great match-ups to decide who would play in the new state tournament. In 1994, Cal-Mum won the Section V Class DD championship and was 10-0. Clyde-Savannah, meanwhile, won the Section V Class D championship and was also 10-0. But instead of having a system that would pit the best D team against the best DD team with a berth in the state tournament on the line, Section V had created a system that picked its state tournament representative according to which team accumulated the highest number of sectional points.

"Why can't kids just play football and not have to worry about all this point business?" said one Cal-Mum booster. "That's the way we used to do it, and we won just as many games as they do now." Well, not quite as many. With the new sectional and state playoff systems, the Raiders could play as many as 13 games per season, nearly half of them in the playoffs.

As the playoffs went on, there were certainly more difficult teams to play, more important games to win. Seeing the best teams in the state play against each other on all four state levels made the new state playoff system worth it in the long run, despite the problems endemic to the Section V playoff system. Also, having the state tournament culminate in a Thanksgiving weekend full of championship games in the Syracuse University Carrier Dome made for some tremendous football. New York was finally doing what most states had been doing for years. The players and coaches deserved the opportunity.

WITHIN THIS CONTEXT of simultaneously contracted and expanded competition, the Red Raider football teams of the era excelled. From 1991 to 1995 Cal-Mum compiled a 58-2 record and won four state titles in a row (1992-1995), three of them on the field. From 1991 to 1997 the Red Raiders won seven straight Section V championships, matching Clyde-Savannah's accomplishment earlier in the decade. In that seven year span, the Red Raiders outscored their opponents by a game average of 30-7.

And in 1993, the first year of the New York State football tournament, the Red Raiders outscored their opponents by an unbelievable 507-83. Even the critics of the playoff system had to admit that this team was one of the most explosive ever to play on Hamilton Field, or anywhere else in Section V or in New York State, for that matter.

The 1993 Red Raiders were the defending state champions, but Monacelli wasn't allowing them to rest on their laurels. "Being number one counts only at the end of the season, not the beginning. And, to be honest with you, Livonia and LeRoy both have loads of experienced talent coming back." Livonia and LeRoy, in fact, had both won sectional titles in their respective classes in 1992.

It's good not to be cocky, but Cal-Mum's experience and confidence served them well. The most common newspaper headline in 1993 was "Cal-Mum rolls over (fill in the blank)." 34-6 over York. 57-7 over Dansville, with eight touchdowns on eight possessions. 27-7 over LeRoy. 54-13 over Avon. 22-0 over Honeoye Falls-Lima. 78-0 over Attica, which set a new record for total points scored by a Red Raiders football team.

Led by the offensive line of Matt Grattan, Pete Moyer, Todd Smith, Eric Thurley and Jamie Vokes—collectively known as "The Beef"—the Raiders amassed staggering totals of 445, 504, 284, 333, 421, 406 and 326 yards. As Monacelli put it later in the season, "the POW in power football begins with our offensive line."

Wade Rowcliffe and Tom Martin were the primary beneficiaries of The Beef's blocking, scoring touchdown after touchdown, often on runs of 40, 50 or 60-plus yards.

The final game of the season was the one everyone in Livingston County looked forward to—undefeated Cal-Mum (averaging 45.3 points scored and 5.5 points allowed per game) against undefeated Livonia (averaging 43.5 points scored and 2.6 points allowed per game). Jack Haley had a good time preparing for this contest, closing his preview with the following non-prediction. "The winner of Friday night's contest between two of the best teams in Livingston County, Section Five and the state of New York will be: (Computer Error. Must Shut Down. Try Again Later)."

The game was everything it was advertised to be. The teams alternated scores for a total of six lead changes. The Beef sprung Wade Rowcliffe for touchdowns of 51 and 59 yards. Six thousand people were at Saunder's Field in Livonia to see the home team barely hold on for a hard-won 25-22 victory. It would be Cal-Mum's only loss in 53 games from the beginning of the 1991 season to the fifth game of the 1996 season. Again, consider the alternate history—had Cal-Mum been able to stop Livonia from scoring just once, or had Cal-Mum been able to score again, the Raiders would have exceeded the undefeated streak of 1976-1981.[*]

What the loss to Livonia seemed to accomplish was sharpen the Red Raiders' focus heading into the sectionals. Once there, they manhandled Barker 60-6 and Warsaw 54-0 to claim their third straight Section V championship. The acquitted themselves just as well in the state tournament, defeating Salamanca 27-0 and Windsor, the previous year's opponent, 34-0. Once again, these games featured the massive and quick offensive line opening up huge holes for Wade Rowcliffe to run through. Rowcliffe scored a total of ten touchdown in these four games—three games, actually, as Tom Martin took center stage in the Warsaw game and scored three touchdowns of his own. The defense was granite, allowing only six points so far in the sectional and state playoffs.

---

[*] More what-ifs. In addition to the hypothetical win against Livonia, had the Red Raiders been able to score two more points against Honeoye Falls-Lima in 1996, Cal-Mum would have won 61 games in a row, shattering the New York State record. None of this is to say that the 1992-1996 teams in any way failed—such a claim would be ludicrous—but rather to show just how good these teams were, as good as any series of teams that have played anywhere in America, before or since.

Monacelli trusted these boys more than most coaches trusted his players. And why not? There were nine seniors on the team who had been there with Monacelli and Fredericks from the beginning.

An illustration of this trust came during the Windsor game. With a fourth-and-one on their own 15-yard line, Monacelli decided to use the same field position strategy that had led to victory against Windsor the year before. The Black Knights called a time-out, and during the break in action several Red Raiders pleaded with their coach to let the offense go for the first down. Like Moses on the mountaintop their arguments prevailed, and the straight-up-the-middle run by Rowcliffe netted 16 yards.

The snow started to fall at Fauver Stadium late in the third quarter. By time the final whistle blew the Red Raiders were celebrating like kids on a day off from school. They were heading east to Syracuse, where the Rye Garnets would be waiting.

Cal-Mum and Rye shared even more similarities than the 1977 Cal-Mum and LeRoy teams had. Both teams had huge offensive lines. Both teams relied on the running game. Both teams had stingy defenses, allowing under six points per game. Both teams were 10-1. Both teams had lost to a larger, Class B school in the final regular season game of the year. Both teams rolled through the playoffs. Something had to give. Who's number one?

The game was close from the beginning. The teams traded touchdowns in the first and second quarters and Cal-Mum scored again with 30 seconds left in the first half. The Red Raiders led 18-13 at halftime, but Raider fans were anxious because this game was taking on the look of the back-and-forth contest against Livonia. On the surface, it seemed like it was turning into the type of game that came down to which team had the ball last.

But there was a subtle difference between this game and the game against Livonia. Cal-Mum had stopped Rye's running game, whereas the Garnets could not reciprocate. The Raiders continued to run in the second half, racking up a total of 349 yards on the ground, 174 of them from game MVP Wade Rowcliffe. Rye, however, had already turned to the air in an attempt to move the ball and stuck with this strategy in the second half. The Garnets finished the game with a respectable 272 yards passing. But they were held to 74 yards rushing. The age-old football mantra held true—take away your opponent's strength and you'll most likely win the game. Cal-Mum did, 38-19.

Monacelli and his boys understood how momentum was being built up, play after play. "We didn't change anything defensively except to adjust to little things," Monacelli said after the game. "We knew it was going to be a bloody-nose type of game. It was nice that it was our defense that forced them out of their offense rather than the other way around."

Stay with what you do best. Don't get fancy. Let your confidence and experience carry you. Keep that "pow" coming at them for a full 48 minutes. These guiding principles led the Caledonia-Mumford Red Raiders to the first on-field statewide championship in New York history.*

As usual, Jack Haley put the game in its proper perspective. "Many years down the road I'll be able to tell my grandchildren that I was there. I was at the first-ever state football championships and I witnessed the mighty Caledonia-Mumford Red Raiders win the first-ever Class C state title." Haley went on to offer a comparison that the 1932 team would have appreciated. "Cal-Mum was the farm boys from Livingston County. You know, the blue collar workers. Rye, from Westchester County, was the city boys, the white collar workers. And the farm boys won it the old fashioned way." Echoing Bill McAlee in the seventies, Haley went on to write, "The Red Raiders didn't do anything they haven't done all season. They just went straight at Rye. Nothing fancy and nothing new. It could have been the same game plan they used in their first game."

IN MANY WAYS, you could easily understand the following season by turning back a few pages and changing all the "1993s" to "1994s." There were some differences, of course. Gone from "The Beef" were Matt Grattan, Todd Smith, Eric Thurley and All-Greater Rochester and All-State honoree Pete Moyer. But Jamie Vokes was still there, and Tim Seifert, Louis Kingsbury, Ron Stephany and the coach's kids, Tony and Dominic Monacelli, were ready to fill in for the departed graduates. Tom Martin was gone, but All-Greater Rochester and All-State Wade Rowcliffe was still there. Ready to take the spotlight were Jeremy Peet and Aaron Edwards. Monacelli was again nervous about the lack of experience. He knew, however, that the confidence was there.

No football game is easy. Nor is the long haul of an entire season ever like taking a leisurely stroll on a cool autumn day. Hard work and preparation, focus and quick thinking, and the cultivation of speed and strength through training are all necessary for peak performance on a football field. That said, the Cal-Mum Red Raiders football season of 1994 was unlike any before it since 1973. Put simply, Cal-Mum obliterated all 11 of its on-field opponents. Only Barker, on the opening weekend of

---

*Technically, it was the second. Earlier in the day, Clyde-Savannah had defeated Tuckahoe, 40-0, for the Class D championship.

the season, was able to corral the Red Raider offense, holding them to a mere two points.*

On the field, Cal-Mum averaged 35.1 points per game. Except for the state championship game against Rensselaer, almost all the points scored against Cal-Mum, a meager 45 in all, came with the games well in hand. The team was consistent, too, scoring more than 42 points or fewer than 25 points only twice. This team was, as one commentator after another said and wrote, a machine.

Wade Rowcliffe was like the exterior of the 1994 machine, the part that gets all the attention. His cumulative numbers were spectacular. 1,855 yards and 31 touchdowns on offense. 51 tackles as a defensive back. 4,262 yards in his high school career, a new Section V record. 500 points scored in his career, also a Section V record. 80 career touchdowns, also a Section V record.** Most Valuable Player in most of the sectional and state playoff games in which he played.

Despite all the oohs and aahs, however, Rowcliffe was more akin to a beat up Ford F-150 than he was to a cherry red Camaro. He'd broken his right arm five times and his left arm twice before ninth grade. He'd broken most of his fingers, his nose several times, and even broke his back during his freshman year. In 1994 he played through the state playoff tournament with a sprained ankle. Rowcliffe was the poster boy for Cal-Mum football of all ages. He would have fit in just as well with Coots and Jackson in 1929, Pullyblank and Shaughnessey in 1950, Tucci and Chiverton in 1973 or Poles and Trojanski in 1978. Rowcliffe, who was honored as the New York State Player of the Year for Class D in 1994, was the epitome of Cal-Mum Red Raider greatness.***

Monacelli received his share of acclaim as well after Cal-Mum defeated Rensselaer for its third state title in a row. As in 1992, he was named the All-Greater Rochester Coach of the year. Later that month, his peers selected him the Class D New York State Coach of the Year. It seemed as if things couldn't have gotten any better, for Monacelli or for his Red Raiders.

---

*Barker, of course, forfeited their game back in the spring, several months before the season began, which, by rule, gave Cal-Mum the 2-0 victory. Once again, no other team was willing to step up and face the Raiders. Said Monacelli, "We make headlines when we win, we make headlines when we lose and now we make headlines when we can't get a game." An even more drastic forfeit came in the first round of sectionals, when the winless Avon Braves decided they'd rather stay home than compete against the undefeated Red Raiders.

**As of this writing, Rowcliffe's yardage record has been eclipsed by 8 players. Only David Zapada from Hornell (2003-2007) has more touchdowns (81) and points (507). Rowcliffe is also second in most points scored in one season (234 in 1994) and third in most touchdowns scored in one season (37 in 1994).

***On November 13, 1999, while playing in his senior year for the University of New Hampshire against the University of Connecticut, Rowcliffe suffered one injury too many. He broke his C-1 vertebrae in a head-to-head collision. He was fortunate to recover—this is one injury that so often leaves athletes paralyzed.

Chapter Eight: 1995

THERE WERE SEVEN returning seniors on the 1995 squad, all of them either three or four year varsity players, all of them champions multiple times over. Dominic Monacelli, Jamie Vokes and Tim Seifert anchored the offensive line. Kevin Donaghue, Mike Leach and Aaron Edwards followed their linemen's blocks from out of the backfield. Louie Kingsbury could both block and catch passes from his tight end position. Together, these seven also formed the core of an experienced and hard-hitting defense.

Put as simply and clearly as possible, the 1995 Red Raiders were unstoppable. No one even came close to beating them. Elba scored 13 points on the Cal-Mum defense in the opening game of the season, the most any opponent would score, but the Red Raiders had already blasted out a 27-point lead by the end of the first quarter, putting the game well out of reach. Every other opponent that season was limited to single digit scoring. LeRoy held the Red Raider offense to 20 points in the third game of the season, and Pine Valley allowed only 18 points in the first round of the state playoffs, but other than that the Cal-Mum offense obliterated every other defense.

Every superlative that comes to mind applies to this team. The team was as great as, some say greater than, the 1929 or 1973 teams. But every superlative also comes in retrospect and on paper—the epic 1995 season was still composed of thirteen football games played on 100-yard football fields in various small towns and cities in upstate New York. Significantly, 1995's success was also more of a team effort than any previous season's success had been. There were stars, of course, especially among the seven seniors mentioned above. Three of them, Mike Leach, Dominic Monacelli and Jamie Vokes, were selected to the All-Greater Rochester team. There was, however, no Jackson or Tucci or Poles or Rowcliffe—no single star of a magnitude that outshone the others. The final assessment of how great the 1995 team was as a team can be made only by looking at the games themselves.

The Raiders opened the season against the Elba Lancers, the first opening weekend game Cal-Mum had played in three years. It was also a rare contest against a predominantly passing offense. Cal-Mum scored 27 points in the first quarter on two touchdown runs each by Kevin Donaghue and Aaron Edwards, complemented by outstanding special teams play. But Elba came back strong in the second quarter with two touchdown passes from third year starting quarterback Joe Bezon. "We rarely see a passing team in Livingston County," Coach Monacelli said. "Our defense wasn't quite sure what to do right away." But the Raider defense figured it out eventually—they allowed only one more touchdown, held Bezon to only four more completions, and sacked the Lancer quarterback a total of six times. Louie Kingsbury, firing away on all cylinders from his defensive end position, had three of those sacks. The Raider offense added three more touchdowns, one from Donaghue and two from Mike Leach. In the end, Cal-Mum thrilled the hometown crowd with a 45-19 victory.

The following week against Dansville, Mike Leach scored two rushing touchdowns and another on an interception return. The defense efficiently silenced any noise the Mustang offense tried to make. Kingsbury, Monacelli, Seifert and Vokes forced Dansville into one three-and-out series after another. The score at the end of the third quarter was also the final score: Cal-Mum 30, Dansville 0.

Cal-Mum hosted LeRoy in game three of the 1995 campaign. It was a battle of sectional champions, with LeRoy returning thirteen starters from its 1994 Class C New York State Championship team. Cal-Mum won the game handily, 20-6. The game was a battle of field position, punctuated by big defensive takeaways, two for LeRoy and four for the Raiders. Two of Cal-Mum's touchdowns came on fumble returns. As Albert Lin of the Rochester *Democrat and Chronicle* put it, "When Cal-Mum made mistakes it merely stalled drives; when the Oatkan Knights committed miscues it resulted in points." The victory was Cal-Mum's sixth in a row against LeRoy, its twenty-first in a row overall.

Notre Dame of Batavia was the next victim. By halftime, Cal-Mum had a 37-0 lead, fed by the ferocious blocking of Monacelli, Vokes, *et. al.*, who sprung Donaghue, Edwards and Leach for over 200 yards and three touchdowns. Leach also scored on a 22-yard fumble return. Louie Kingsbury blocked a punt out of the end zone for a safety. The teams traded touchdowns in the second half, and the Red Raiders went home with a comfortable 43-6 victory.

Attica fared no better the following week. Cal-Mum scored three touchdowns in the first half of this game, one each from Donaghue, Edwards and Leach. The defense was perhaps more impressive than it had been so far all season, shutting out the Blue Devils and allowing only 112 total yards. Jamie Vokes impressed everyone with his dominating performance, making six tackles and dropping the Attica quarterback to the turf for two sacks. Cal-Mum won 29-8.

The following week, Cal-Mum hosted Honeoye Falls-Lima on Senior Night. All seven Red Raider seniors—"cagey veterans," as Monacelli called them—excelled during the 49-8 dismantling of the Cougars. Kevin Donaghue outshone them all, however, and outshone the full moon that hung over Hamilton Field, with his 112-yard, three-touchdown rushing performance. Donaghue provided an encore to his masterful performance with a 32-yard interception return. No one could have guessed that Honeoye Falls-Lima would play a much, much different type of game the following year.

The annual tussle against the Livonia Bulldogs was the final scheduled game that season. It started out close, as Cal-Mum scored twice on touchdown runs by Edwards and Leach, followed by a Livonia touchdown to make the score 16-8 early in the second quarter. The Red Raiders hit the throttle and never looked back after that, however, scoring 35 unanswered points in a 51-8 rout. The big lead gave Monacelli a chance to play his second string, which scored two touchdowns in the fourth quarter and earned the honor of being on the field as another undefeated regular season came to end.

Could anyone stop the Red Raider juggernaut? York, which had had some success in past years, was the first sectional opponent. At least the Golden Knights didn't forfeit as Avon had the year before. "We did not think we couldn't win the game," York coach Dan Caraher said. "We would have had to play a perfect game and they would have had to do something wrong. But we honest to God felt that we had a shot at it if we did everything right."

After the game, Monacelli praised the Golden Knights' effort. "I give York a great deal of credit for playing a game in which a lot of people had decided they shouldn't play in," he said. "Dan [Caraher] always said they would play anyone at any time."

Cal-Mum ran for 226 yards in the first half and scored 27 points on four rushing touchdowns. The most dramatic score, perhaps the most dramatic play all season, came when Mike Leach took a direct snap on fourth and 6 and ran the ball for a 43-yard touchdown. What made the play dramatic was that Monacelli and Fredericks knew nothing of it before they saw it develop—they had called for a punt. Monacelli wasn't angry; how could he be. He explained after the game that "You coach the kids to do certain things if they see it and you give them that leverage to do it when they see it. If it's there, then it's their call."

York continued to play hard. They dominated the third quarter, moving the ball 90 yards on an eleven-minute drive that was capped by a touchdown scored by the coach's son, Jeff Caraher. The Golden Knights might not have had a snowball's chance in the Devil's kitchen that night at Hamilton Field, but through their effort, their perseverance and their sportsmanship, the team demonstrated a basic truth about interscholastic athletic competition—trying as hard as you can is the true meaning of winning.

The second round of the sectional tournament featured a match up that fans had wanted to see the year before, Cal-Mum versus Clyde-Savannah. The result of the 1995 game, however, made it even more unfortunate that administrators' rules had kept the teams from playing the previous year. While the 1995 Red Raiders were just as good, if not better, than they had been in 1994, the same cannot be said for the Golden Knights. "These are different teams and a different era in Clyde's football history," a diplomatic Monacelli said after Cal-Mum's 50-0 victory. "We were severely out-manned across the front line," said Clyde-Savannah coach Joe McClinton, in his first year after Ron Vitticore's retirement. Kevin Donaghue ran for 168 yards and three touchdowns, and threw for another, a 71-yard strike to Louie Kingsbury. Aaron Edwards contributed 134 yards rushing, and Mike Leach played what was perhaps the best game of his career, not by his rushing, which Clyde-Savannah actually stopped, but rather by his fierce blocking on the many traps and counters that Coach Fredericks called. Leading the way through the gaping holes opened up by Vokes and Monacelli, Leach knocked down, bowled over and caused to flee, defender after defender.

Three of the defensive stars were also somewhat quieted that day, as Monacelli, Seifert and Vokes were all targeted by the Golden Knights' blocking scheme of plugging the middle of the Red Raider defense. That left Louis Kingsbury free to roam, however, and he did so by harassing Clyde's quarterback, David Drahms, play after play. Here's how Jack Haley put it, breathlessly in awe after the shellacking. "Saturday afternoon was a very cloudy day in Hornell and no one knew that better than Clyde-Savannah quarterback David Drahms as the senior signal-caller spent much of the afternoon lying on his back looking up at the sky with Cal-Mum defensive end Louie Kingsbury laying on top of him as the two-time defending state champion Red Raiders crushed the Golden Eagles 50-0 in the Class DD semifinal contest at Maple City Park."

"They are strong," McClinton said, also in awe of the team that had just defeated his boys. "There weren't any fatboys out there. They were all chiseled and hard-working kids." The only question was whether the strength would hold, whether the hard work would pay off in additional Section V and New York State championships.

The Section V Class DD championship, Cal-Mum's fifth sectional title in a row, was won against Red Jacket, 33-6 at Fauver Stadium. As usual, the victory was a team effort, with Vokes, Monacelli, Seifert and Donaghue winning the various MVP awards. The Raiders effort was business-like, the victory efficient. The team's post-game celebration was subdued, because they all knew that there were more victories to win, more history to write. "We're not so sure we have really peaked yet," Monacelli noted. These were ominous words for any opponent, from wherever in New York State they would come, who stood in the juggernaut's way.

Those opponents, as the games turned out, ended up being the same opponents that the Red Raiders had encountered in the 1994 New York State championship season.

First came Pine Valley, a team coached by Cal-Mum alumnus Bob Krenzer. The Panthers had been averaging just over 50 points per game. They had defeated Westfield 46-0 to win the Section VI Class D championship. They were big, fast and tough. They could even boast of having a criminal on the team, a running back who'd been on probation for two years and who had gotten into more trouble the week before the game against Cal-Mum by missing an appointment with his probation officer.

Jamie Vokes, for one, was not intimidated. Early in the game, with Pine Valley leading 3-0 as a result of a botched punt return, Kevin Donaghue ran the ball up the middle for a one-yard gain on third and four. Donaghue's run wasn't particularly noteworthy—what was worth noting was Vokes' block on the Panthers' nose tackle, across the line of scrimmage, past the middle linebacker and deep into the defensive secondary, where Vokes deposited his overmatched opponent on his rump. This caught Monacelli's and Fredericks' attention. They called for their backs to follow Vokes for the rest of the drive, which resulted in a 7-yard Donaghue touchdown.

The game remained 6-3 through the third quarter, with both defenses holding the opposing offense to near nothing. True, Pine Valley was playing without its number one rusher, Josh Roth, who had sprained a knee in the victory over Westfield. It was still a powerhouse, though, and the Cal-Mum defense completely shut it down after allowing the initial field goal. "We have a great deal of trust in that defense," Monacelli said. "They're pretty tough men in there, and I say men because you could walk down a dark alley with any of those guys and not be afraid." The Cal-Mum defense came through with its usual big play early in the fourth quarter. On second down at the Pine Valley 36-yard line, Panther quarterback Max Blair tried to connect with one of his receivers, but his pass was picked off by a leaping Matt Cappotelli, who ran the ball back 42 yards for a touchdown. The Raider defense continued to hold. Jamie Vokes again opened the holes for the Raider running backs, who scored another touchdown to make the final score 18-3. As in 1994, so too in 1995—the Cal-Mum Red Raiders proved that they were the number one high school football team in western New York.

As in 1994, so too in 1995—the next opponent for the Cal-Mum Red Raiders was from the Southern Tier, the Deposit Lumberjacks. A late autumn snow storm fell in western New York the week before the game. Cal-Mum was forced to practice inside the gym, a situation that made Monacelli nervous due to the inability to recreate game-like conditions. The hardship didn't stop the Red Raiders offense, however, which began its first possession on its own ½-yard line after an excellent Lumberjack punt. Cal-Mum fired up its machine-like rushing rotation of Leach and Edwards and Donaghue, with the offensive line driving Deposits defenders back and back and back, preventing the defense from making tackles until after 5, 10, 12, or 15 yards had been gained. Six minutes later, Leach took the ball in for the first Cal-Mum score. The 99 ½-yard drive set a new New York State playoff record.

Deposit played hard and scored a touchdown of its own late in the first quarter. But the Raider offense was relentless, the players perhaps taking out their anger at having been limited to 18 points the previous week on this week's opponent. Leach, who ended up winning the most valuable player award,[*] scored two more touchdowns in the second quarter to give Cal-Mum a 20-6 lead. The defense, appropriately enough, would add another score in the fourth quarter when Brian Grattan recovered a fumble in the end zone. When the final whistle sounded, Cal-Mum had carried the ball 61 times and gained a total of 362 yards on the ground, both numbers setting new state playoff records.

The song remained the same in the New York State Class D championship game against the Rensselaer Rams. The defense completely shut down the Rams' running star D.J. Whitman, who had gained 1,692 yards and had scored 29 touchdowns that year. Nor could Rensselaer's quarterback Gene Bradley do much of anything, despite his 1,200 yards and 13 touchdowns in the previous twelve games. Cal-Mum allowed zero points from the potent Rams offense. Even the second team defense stopped the Rams from scoring by stuffing Whitman at the one-yard line as time ran out. The Cal-Mum defense, in fact, scored two touchdowns of its own, one on Tim Seifert's blocked punt recovery for a touchdown (Mike Leach blocked the punt) and another on a Leach 42-yard fumble return. Another punt blocked by Jamie Vokes set up the first touchdown of the game. Monacelli, Vokes and Tim Seifert, who won the Defensive Most Valuable Player award with eight tackles, totally outplayed the Rams' offensive line for all forty-eight minutes of the game. Whitman ended the game with a mere 40 yards and Bradley completed only 7 of 21 passes.

---

[*]The football game award was not the only one Leach received that day. Later that evening, he was also honored with the Junior Showmanship Award from the Western New York Draft Horse and Pony Club. Since he was a young boy, Leach had raised and shown horses for the Estes family's Honey Locust Farms.

Offensively, it was Leach's turn to shine. He ran the ball 13 times for 120 yards, earning the Offensive Most Valuable Player award. He was humble in his acceptance of the award, though, because, as a blocker himself, he knew that his offensive line deserved the prize as much as he did. All told, the Red Raider offense gained 275 yards in its 41-0 victory, all of them on the ground.

In 1995, the Cal-Mum Red Raiders football team won its third New York State championship in a row and was ranked number one in New York State for the fourth straight year. The 1995 team had achieved Cal-Mum's second undefeated season in a row and its third undefeated season in four years. The 1995 season ended with the Red Raiders in the midst of a thirty-one game winning streak, the second longest in Cal-Mum football history.

As we'll see, plenty of great moments were still to come after 1995. Several very good teams and one great one had yet to play on Hamilton Field.

Yet 1995 was the end of an era, and not only because of the devastating losses that the Red Raiders would suffer in 1996.* The players sensed it, and not only because the most important team leaders were graduating.

"It's good that it's over," said an exhausted but ebullient Leach.

"I'm glad it ended this way," added Dominic Monacelli, who would later be named the New York State Class D Player of the Year.

"It's a great way to go out," Jamie Vokes said.

"It hasn't hit me yet, but we won and that is all that matters right now." Tim Seifert explained, "We know how much it means to play good together all the time. It will probably set in five years, but now we know what we've done."

Dominic Monacelli echoed Seifert's sentiments. "The problem right now is we don't really know what it is all about—the greatness of it. When we look back on it in college or out of college we'll look back and say, 'Hey, we were a great team and a great dynasty.'"

Coach Monacelli had the following thoughts to offer after the victory. "If you sit down and think about what we were able to do, it is a staggering thought when you are talking about the competition levels. It is just unfathomable to understand how you can make it this far." What did the future hold for Monacelli, now that the last of

---

*Devastating loss #1: HF-L 23, Cal-Mum 22, in which Cougar coach Bill Donegan, former Cal-Mum player during The Great Streak, puts an end to the lesser thirty-five game streak. Devastating loss #2: LeRoy 35, Cal-Mum 14, in which Oatkan Knight coach Brian Moran turns the corner in his struggle to beat his Red Raider rivals. Devastating loss #3: Valhalla 12, Cal-Mum 8, in which the Viking defense stops the Cal-Mum offense cold at the 4-yard line with under three minutes left in the game to win the 1996 New York State Class D championship.

his three sons was graduating? "I can enjoy coming home for now anyways, cook supper for my family and relax." *Buon appetito*, coach—you deserve it!

The 1995 team, especially the seniors, clearly understood that there's pressure at the top. They felt it, but they also dealt with it through the discipline of hard work, reliance on each other, respect for each other and for their coaches, and pride in having the privilege to wear the maroon and white jersey of Cal-Mum Red Raider football.

They also knew they were not the first to wear the maroon and white as champions. They knew they were not the first to accomplish greatness on a scale that few others thought possible. They knew well who their companions in the high school football pantheon were. The undefeated, untied, unscored-upon team from 1929. The undefeated teams under Coach Robert Freeman in the late 1940s and early 1950s. Coach Bill McAlee's 1973 and 1974 teams, which the 1992-1995 teams most closely resembled. The teams of The Great Streak in the late 1970s and 1980. Now, two decades after their unparalleled championship run began, Coach Mike Monacelli's early 1990s Red Raider teams are remembered as among the best, if not the best, above all others.

Here is Jack Haley's final homage to the greatness that was the 1995 Cal-Mum Red Raiders football team.

> After the awards were handed out the Red Raiders went to the sidelines and cheered on the LeRoy players as they came out to try and duplicate what Caledonia-Mumford had just accomplished.
>
> Maybe this was the passing of the torch, after all we do have to realize that the Red Raiders won't win every single state championship. Eventually the day will come that a team takes to the same field and comes out with a victory.
>
> But let's not think about that right now. Today, tomorrow and next week is a time to still enjoy the success that the Red Raiders have had. It really is amazing what they have accomplished. Maybe, it will take five years for everyone to really realize what they have done.
>
> They have given us hours of enjoyment watching them play the game better than most. They almost make it look easy, but we do know they have worked hard for this.
>
> You can love them or you can hate them, but remember that you must respect them for they have earned that.
>
> They have earned the right to be called champions and they have earned the right to be called the very best. Thirteen other teams have had

the chance, but they couldn't get it done. In fact 31 teams have tried to defeat them but the smoke has cleared, the dust has settled and the best are standing tall.

Congratulations men, you have earned it.

Chapter Nine:
Destroy LeRoy

THE LEROY OATKAN KNIGHTS also won a New York State football championship in 1995. They rolled through their Class C opponents in both the sectional and state playoff tournaments. They defeated Saranac Lake 37-27 in the Carrier Dome right after Cal-Mum had dismantled Rensselaer. Players from the two teams mingled on the sidelines between the games, as Jack Haley had mentioned in his post game column. The LeRoy players congratulated the Red Raiders on their accomplishment. The Cal-Mum players wished the Oatkan Knights good luck in their upcoming contest.

The behavior of the players on the sidelines was mirrored by the behavior of the fans in the communities—fraternization between Red Raider and Oatkan Knight fans was a constant feature of New York State's best high school football rivalry. When the village of LeRoy and the school administration "banned" tailgate parties before the 1996 game at Hartwood Park, friends from one town started to make calls to friends from the other. Tucker Callan from Caledonia called Rock Wright, who lived across the street from Hartwood Park, and arranged for a party on Wright's front lawn.

"The guy who owns this house has no problem letting us have some fun in his yard before the game, even though he's from LeRoy and I'm from Caledonia," explained Callan, one of the most vocal sideline-roaming super fans of the Raiders. "That's what's so great about this. For two hours once a year we can get on each other and really have some fun. But in the end, we're all just good friends."

Friendly competition was the essence of this great rivalry. My uncle Gus Krenzer used to tell me stories of carrying his football gear to a farmer's field that was half in LeRoy and half in Caledonia, where boys would play unofficial games amidst cornstalks that served as yard lines on a makeshift gridiron. They simply couldn't get enough of Cal-Mum versus LeRoy.

Pullyblank family lore tells of a momentous decision made long ago that sent half the family's children to Caledonia's school and the other half to LeRoy. In this story, the town line ran right through the Pullyblank family's kitchen.

The Cappotelli and Shaughnessey families also had branches in both districts. Junior Poles coached at LeRoy for a while after his attempt at a National Football League career was thwarted by last minute roster moves. Chris Cappotelli also coached there.

In the 1990s and 2000s, Cal-Mum coach Mike Monacelli and LeRoy coach Brian Moran were close friends for 364 or 363 days of the year, on non-game days, that is.

The cries of "Destroy LeRoy!" that could be heard from Cal-Mum players, cheerleaders and fans were the cries of a good-natured family dispute.[*]

It was, perhaps, that closeness the rest of the year that fed into the competitiveness on game night. "You're dealing with probably as long of a span of two teams playing against each other as there is in Western New York," said Mike Monacelli, referring to the historical nature of the rivalry, covered in this book back in chapters one and two. "You're dealing with two communities that are very passionate about athletics, but are extremely passionate about football."

Eddie Coots, who played on the 1929 team and served on the Hamilton Field chain gang for decades, said that "it's just an old grudge game. They always seem to have a good team and we always seem to have a good team."

Even when one or both teams have not been all that good, the anticipation for the big game was in the air. "If both teams were 0-7 and playing in the last game of the season," said Fred Hermansen, a long-time Caledonia fan and Section V statistician, "there's no doubt that the intensity and great spirit of competition would still be there."

"This is Cal-Mum/LeRoy," Oatkan Knight head coach Brian Moran affirmed. "It could be two teams going in 0-7 and it wouldn't matter."

A case in point was in 1991, when Cal-Mum defeated a tough but underwhelming LeRoy team 22-18 to end the regular season 7-0 en route to a Section V championship. "That's what a great high school rivalry is all about," Monacelli said after the hard-fought game that ended with a Cal-Mum defensive stand at the one-yard line. "Take the record and throw it out the window, and just go out and go bang. That's what these two teams do year in and year out."

---

[*]Is it LE-Roy or Le-ROY? Cal-Mum cheerleaders and fans use the former pronunciation because it rhymes with DE-story and therefore makes the chant work. Residents of the village that lies 6.7 miles to the West of Caledonia on Route 5 use the latter pronunciation, and claim that anyone who emphasizes the first syllable is a barbarian. Most outsiders agree with the second point of view.

Year in and year out. The Cal-Mum vs. LeRoy rivalry has already been an important thread running through this whole history. Before turning to the games that came after Cal-Mum's 1991-1995 run of success, including several of the games that were perhaps the greatest of them all, it should be useful to recap the series as a whole, dating back to its beginnings at the turn of the twentieth century.[*]

The rivalry can be roughly divided into several eras. First, in the very early 1900s, Caledonia and LeRoy often played officially-sanctioned games at least twice per season. In 1900 Caledonia won twice 16-0 and LeRoy won once 16-5. In 1902 LeRoy won twice 11-0. In 1904 Caledonia won the only game 16-0. In 1905 LeRoy won 6-5 and Caledonia won 11-10. In 1911 Caledonia won twice 10-6 and 19-0. Little more is known of these games besides the scores. Suffice it to say that the players who took the field under Mike Monacelli and Brian Moran in the 1990s and early 2000s would have hardly recognized the type of game that was being played a hundred years before.

The second era of the rivalry came in the years 1927-1932, years that were explored in chapter two of this book. LeRoy won three out of five of the games played during this era by scores of 2-0 and 6-0 in 1927 and 1930, respectively, and 18-7 in 1932, the game for which revenge was very sweet for me and my teammates in 1985. Caledonia won 6-0 in 1929. The teams tied 6-6 in 1931. They did not play against each other in 1928. The point worth making about these games is that they were uncharacteristically low scoring at a time when Caledonia and LeRoy both racked up huge offensive numbers. Throw the records out the window indeed, even back then.

The third era of the rivalry came in the late 1940s and early 1950s, the era discussed in chapter three, "Football Families." As I wrote there, the years that Caledonia/Cal-Mum played LeRoy were also the years that the Red Raiders achieved their greatest success. I'll pick up this theme again at the very end of this book—playing LeRoy simply made Cal-Mum a better team. LeRoy won four out of the seven games in this span, while Cal-Mum won in 1948 and, of course, in the undefeated 1950 and 1954 seasons.

The fourth era of Cal-Mum/LeRoy football began in 1965 and ended with Frank Ruane's inglorious exit from Cal-Mum in 1972.[**] The notable games of this era include the 0-0 tie in 1970, and the crushing victories for LeRoy in 1971 and 1972 that possibly hastened Ruane's departure.

---

[*] A complete list of Caledonia/Cal-Mum versus LeRoy scores can be found in Appendix G.
[**] The two teams have played at least once every year since 1965, so the eras of the rivalry hereafter described certainly overlap and might look different to another observer.

Next came the McAlee/Santini and then the McAlee/Ruane years, which spanned from 1973 through the 1981 season. Many Cal-Mum fans consider these the glory years of the rivalry, which included the 1977 19-0 victory that opened this book, the 1980 26-21 triumph in the sectional title game, which was described in depth in chapter five, and the 1981 21-20 miraculous last minute victory at Hartwood Park. Turn back to the opening chapter to see why these years of the rivalry were so intense.

If we were using terminology derived from the history of Egypt, the next era of the rivalry might be called the "first intermediate period" or something like that, as neither team from 1982 through 1990 was able to dominate for long. 1982 and 1984 belonged to two Section V champion Oatkan Knight teams. 1985 saw Roland Poles run for 297 yards, elevating him to the level of greatness that his brothers had achieved. McAlee won his last two match-ups against LeRoy in 1987, and Monacelli won his first as varsity coach in 1990.

But Cal-Mum took the upper hand in the rivalry from 1991-1995, which brings us up to date, tailgating with Tucker Callan and friends on an Oatkan Knights fan's front lawn, waiting to see if Cal-Mum can extend its six-game winning streak against LeRoy, even though the 35 game winning streak which began back in 1993 had ended two weeks before against Honeoye Falls-Lima.

THE RED RAIDERS were not able to do so. Instead, the Oatkan Knights galloped out to a 35-0 lead, taking full advantage of an average drive-start from the Cal-Mum 30-yard line. Cal-Mum did score two touchdowns to make the final score 35-14, but the end result fell well short of respectable from the Red Raider perspective. From then on, it would have been a good idea for Tucker Callan to stay away from those LeRoy fans' front yards and get takeout instead.

Also from that game on, however, Cal-Mum and LeRoy would follow parallel paths to the Carrier Dome, winning the Section V Class D (Cal-Mum) and Class C (LeRoy) championships and winning their quarterfinal and semifinal games in the state tournament.

But both teams suffered close defeats in their respective New York State championship games. Cal-Mum lost to Valhalla 12-8, stopped on fourth down deep in Valhalla territory at the end of the game. LeRoy lost to Watervliet, 20-19 in a game that was equally heartbreaking. Their destinies were becoming more closely connected than ever, as the unparalleled 1997 contests would prove.

Destroy LeRoy

The annual Cal-Mum/LeRoy tilt scheduled for October 3, 1997, at Hamilton Field was one of the most anticipated match-ups in years. Not only were both teams hungry for championships after coming oh-so close the year before, they were also in the same sectional class for the first time in many years, which meant that the regular season game might be act one of a two-part drama. LeRoy was ranked third among Class C schools in the state coming into the game, Cal-Mum was ranked ninth.

Additionally, Cal-Mum's Matt Cappotelli, the New York State Class D Player of the Year in 1996—the third Red Raider in a row to receive that honor—wanted revenge for the drubbing his team had taken during his junior year. Many Red Raiders fans said that Cappotelli was the best of the bunch among the long line of fine running backs that Cal-Mum had produced over the years. He was fast up and down the field and quick in his cutbacks. Coach Monacelli added that "you'd better put your mouthpiece in when you're trying to tackle him because he also can knock your teeth out onto the football field." Cappotelli did plenty of teeth-knocking from his defensive back position as well.

On their side, the Oatkan Knights featured second-year starting quarterback Justin Ausher, who passed for 14 touchdowns in 1996. The Cal-Mum linemen on both sides of the ball would also have to contend with Pat Ashley, a monstrous yet quick offensive and defensive tackle. When Cal-Mum was on offense, Jeremy McIlwayne, who outweighed even the 300-pound Ashley, would have to use all his leverage to hold the LeRoy star at bay.

LeRoy started the game with the line of scrimmage firmly in its control. The Oatkan Knights ate up seven minutes off the clock on their opening drive, but turned the ball over on downs at the Cal-Mum 15-yard line. They got the ball at the beginning of the second quarter, however, and Chad Clark ran it right up Cal-Mum's gut for a 51-yard touchdown and the first points of the game. Cal-Mum responded in kind in the third quarter when the offensive line broke open a hole for Matt Cappotelli, who ran the ball for 52 yards and a Cal-Mum score. The two point conversion was successful. Cal-Mum scored again in the third quarter to make the tally 14-7, but LeRoy's Ashley got through on the two point conversion and sacked quarterback Ryan Zimber. Then LeRoy took the ball and tied the game 14-14, taking the ball into the end zone on a fourth-and-goal from the one. The game stayed even for the duration.

About half the fans stayed, too. They were the ones who knew that Section V had a new sudden death overtime rule for regular season games. What Jack Haley called the best football game ever played wasn't quite over yet. Many of the hundreds of fans who left the stadium rushed back to see Chad Clark score again on fourth down from the 4-yard line to break the tie in LeRoy's favor. Then the Oatkan Knights held

Cal-Mum on three downs, forcing the Red Raiders to convert on fourth down as well.

The play Monacelli and Fredericks called was the same play they had called on fourth down and goal against Valhalla in the state championship a year before—a halfback option pass from Matt Cappotelli to any one of three open receivers he could find. The result was the same, too, as the ball fell short of the receiver's hands.

"It was almost the exact same play as in the state finals," a teary-eyed Cappotelli said after the game. "They tell you it's not your fault," he added, feeling the weight of the rivalry's history upon his shoulders. "When it happens you can't accept that."

There's an old saying that in order to truly know pleasure, you must first experience pain. After the way the game against LeRoy ended, Matt Cappotelli was halfway there.

The brunt of Cappotelli's suffering fell on the remainder of Cal-Mum's opponents. Dansville, Bishop Kearney and Letchworth all went down in defeat as Cappotelli amassed over 1,400 yards on the ground. Alexander refused to even step on the same field as the Red Raiders, forfeiting the final game of the season instead.

LeRoy kept winning, as well. The stage was set for act two of this neighborly drama—a Section V Class B championship game showdown on November 8, 1997. The game at the University of Rochester's Fauver Stadium would be the first time Cal-Mum and LeRoy met with a sectional title on the line since 1980, the year Ronnie Poles made his thrilling touchdown run to beat the Knights 26-21.

Could Cappotelli repeat Poles' performance? "We'll be ready for them this time," he promised.

Three thousand fans showed up for the title game on that brisk November Saturday, about half as many as usually attended a Cal-Mum/LeRoy tilt at either team's home field. Those who were there witnessed a first half that was very similar to so many past games between these two powers—good offensive play held in check by even better defensive play. Both teams got big interceptions—Cal-Mum's was made by Adam Cappotelli, Matt's younger brother. Both teams got excellent punt coverage. Both teams moved the ball fairly well, but not quite well enough to put big numbers on the scoreboard. Justin Ausher rammed the ball into the end zone for LeRoy's first score with just over eight minutes left in the second quarter. LeRoy took its 7-0 lead into the locker room at halftime. Matt Cappotelli, suffering from the flu and praying for strength throughout the game, gained only 20 yards on seven carries in the first half. Raider fans were getting nervous as they quietly waited in the concession line for their coffee and hot chocolate.

But Cal-Mum and Cappotelli got the ball moving in the second half, taking it all the way to the LeRoy seven-yard line before turning it over on downs. Then, as always, Monacelli and Fredericks were hesitant to attempt field goals. The first big break for Cal-Mum came in the ensuing possession when Ausher fumbled the ball in the end zone and the hard-hitting senior Mike Cox pounded his way through one Oatkan Knight after another to recover it for a touchdown. Adam Cappotelli gave Cal-Mum its second big break when he picked off Ausher again at the beginning of the third quarter and ran the ball back to the LeRoy 25. That set up a series of runs by older brother Matt, including a one-yard dive into the end zone which gave the Red Raiders a 12-7 lead.

LeRoy got its own turnover soon after that, though. The Red Raider defense had held the Oatkan Knights to a quick three-and-out series, but on the first play from scrimmage of the drive that Raider fans hoped would put the Knights away, the ball was knocked out of Josh Hayes' hands and was recovered by Tom Shaughnessey. Andy Paladino scored on a six-yard run, the two-point conversion succeeded, and LeRoy had the edge again, 15-12, with only 2:25 remaining in the game.

"We were fighting and they were fighting and that's the way football is," Mike Monacelli said. "I said [to my players] let's try and get a good kickoff return, and then play football. There's still two minutes left to go, we have some good players, we can move the football."

Adam Cappotelli listened well. He took the kickoff and ran it back to the LeRoy 43. Cal-Mum's blocking was superb on the return as one Oatkan Knight after another was leveled, pushed out of Cappotelli's way or simply detoured from the angle that would have gotten the tackle. Quarterback Chris Jones and Adam Cappotelli combined on two excellent pass plays during the next drive, one of thirteen yards and another of nine.

Appropriately enough, it was Matt Cappotelli—dehydrated, exhausted, dizzy and dazed—who did the rest. He found a way to follow his blockers across the line of scrimmage on trap plays and counter plays and simple runs up the gut from the Power I. Then, at the one-yard line, with 19 seconds left in the game and the clock ticking, Cappotelli took the ball straight up the middle and into a pile of players wearing both maroon and white and white and black. Someone in that pile, either Red Raider or Oatkan Knight, knocked the pigskin out of his hands with an elbow or knee—nobody knew exactly what happened. But the ball bounced Cappotelli's way this time, right back into his arms as he lay on the end zone turf. Cal-Mum now had an 18-15 lead. The Raiders scored on the two point conversion. The Knights were unable to move the ball after the ensuing kickoff. Matt Cappotelli once again collapsed onto the ground as he had done after losing both the New York State championship game against Valhalla the year before and act one of the war against LeRoy earlier that season.

Only this time he collapsed victorious, smiling, laughing, giving thanks instead of asking for divine intervention. "This is by far the biggest game I have ever played in," Cappotelli said afterwards. The biggest game—even bigger than the three state championship games he had played in during his freshman, sophomore and junior seasons. Some might find the comment odd, but Matt Cappotelli knew better, as did every other player on the field that day, as do we all. This was Cal-Mum versus LeRoy. It doesn't get any better than this.[*]

CAL-MUM AND LEROY played twice per year in 1998, 1999 and 2000. As in 1997, the team who lost the regular season game won the sectional playoff game, LeRoy in 1998 and 1999, Cal-Mum in 2000. Before each game, the local newspapers from Rochester, Geneseo or Batavia published a preview article that reviewed the rivalry, quoted the thoughts of the coaches, and concluded that the game, as always, was up for grabs. Both teams were very good during those years, the sectional game winner making it into the state tournament, but never getting into the state championship game. Players and coaches both talked up the games as being important ones. They were emotional games, games that everyone in both towns circled on the schedule when it came out in May.

Cal-Mum had some standout players who played exceptional games against LeRoy in these years. Adam Cappotelli took over right where his older brother Matt left off, running the ball with much success in the 1998 and 1999 regular season games. Mike Fox continued to perform as well, earning a spot on the 1999 All-Greater Rochester team and the honor of being named the Class C Section V defensive Player of the Year. Fox's 70 solo tackles in 1999 were as impressive as any defensive accomplishment of any previous Raider. Troy Anderson was the go-to guy on the 2000 team, scoring all three touchdowns in Cal-Mum's upset victory against LeRoy in the sectional semifinals.

The 2000 team provides an especially good tale, both in terms of the LeRoy games and in the larger story of the season. The players came into the late August training camp very undersized and with very limited experience. Sean Ramsey, reflecting back on that year, had this to say: "We got our butts kicked in scrimmage, lost to LeRoy big [24-0, in fact], and lost against Perry for the first time ever. Many people

---

[*]After losing to Christian Brothers Academy of Syracuse 40-20 in the state tournament semifinals, Cal-Mum ended the 1997 season ranked #4 in New York State. Matt Cappotelli was named to the All-Greater Rochester team again. He was also honored as the Class C New York State Player of the Year for the second year in a row. He ended his Red Raider career with 3,602 yards rushing and 40 touchdowns. His life took some dramatic turns after graduating from CMCS, as a Google or Wikipedia search will quickly reveal.

throughout the town did not believe in us, and every player saw their state playoff run dwindling."

Ramsey continues, "Then something happened. Players like James Beaumont, Troy Anderson, Justin Rodgers, and Chris Brown never let us give up." The 24-17 sectional victory over LeRoy, in which the whole team, but especially Troy Anderson, excelled, was "maybe the biggest upset" in the history of the rivalry, Ramsey said. Others would agree.

Ramsey's final assessment of the 2000 season speaks volumes about what it meant for all of us to wear the maroon and white, and for what it still means today. "To me, what makes [the 2000 season] special is that although we did not have the star players, we did what every Cal-Mum football player seems to do and that is keep fighting till the end. Football is a way of life in this town and I am just glad to be part of this great tradition!"

The question must be asked, however—were all these Cal-Mum/LeRoy games too much of a good thing? Did two meetings per season tarnish the luster that competition between the teams had buffed to a brilliant shine over the years? Was 1997 the high point of the rivalry, to which it would not return as long as both teams were in the same sectional classification?

Part of the problem was, as usual, the sectional tournament format, which made the regular season game less important than it had been in years past. LeRoy coach Brian Moran admitted as much before the 1998 regular season game. "We're in a bracket with eleven teams and they take eight of them for the playoffs," he said. "Obviously you've got to win some games, but [the first game against Cal-Mum] is not as important as it was in the past when they only took the top four teams." Some fans found the pattern of one team winning game one and the other team winning game two, the sectional game, tiresome in its predictability. "It's the jinx of the regular season game," Brian Moran said after his team lost to the Troy Anderson-led Cal-Mum team 24-17 in the 2000 sectional semifinals.

In an effort to forestall the jinx, or at least provide some gap between the regular season and any eventual sectional contest, the Livingston County schedule makers shifted the rivalry to the beginning of the season in 2001. It was to be the second game of the season to be precise, scheduled for Friday, September 14, 2001.

"WILL THEY PLAY?" That was the question that passed between dozens of Red Raider and Oatkan Knight fans amidst the shock and grief that came upon us on 9/11. It was, after all, just a football game, a mere contest between boys having fun that was far outweighed by the enormity of what had happened in New York City, Washington, D.C., and Shanksville, Pennsylvania. Major League Baseball cancelled its games up to September 21 and adjusted its regular season schedule back a week. The National Football League postponed its games from September 16 and 17 to January. Many colleges cancelled or postponed their games. But their was a difference between the pros and college on the one hand and high school sports on the other hand—the pro and collegiate teams had to fly to their game destinations, a mode of transportation that was shut down for a week after the attacks. Some people in both communities believed that high schools should follow the example of the colleges and pros. Friday, September 14 was declared a national day of mourning and prayer. It was not a day for a football game.

Officials from LeRoy and Cal-Mum, however—and, to be fair, from many other schools in Section V and around the state—saw things differently. Cal-Mum superintendent Dave Dinolfo said, "I couldn't think of a better place to be than right here with both of our communities cheering our children, who really are the hope of our country." There was a time of silence and a reading of prayers. The crowd sang the national anthem with much gusto and many tears. And at 7:30, Cal-Mum and LeRoy played their football game. Two communities that were tied together through competition now cooperated to show how to get through a time of crisis. Both communities had made it through two world wars, a great depression and two wars in Southeast Asia since the time their football rivalry started. The message on September 14, 2001, was plain and clear: we'll make it through this crisis too.[*]

AS OF THIS WRITING, the 2003 Red Raiders were the last great undefeated team in Cal-Mum football history.[**] Like the great teams before them, they dominated the competition, scoring 241 points and allowing only 18 during the regular season, and amassing a staggering 196 in the five playoff games prior to the New York State Class C championship game against the Hoosick Falls Panthers, giving up only 21 during that run to the Carrier Dome. No one could stop them, no one came close until the state tournament, when both Portville, in the quarterfinals, and Hoosick Falls, in the

---

[*] LeRoy won the game 28-0. That was not, however, the most excruciating loss for Cal-Mum that year. Avon, back in the competitive mix after several years of mediocrity, beat the Red Raiders 34-28 in overtime to close out the 2001 regular season. Then, in the sectional semifinals, Avon won again 34-28, this time on Germaine Dixon's incredible 75-yard interception return for a score as time ran out. Avon lost the sectional championship game to LeRoy, getting shellacked 49-6.

[**] The 2010 team came close, winning the Section V championship against Avon and winning state playoff games against old foes Silver Creek and Walton. The Raiders lost to Tuckahoe in the Class D State Championship game, however. Tuckahoe was also a perennial football powerhouse, perhaps because of its own traditional rivalry against nearby Chester.

championship game, challenged the Raiders' on-field superiority. As we'll see, it was an extremely talented group of football players that year. The team had athletes who could throw, catch, run, block and, especially, tackle on a level with any of the great Raider players of years past.

There was another reason for their success, however, an intangible one—the boost in performance provided by the town border rivalry with the LeRoy Oatkan Knights, which reignited in spectacular fashion the year before, in 2002. There is no doubt that the 2002 Section V Class C championship game and the 2003 rematch fueled the 2003 team's march to glory.

The 2002 Red Raiders had only 24 players on the roster. Still, with Ricky Riddle, Jon Harrington and Jeremy Darron in the backfield following the blocks of John Zelinski, Craig Pullyblank and Jeff Boop, the team opened fans' eyes across Livingston County by whipping Warsaw 66-0 in the first game of the season. But Joe Shaughnessey and the LeRoy rushing attack were too much for Cal-Mum's defense. The Oatkan Knights won the regular season game handily, 21-0. Both teams rolled over the rest of the Livingston County and Section V Class C competition, however. They were all set to meet again in the Class C sectional championship game on Saturday, November 10, 2002, at Fauver Stadium.

The game would turn out to be the best contest between the schools since the classic 1997 games. As in so many other Raider/Knight rumbles of the past, the teams played dead-even football for the first twenty-four minutes. LeRoy's ace kicker Brendan Fulmer missed two field goals, and the defenses held fast on both ends of the field to preserve a 0-0 tie.

Cal-Mum's offense struck first. With four minutes to go in the third quarter, Jeremy Darron bulled his way through the LeRoy offensive line and knocked the ball out of Joe Shaughnessey's hands. Ryan Sherman pounced on the pigskin at the LeRoy 9-yard line, giving the Red Raiders and excellent opportunity to score. The Raiders took full advantage, scoring on a Jon Harrington run and a Rick Riddle conversion to take an 8-0 lead.

The Red Raiders' defense continued to apply the pressure. Jeff Boop sacked Shaughnessey to force a third-and-long. Shaughnessey responded, however, by throwing a perfect strike to Brendan Fulmer, who dashed the rest of the way for a 47-yard touchdown. Ricky Riddle swatted away the two-point conversion attempt, and Cal-Mum held on to its 8-6 lead.

Both defenses held firm throughout much of the fourth quarter. Then Shaughnessey took over. He returned a punt to the LeRoy 37. He scrambled out of Jeff Boop's grasp for a 12-yard gain. Then, with just over three minutes left in the game and again pressured by Boop's relentless blitz, he threw a perfectly placed pass to

Jake Whiting, who caught the ball over a leaping Ricky Riddle and carried two other Raider defenders into the end zone for the go-ahead touchdown. LeRoy's victory was sealed when Branden Fulmer intercepted quarterback Paul Keeley's pass with under two minutes to go.

"This hurts," one Red Raider player after another said through their tears as they shook the Oatkan Knights players' hands. Monacelli too was in tears, perhaps having come to expect that the "regular season jinx" would hold. "You can't underestimate the heart of a ballplayer," he said in reference to his overachieving team. "My kids had the cards stacked against them since August with the low roster numbers. We shuffled the deck a number of times throughout the season. I am very proud to be a part of what I saw out there today."

After the game, Monacelli practiced the good sportsmanship that he always preached to his players. He consoled his team, then went to the LeRoy locker room and, with Coach Moran's permission, offered the Oatkan Knights his personal congratulations and wished them success in the state tournament.[*]

I HAVE ARGUED throughout this book, and especially in this chapter, that the rivalry between the Cal-Mum Red Raiders and the LeRoy Oatkan Knights has, over the years, made both teams better. For Cal-Mum, the years 1929-1932, 1950-1954, 1977-1981 and 1997 were all years when the team's overall success was heightened by the fierce competition provided by LeRoy.[**] The teams seemed to share a symbiotic relationship, feeding off each other and, through the nourishment that the rivalry provided, growing strong enough so that neither school was intimidated by other, perhaps more talented teams from elsewhere in New York State.

Cal-Mum's 2003 New York State championship season was the culminating example of this trend, for the success of the entire season flowed outward from the success of one game, the opening week battle versus LeRoy.

---

[*] LeRoy lost to Onondaga 13-10 in the 2002 state semifinal game when superstar Mike Hart made his unbelievable last minute touchdown run that can be revisited on YouTube. Fortunately for Cal-Mum, Onondaga moved to Class D for the 2003 season. Hart set several national high school rushing records in 2003. In the 2003 New York State Class D championship game against Cambridge, Hart ran for 390 yards and 6 touchdowns. Cal-Mum won the Class C championship later that day. The (thankfully) hypothetical question is: could the 2003 Cal-Mum defense have stopped Hart?

[**] The exception to this rule, of course, was the run of success from 1991-1995. In 1996, in fact, LeRoy head coach Brian Moran successfully used his teams "zero for the nineties" record against Cal-Mum for motivation. From then on, LeRoy more than Cal-Mum drew the benefit of what the rivalry provided, winning nine Section V championships.

During the off season, all the 2003 seniors thought endlessly about the 2002 loss. They watched the game on tape over and over. They talked about it while out running. They yelled about it in the weight room. They heard about it, "every day" according to quarterback Paul Keeley, from their acquaintances and cousins who lived in LeRoy. "We want to remember how close we were," Keeley said as the 2003 opening day game approached. The other 13 returning starters, especially Jeff Boop, who had Joe Shaughnessey in his grasp so many times that game, agreed.

Therefore, when the ball was kicked off at 7:30 PM on Friday, September 5, 2003, at Hamilton Field in Caledonia, everyone wearing maroon and white was hungry for revenge. Jeff Boop and Nate Rodgers got theirs by devouring every Oatkan Knight ball carrier that came within ten yards. They ended up with a combined total of 30 tackles that night. Jamie Fitch got his by running hard every time he received the ball. He ended up with 127 yards and three touchdowns that night. Ryan Sherman and Paul Keeley got theirs by playing opportunistic football. Each ended up with an important fumble recovery that night. The Red Raider faithful got theirs by watching their home team score two touchdowns in the fourth quarter, when emotions always ran the highest anyway. That night, they cheered louder than they ever had before.

And Monacelli never looked back. He watched his team get better each week through the regular season. The offense amassed 58, 52 and 50 points on its most potent nights. The defense remained rock-solid, holding five of seven opponents, including LeRoy, to zero points.

In the sectionals, Perry, Avon and Pembroke were no match for what the Raiders could do. In the state tournament, the defense won the game against an excellent Portville Panthers team on a couple of timely turnovers. First, Chris Harmon caused a fumble that led to a Jeremy Darron touchdown to give Cal-Mum a 12-7 lead. Then Kyle Mynter tipped a pass that was intercepted at the Cal-Mum one-yard line by Bob Toland. The lead held. The Raiders moved on. They were able to breathe a little bit in the semifinal game by taking a 34-0 lead over General Brown into the locker room at halftime and by finishing the game as 48-7 victors. Once again, the Cal-Mum Red Raiders were on their way to a New York State championship game.

Appropriately, Coach Monacelli called upon the ghosts of Red Raider past before the game at the Carrier Dome against Hoosick Falls. He brought his team together after Friday's practice and had them huddle up. "I showed them the scrapbook from the '93 team, the '94 team and the '95 team," Monacelli said. "And then I showed them the fourth scrapbook—and it was empty. I said to them, 'what are you gonna put in yours?'"

Paul Keeley knew. The quarterback was ecstatic after the 30-26 victory over Hoosick Falls, high-fiving and hugging his teammates and coaches, roaming the sidelines pointing up to his family and friends in the stands. Like so many of us, he was also rooted deeply enough in the rich soil of his football team's history to understand what the victory *really* meant.

"We're going to be right up there with the great teams in Cal-Mum history," Keeley said, offering some indication that he and his teammates had discussed the topic before. "The 1929 team that was unbeaten and unscored-upon, the streak teams and the 1995 team that had a great defense and a running game like ours."[*]

Backwards and forwards the story goes, back into years past, forwards into the future. The history of Cal-Mum Red Raider football helps create success precisely because it reminds us, again and again, of what greatness is and provides a blueprint for how that greatness can be achieved. The voices from the past are still talking. All we have to do is listen to what they're telling us.

So get on your feet, Raider fans—as long as our boys in maroon and white keep suiting up on fall Friday nights and giving everything they've got, we'll always have a reason to cheer.

---

[*]2003 was also Cal-Mum's sixteenth official undefeated season, dating back to 1904. As of this writing, according to the National High School Sports Record Book at www.nfhs.org, the Red Raiders rank eighth in the nation in total number of undefeated seasons.

Sources/References

Chapter One: Who's Number One?

Rick Woodson, "Mac spells football F-U-N," Rochester *Times Union*, October 23, 1977.

Tom Fitzgerald, "Joy in LeRoy," Rochester *Democrat and Chronicle*, October 24, 1977.

Tom Batzold, "Victory is Sweet for Cal-Mum," Rochester *Times Union*, October 29, 1977.

Tom Fitzgerald, "Cal-Mum pounds LeRoy," Rochester *Democrat and Chronicle*, October 29, 1977.

Chapter Two: 1929

History of Caledonia from "The History of Livingston County" by James H. Smith. privately published, 1881.

School history from the web article "Caledonia, hear us praise thee! An historical account of the Caledonia-Mumford School" at *http://www.cal-mum.com/school_history.htm*, accessed November 14, 2011.

Caledonia High School yearbooks, various years. Coach Mike Monacelli put together a thorough collection of yearbook entries from these early years. He gave copies of this "Cal-Mum Football Yearbook" to several fans and amateur archivists in town. This collection serves as the best source of information for the nuts and bolts of Cal-Mum football history.

On the other undefeated, unscored-upon teams, see the following: Hal Wilson's *www.pafootballnews.com*; the Waco Tigers page at *texashsfootball.com/board/index.php?showtopic=73048*; the very impressive *http://michigan-football.com.htm* pages; Don Rowe, "Hamilton Lions will honor undefeated team of 1977," from the 11/21/11, Columbus, MS *Dispatch* at *http://www.cdispatch.com/sports/article.asp?aid=7797*; Dave Kane, "40 years later: Pittsfield football players reflect on most dominant season ever" from the 9/23/10, Springfield, IL, *State-Journal Register* at *http://www.sj-r.com/sports/x35355855/Players-reflect-on-most-dominant-season-of-Saukees-dynasty*; and Kevin Askeland's list of the "Top 10 most untouchable high school football records" at *http://www.maxpreps.com/news/LJHxhdKiEd-YiQAcxJSkrA/top-10-most-untouchable-high-school-football-records.htm*. See also the National High School Sports Record Book 2011, which can be downloaded from *http://www.nfhs.org/content.aspx?id=3230*.

Caledonia vs. Aquinas from the Rochester *Democrat and Chronicle*, Sunday, October 16, 1932, and the Rochester *American*, also Sunday, October 16, 1932. Authors and page numbers cannot be identified. I found both articles in the pages of Eddie Coots' scrapbook.

Chapter Three: Football Families

Yearbooks from the 1940s, 1950s and 1960s were used to gather information on rosters and game scores.

The article on the lights came from the Caledonia *Advertiser*, October 19, 1950. Author unknown.

The article on Ed Matthews joining the Cal-Mum faculty came from the Caledonia *Advertiser*, unknown date, 1959. Author unknown.

Information on Coach Frank Ruane's system came from Rob Martin's notebooks. I owe a debt of thanks to Shannon Martin for allowing me access to her late husband's voluminous Cal-Mum football history collection.

Charles Loftus' essay is from James Gibson Holgate's *Fundamental Football* (New York, NY: Ronald Press, Company, 1958), pp. vii-x. Coach Ruane gave copies of the essay to all his players, which they were to staple to the inside cover of their spiral-bound, fifty-sheet, college-ruled football notebook.

Sources/References

Chapter Four: The Big Mac Attack

Steve Monroe, "Cal-Mum rolls over LeRoy," Rochester *Democrat and Chronicle*, October 27, 1973.

Bob Matthews, "McAlee's 3-month miracle," Rochester *Democrat and Chronicle*, November 17, 1973.

Tom Fitzgerald, "Cal-Mum football's fun," Rochester *Democrat and Chronicle*, October 30, 1974.

Bob Matthews, "Cal-Mum finds new coach, hope," Rochester *Democrat and Chronicle*, September 25, 1973.

Rick Woodson, "Mac spells football F-U-N," Rochester *Times Union*, Monday, October 23, 1977.

Gary Fallesen, "Cal-Mum's McAlee will retire never having played role of underdog," Rochester *Democrat and Chronicle*, October 7, 1987.

Chris Metcalf, "1973 Red Raider football quad reunites," Livingston County *News*, July 24, 1995.

Quotes about the 1973 team come from personal interviews and from Jim Vokes' Cal-Mum football page at *http://www.cal-mum.com/vokes/index.htm*.

The 1974 Cal-Mum vs. LeRoy game was covered in Tom Fitzgerald's articles, "LeRoy: the unbeaten underdog" and "Cal-Mum football's fun," Rochester *Democrat and Chronicle*, October 30, 1974; "Cal-Mum finishes undefeated again," Rochester *Democrat and Chronicle*, November 2, 1974; Caledonia *Advertiser*, November 7, 1974.

On Livonia coach Mike Haugh, see Rudy Martzke, "Livonia: new challenger to Cal-Mum domination," Rochester *Democrat and Chronicle*, September 5, 1978.

Tom Fitzgerald, "Livonia stops the Raiders," Rochester *Democrat and Chronicle*, October 19, 1975.

Bill Koenig, "LeRoy's Ruane: 'I seek no revenge,' " Rochester *Democrat and Chronicle*, October 18, 1977.

Chapter Five: Monumental Meetings, 1978-1981

Mary Place Boyd, "History of the Soldiers' Monument" at *http://www.cal-mum.com*.

Bob Pullyblank quote in Chris Metcalf, "Cal-Mum has longstanding tradition," Livingston County *News*, September 8, 2010.

Tom Batzold, "Cal-Mum size worries Alena," Rochester *Democrat and Chronicle*, November 18, 1978.

Greg Boeck, "Junior," Rochester *Democrat and Chronicle*, January 14, 1979.

Greg Boeck, "Cal-Mum finishes undefeated again," Rochester *Democrat and Chronicle*, November 19, 1978.

"Cal-Mum retains crown with tie-breaker victory," Rochester *Democrat and Chronicle*, November 18, 1979. Author unknown.

Jennie Rees, "Another Cal-Mum, LeRoy battle," Rochester *Times Union*, November 13, 1980.

John Kolomic, "Surprise play lifts Cal-Mum to 26-21 win," Rochester *Democrat and Chronicle*, November 15, 1980.

Dick Patrick, "It's the end of an era," Rochester *Democrat and Chronicle*, November 9, 1981.

Bob Minzesheimer, "Life after Cal-Mum loss? Yes.," Rochester *Democrat and Chronicle*, November 10, 1981.

Gary Fallesen, "Cal-Mum wins 43d," Rochester *Democrat and Chronicle*, September 19, 1981.

Dick Patrick, "LeRoy victim of air raid," Rochester *Times Union*, October 12, 1981.

Joe Robbins, "Cal-Mum rally overcomes Livonia, 17-14," Rochester *Democrat and Chronicle*, October 17, 1981.

Bob Minzesheimer, " 'It's the only game in town,' " Rochester *Democrat and Chronicle*, October 16, 1981.

Gary Maloney, "McAlee can feel pressure from Cal-Mum streak," Olean *Times Herald*, October 23, 1981.

Sources/References

Gary Maloney, "Cal-Mum walks the tightrope," Olean *Times Herald*, October 24, 1981.

Dan Galante, "A weekend to remember," Rochester *Democrat and Chronicle*, November 10, 1981.

Chapter Six: Under Pressure

Gary Fallesen, "No streak, but Cal-Mum still appears the strongest," Rochester *Democrat and Chronicle*, September 16, 1982.

John Kolomic, "Cal-Mum wallops Notre-Dame, 35-0," Rochester *Democrat and Chronicle*, September 18, 1982.

Leo Roth, "Roland Poles fools skeptics on, off field," Rochester *Times Union*, October 17, 1985.

Gary Fallesen, "Cal-Mum's Poles develops unwavering faith in inner ability," Rochester *Democrat and Chronicle*, October 17, 1985.

Gary Fallesen, "Two late touchdowns lift Cal-Mum over Avon," Rochester *Democrat and Chronicle*, October 22, 1983.

Brett Avery, "Cal-Mum's late pass tops Avon," Rochester *Democrat and Chronicle*, October 13, 1984.

Brett Avery, "Cal-Mum keeps ball on ground, stops Avon 7-0," Rochester *Democrat and Chronicle*, October 12, 1985.

John Moriello, "Cal-Mum, McAlee reach pinnacle," Rochester *Democrat and Chronicle*, November 17, 1987.

Chapter Seven: Monacelli Moments

Jack Haley, "Is it two or is really three?," Livingston County *News*, December 1, 1994.

Allen Wilson, "Bruise Brothers make their mark for Cal-Mum," Rochester *Democrat and Chronicle*, November 14, 1991.

Jack Haley, "Raiders run to victory," Livingston County *News*, November 21, 1991.

Jack Haley, "A bad call should not play part in an important football game," Livingston County *News*, November 21, 1991.

Jack Haley, "Moving apart," Livingston County *News*, September 4, 1992.

John Smallwood, "Cal-Mum defense does it," Rochester *Democrat and Chronicle*, November 23, 1992.

Jack Haley, "Still no takers for Cal-Mum," Livingston County *News*, September 2, 1993.

Donna MacKenzie, "Cal-Mum has a line on another title," Rochester *Democrat and Chronicle*, September 3, 1993.

Jack Haley, "Get ready for war on Friday," Livingston County *News*, October 21, 1993.

Jack Haley, "Red Raiders run to state title," Livingston County *News*, December 2, 1993.

Jack Haley, "A day to never forget," Livingston County *News*, December 2, 1993.

Chapter Eight: 1995

Albert Lin, "Cal-Mum runs winning streak to 21," Rochester *Democrat and Chronicle*, September 9, 1995.

Jack Haley, "Seniors help Red Raiders roll on," Livingston County *News*, October 14, 1995.

Jack Haley, "Cal-Mum runs past Knights," Livingston County *News*, October 21, 1995.

Jeff DiVeronica, "Cal-Mum runs from overmatched Clyde," Rochester *Democrat and Chronicle*, November 4, 1995.

Sources/References

Albert Lin, "Cal-Mum defense silences formidable Pine Valley offense," Rochester *Democrat and Chronicle*, November 25, 1995.

Eric Mack, "The Red Raiders make it a three-peat," Livingston County *News*, November 28, 1995.

Jack Haley, "Simply the best around," Livingston County *News*, November 28, 1995.

Chapter Nine: Destroy LeRoy

Ben Carlson, "Tailgating a part of the Cal-Mum/LeRoy game," Livingston County *News*, October 18, 1996.

Steve Bradley, "Cal-Mum vs. LeRoy: A century of football," Batavia *Daily News*, October 1993.

Paul Hartwick, "LeRoy, Cal-Mum set to renew rivalry," Batavia *Daily News*, October 1992.

Dave Staba, "Red Raiders run their record to 7-0," Livingston County *News*, October 1991.

James Johnson, "LeRoy outlasts Cal-Mum in Overtime," Rochester *Democrat and Chronicle*, October 4, 1997.

James Johnson, "Cappotelli caps rally for Cal-Mum," Rochester *Democrat and Chronicle*, November 9, 1997.

Eric Keppler, "The rivalry: part 58," Batavia *Daily News*, October 1998.

Chris Metcalf, " LeRoy rallies past Cal-Mum," Batavia *Daily News*, November 13, 2002.

James Johnson, "Cal-Mum on top," Rochester *Democrat and Chronicle*, November 29, 2003.

Appendix A:
Game-by-Game Scores, 1925-2011

THE BIRTH of Caledonia football came in 1900, when Caledonia beat LeRoy twice and lost to LeRoy once. There were several other games against LeRoy before 1925. These early games are discussed in Chapter Two and are noted in Appendix E. Also, there were several other known games in the infancy of Caledonia football, including victories against Sodus in 1904 and Holley in 1905. Apparently, Caledonia was undefeated in 1904, and played a total of nine games in 1905, although only the games against Holley and LeRoy are recorded. Reliable information for the early years of Caledonia football is otherwise lacking. Therefore, this game-by-game tally of scores offered below begins with the year 1925, the first year for which reliable information is available.

Scores begin on the following page and are listed year-by-year, with opposing teams in the left column, followed by the game's final result (Win, Loss, or Tie), the points scored by Caledonia (PF = Points For) and the opponent (PA = Points Against), and any interesting notes relating to the particular game. The season's total points scored by Caledonia and the opposing teams appear under the game scores.

Appendix A: Game-by-Game Scores, 1925-2011

1925: 6-0-1

Opponent	Result	PF	PA	Notes
Albion	Win	31	3	
Geneseo	Win	6	0	
Bergen	Win	12	0	
Webster	Win	12	0	
Scottsville	Win	6	0	
Scottsville	Tie	6	6	
Bergen	Win	7	0	
		83	**9**	

1926: 4-3-0

Opponent	Result	PF	PA	Notes
Greigsville	Win	12	7	Margaret McCabe writes the Caledonia alma mater
Bergen	Win	7	3	
Greigsville	Loss	12	13	
Scottsville	Win	20	0	
Albion	Loss	6	12	
Scottsville	Win	16	0	
Webster	Loss	0	32	
		80	**73**	

1927: 6-2-1

Opponent	Result	PF	PA	Notes
Genesee Weslyan	Loss	0	6	
Albion	Tie	0	0	
Greigsville	Win	6	0	
Bergen	Win	31	0	
Scottsville	Win	13	6	
Livonia	Win	19	0	
Scottsville	Win	21	0	
LeRoy	Loss	0	2	
Avon	Win	38	0	22-game winning streak begins
		108	**14**	

1928: 9-0-0

Opponent	Result	PF	PA	Notes
Avon	Win	6	0	
Perry	Win	6	0	
Batavia Reserves	Win	38	0	
Greigsville	Win	12	6	
Warsaw	Win	13	0	
Dansville	Win	12	6	
Albion	Win	6	0	
Attica	Win	37	6	
Livonia	Win	7	0	13-game shutout streak begins
		138	**18**	

1929: 9-0-0

Opponent	Result	PF	PA	Notes
Attica	Win	35	0	
Batavia Reserves	Win	28	0	
Livonia	Win	47	0	
Warsaw	Win	21	0	
Dansville	Win	48	0	
Greigsville	Win	40	0	
LeRoy	Win	6	0	Honeoye Falls military band plays
Avon	Win	21	0	
Geneseo	Win	28	0	
		274	0	

1930: 6-2-0

Opponent	Result	PF	PA	Notes
Attica	Win	39	0	
Perry	Win	12	0	Jim Jackson scores on 2 interception returns
Livonia	Win	28	0	
Dansville	Loss	0	6	22-game winning streak & 13-game shutout streak end
Greigsville	Win	6	0	
LeRoy	Loss	0	6	
Avon	Win	47	0	
Geneseo	Win	45	0	
		177	12	

1931: 6-1-1

Opponent	Result	PF	PA	Notes
Fairport	Loss	0	6	Raiders start wearing maroon and white
Mynderse Academy	Win	22	6	
Greigsville	Win	20	0	
Livonia	Win	55	0	
Geneseo	Win	14	0	
LeRoy	Tie	6	6	
Avon	Win	51	0	
Dansville	Win	21	7	
		195	**25**	

1932: 8-1-0

Opponent	Result	PF	PA	Notes
St. Thomas Indian	Win	44	0	Cattaraugas Reservation school
Dansville	Win	38	0	
Avon	Win	34	0	
Aquinas	Win	43	6	Jim Jackson scores 5 touchdowns
Mt. Morris	Win	7	0	
Greigsville	Win	39	0	
LeRoy	Loss	7	18	
Geneseo	Win	25	0	
Nunda	Win	67	0	Highest point total until 1993
		304	**24**	

Appendix A: Game-by-Game Scores, 1925-2011

1933: 4-2-1

Opponent	Result	PF	PA	Notes
Avon	Win	27	6	
Mt. Morris	Win	31	0	
Wayland	Win	12	7	
Geneseo	Win	26	13	
Aquinas	Tie	7	7	
Dansville	Loss	0	8	
Batavia	Loss	6	7	
		109	**48**	

1934: 4-1-1

Opponent	Result	PF	PA	Notes
Mt. Morris	Tie	0	0	
Wayland	Win	13	0	
Bath	Win	24	0	
Geneseo	Win	13	7	
Dansville	Loss	7	18	
Avon	Win	12	6	
		69	**31**	

1935: 4-2-0

Opponent	Result	PF	PA	Notes
Wayland	Win	19	0	
Bath	Win	18	0	
Geneseo	Win	28	0	
Dansville	Lose	6	13	
Mt. Morris	Win	13	0	
Avon	Lose	6	13	
		83	**26**	

1936: 5-1-0

Opponent	Result	PF	PA	Notes
Wayland	Win	44	0	
Perry	Win	31	0	
Dansville	Win	34	0	
Warsaw	Win	33	0	
Avon	Loss	15	21	
Corning	Win	12	0	
		157	21	

1937: 1-3-0

Opponent	Result	PF	PA	Notes
Warsaw	Win	25	0	
Perry	Loss	7	25	
Avon	Loss	0	7	
Dansville	Loss	6	7	
		38	39	

1938: 2-3-0

Opponent	Result	PF	PA	Notes
Avon	Loss	6	7	
Dansville	Win	27	0	
Wellsville	Loss	0	6	
Warsaw	Win	12	6	
Perry	Loss	6	19	
		51	38	

Appendix A: Game-by-Game Scores, 1925-2011

1939: 3-2-0

Opponent	Result	PF	PA	Notes
Warsaw	Win	7	0	Robert Freeman coaches his first game
Perry	Loss	12	33	
Avon	Win	7	6	
Dansville	Win	6	0	
Wellsville	Loss	6	19	
		38	**58**	

1940: 4-2-0

Opponent	Result	PF	PA	Notes
Canisteo	Win	12	6	
Warsaw	Win	12	6	
Perry	Loss	0	40	
Avon	Loss	7	27	
Dansville	Win	13	6	
Irondequoit	Win	19	0	
		63	**85**	

1941: 4-1-1

Opponent	Result	PF	PA	Notes
Dansville	Loss	0	25	
Canisteo	Win	25	0	
Warsaw	Win	13	0	
Perry	Win	19	0	
Avon	Win	19	0	
Irondequoit	Tie	13	13	
		89	**38**	

1942: 0-0-0

Opponent	Result	PF	PA	Notes
--	--	--	--	No football due to lack of transportation during World War II
		0	0	

1943: 4-2-0

Opponent	Result	PF	PA	Notes
Dansville	Loss	0	14	
Industry	Win	7	6	
Avon	Win	17	13	
Industry	Win	13	0	
Dansville	Win	27	0	
Avon	Loss	0	34	
		64	67	

1944: 3-3-0

Opponent	Result	PF	PA	Notes
Irondequoit	Win	6	0	
Dansville	Win	14	0	
Avon	Loss	0	6	
Irondequoit	Loss	0	13	
Dansville	Win	7	0	
Avon	Loss	20	33	
		47	52	

Appendix A: Game-by-Game Scores, 1925-2011

1945: 1-2-2

Opponent	Result	PF	PA	Notes
Avon	Tie	6	6	
Dansville	Loss	6	7	
Avon	Loss	2	7	
Dansville	Tie	13	13	
Industry	Win	26	7	
		49	40	

1946: 5-2-0

Opponent	Result	PF	PA	Notes
Warsaw	Win	40	13	
Dansville	Win	26	7	
Perry	Win	13	0	
Avon	Win	18	0	
Dansville	Loss	6	12	
Oakfield	Win	38	0	
Avon	Loss	13	20	
		154	52	

1947: 7-0-0

Opponent	Result	PF	PA	Notes
Industry	Win	38	7	
Industry	Win	27	7	
Livonia	Win	32	0	
Warsaw	Win	34	6	
Avon	Win	34	7	
Dansville	Win	27	0	
Perry	Win	47	6	
		239	33	

1948: 6-1-0

Opponent	Result	PF	PA	Notes
LeRoy	Win	18	2	
Bath	Loss	13	20	
Warsaw	Win	40	12	
Avon	Win	14	0	
Dansville	Win	33	6	
Perry	Win	20	6	
Livonia	Win	56	0	
		154	**46**	

1949: 5-2-0

Opponent	Result	PF	PA	Notes
LeRoy	Loss	6	25	
Bath	Loss	0	7	
Avon	Win	26	6	
Dansville	Win	22	6	
Perry	Win	34	6	
Livonia	Win	29	7	
Warsaw	Win	35	13	
		152	**70**	

Appendix A: Game-by-Game Scores, 1925-2011

1950: 7-0-0

Opponent	Result	PF	PA	Notes
Warsaw	Win	41	6	
Dansville	Win	13	7	
Perry	Win	27	13	
Livonia	Win	28	6	
York	Win	33	12	First Hamilton Field game with lights
Avon	Win	33	0	
LeRoy	Win	31	6	
		206	**48**	

1951: 5-3-0

Opponent	Result	PF	PA	Notes
LeRoy	Loss	6	25	
Perry	Win	13	6	
Livonia	Win	7	0	
Warsaw	Win	25	0	
Attica	Win	19	0	
Avon	Loss	13	15	
Dansville	Loss	6	20	
John Marshall	Win	25	13	
		114	**79**	

1952: 5-3-0

Opponent	Result	PF	PA	Notes
Avon	Win	14	0	
LeRoy	Loss	13	19	
York	Win	32	12	
Mt. Morris	Loss	7	19	
Geneseo	Win	14	7	
Dansville	Win	35	0	
Livonia	Loss	7	19	
Charlotte	Win	27	14	
		149	90	

1953: 4-2-1

Opponent	Result	PF	PA	Notes
LeRoy	Loss	0	12	
York	Win	34	6	
Mt. Morris	Win	19	0	
Geneseo	Win	14	0	
Dansville	Win	33	25	
Livonia	Loss	0	21	
Avon	Tie	6	6	
		106	70	

Appendix A: Game-by-Game Scores, 1925-2011

1954: 7-0-0

Opponent	Result	PF	PA	Notes
York	Win	25	6	
Mt. Morris	Win	13	6	
Geneseo	Win	26	7	
Dansville	Win	22	7	
Livonia	Win	21	6	
Avon	Win	27	6	
LeRoy	Win	20	0	
		155	**38**	

1955: 6-1-0

Opponent	Result	PF	PA	Notes
Mt. Morris	Win	46	6	
Geneseo	Win	32	6	
Dansville	Win	26	0	
Livonia	Win	33	0	
Avon	Win	31	6	
Madison	Loss	6	7	
York	Win	42	0	
		216	**25**	

1956: 4-2-0

Opponent	Result	PF	PA	Notes
Brockport	Loss	26	27	
Dansville	Win	26	0	
Livonia	Win	28	7	
Avon	Loss	0	25	
York	Win	42	0	
Mt. Morris	Win	20	0	Coach Freeman's last game
		142	59	

1957: 3-3-1

Opponent	Result	PF	PA	Notes
Brockport	Loss	0	20	
Dansville	Win	7	6	
Avon	Loss	6	22	
York	Win	20	6	
Livonia	Loss	6	7	
Mt. Morris	Tie	0	0	
Albion	Win	12	6	
		51	69	

Appendix A: Game-by-Game Scores, 1925-2011

1958: 4-3-0

Opponent	Result	PF	PA	Notes
Brockport	Loss	6	14	
Dansville	Win	33	7	
Avon	Win	14	0	
York	Win	27	6	
Livonia	Loss	12	39	
Mt. Morris	Win	21	0	
Albion	Loss	6	26	
		119	**92**	

1959: 2-3-2

Opponent	Result	PF	PA	Notes
Perry	Win	13	6	
York	Loss	0	13	
Mt. Morris	Win	19	6	
Dansville	Tie	6	6	
Livonia	Tie	6	6	
Avon	Loss	0	25	
Albion	Loss	7	27	
		51	**89**	

1960: 0-6-1

Opponent	Result	PF	PA	Notes
Perry	Loss	0	20	
Mt. Morris	Loss	0	33	
Dansville	Loss	0	28	
Livonia	Loss	7	20	
Avon	Loss	0	19	
York	Tie	20	20	
Albion	Loss	13	14	
		40	154	

1961: 2-5-0

Opponent	Result	PF	PA	Notes
Alexander	Win	7	0	
Dansville	Loss	13	20	
Livonia	Loss	0	19	
Avon	Loss	0	24	
York	Loss	12	25	
Mt. Morris	Loss	0	26	
Perry	Win	19	13	
		51	127	

1962: 4-3-0

Opponent	Result	PF	PA	Notes
Mt. Morris	Loss	7	26	
York	Win	7	6	
Avon	Win	13	6	
Livonia	Loss	0	13	
Perry	Loss	6	12	
Dansville	Win	14	7	
Geneseo	Win	19	14	
		66	**84**	

1963: 5-2-0

Opponent	Result	PF	PA	Notes
York	Win	16	13	
Avon	Win	9	6	
Livonia	Win	32	19	
Canisteo	Win	13	6	
Dansville	Loss	0	21	
Geneseo	Win	12	0	
Mt. Morris	Loss	19	31	
		101	**96**	

1964: 4-3-0

Opponent	Result	PF	PA	Notes
Avon	Loss	0	13	
Livonia	Win	21	6	
Canisteo	Win	19	6	
Dansville	Loss	16	32	
Geneseo	Win	48	6	
Mt. Morris	Loss	7	19	
York	Win	19	7	
		130	**88**	

1965: 7-1-0

Opponent	Result	PF	PA	Notes
Livonia	Win	40	0	
Canisteo	Win	14	0	
Dansville	Win	21	0	
Geneseo	Win	6	0	
Mt. Morris	Win	39	7	
York	Win	33	20	
Avon	Win	26	10	
LeRoy	Loss	7	12	
		176	**49**	

Appendix A: Game-by-Game Scores, 1925-2011

1966: 5-3-0

Opponent	Result	PF	PA	Notes
Canisteo	Win	27	6	Frank Ruane's first game
Dansville	Loss	7	22	
Geneseo	Loss	6	7	
Mt. Morris	Win	13	0	
York	Win	26	6	
Avon	Win	26	0	
Livonia	Win	6	0	
LeRoy	Loss	0	39	
		111	**80**	

1967: 7-1-0

Opponent	Result	PF	PA	Notes
Dansville	Loss	18	19	
Geneseo	Win	6	0	
Mt. Morris	Win	26	0	
York	Win	32	13	
Avon	Win	41	0	
Livonia	Win	6	0	
Canisteo	Win	20	0	
LeRoy	Win	31	0	
		180	**32**	

1968: 7-1-0

Opponent	Result	PF	PA	Notes
Geneseo	Loss	13	33	
Mt. Morris	Win	31	7	
York	Win	13	0	
Avon	Win	24	7	
Livonia	Win	40	0	
Canisteo	Win	34	0	
Dansville	Win	34	14	
LeRoy	Win	7	0	
		206	**61**	

1969: 7-1-0

Opponent	Result	PF	PA	Notes
Letchworth	Win	21	6	
York	Win	8	6	
LeRoy	Win	6	0	
Avon	Loss	0	20	
Livonia	Win	41	0	
Geneseo	Win	22	13	
Dansville	Win	24	0	
Canisteo	Win	14	0	
		136	**45**	

Appendix A: Game-by-Game Scores, 1925-2011

1970: 5-2-1

Opponent	Result	PF	PA	Notes
Dansville	Win	20	6	
Mt. Morris	Win	36	0	
York	Win	24	6	
Livonia	Win	43	0	
Geneseo	Loss	0	13	
Avon	Loss	0	20	
LeRoy	Tie	0	0	
Canisteo	Win	20	0	
		143	**45**	

1971: 4-4-0

Opponent	Result	PF	PA	Notes
Canisteo	Win	30	26	
York	Win	24	0	
Livonia	Win	28	26	
Geneseo	Loss	0	28	
Avon	Loss	18	19	
Mt. Morris	Win	28	12	
Perry	Loss	6	18	
LeRoy	Loss	0	32	
		134	**161**	

1972: 3-5-0

Opponent	Result	PF	PA	Notes
Warsaw	Win	12	0	
Livonia	Loss	6	14	
Geneseo	Loss	12	14	
Avon	Loss	8	26	
Mt. Morris	Win	60	0	
York	Win	28	0	
Letchworth	Loss	20	22	
LeRoy	Loss	0	48	Coach Ruane's last game
		146	**124**	

1973: 8-0-0

Opponent	Result	PF	PA	Notes
Dansville	Win	55	0	Bill McAlee's first game; 21-game winning streak begins
York	Win	66	26	
Livonia	Win	62	0	
Geneseo	Win	43	0	
Avon	Win	34	19	
Mt. Morris	Win	34	0	
LeRoy	Win	42	16	"Remember!"
Canisteo	Win	53	6	
		389	**67**	

Appendix A: Game-by-Game Scores, 1925-2011

1974: 8-0-0

Opponent	Result	PF	PA	Notes
Canisteo	Win	34	0	
Livonia	Win	40	8	
Geneseo	Win	42	0	
Avon	Win	43	0	
Mt. Morris	Win	34	0	
York	Win	42	8	
Perry	Win	42	0	
LeRoy	Win	22	14	"What a feeling!" McAlee says after the big home win
		308	30	

1975: 8-1-0

Opponent	Result	PF	PA	Notes
Warsaw	Win	40	6	
Geneseo	Win	32	6	
Avon	Win	39	8	
Wellsville	Win	33	6	
York	Win	43	16	
Livonia	Loss	6	14	21-game winning streak ends
Letchworth	Win	38	8	
LeRoy	Win	22	6	
Dansville	Win	24	6	
		277	76	

1976: 7-1-0

Opponent	Result	PF	PA	Notes
Warsaw	Win	34	6	
LeRoy	Loss	7	28	The lights go out at Hamilton Field
Livonia	Win	28	18	49-game winning streak, "The Great Streak," begins
Letchworth	Win	39	0	
York	Win	49	0	
Dansville	Win	18	0	
Honeoye Falls-Lima	Win	39	6	
Avon	Win	13	12	
		226	71	

1977: 8-0-0

Opponent	Result	PF	PA	Notes
Geneseo	Win	27	6	
Avon	Win	24	6	
Dansville	Win	41	14	
Canisteo	Win	30	2	
Perry	Win	37	0	
Livonia	Win	21	13	
LeRoy	Win	19	0	Who's number one? McAlee's most memorable game
Honeoye Falls-Lima	Win	34	6	
		233	47	#1 in NYS small school poll

Appendix A: Game-by-Game Scores, 1925-2011

1978: 9-0-0

Opponent	Result	PF	PA	Notes
Letchworth	Win	55	12	
Livonia	Win	34	0	
York	Win	45	0	
Avon	Win	14	7	
Warsaw	Win	32	0	
Dansville	Win	13	10	Poles and Trojanski "power the I"
Honeoye Falls-Lima	Win	40	0	
LeRoy	Win	13	3	
Lyons	Win	42	0	Section V Class B championship; monumental meeting
		288	32	#1 in NYS small school poll

1979: 9-0-0

Opponent	Result	PF	PA	Notes
Canisteo	Win	23	0	
Avon	Win	28	2	
Dansville	Win	34	7	
Perry	Win	34	0	
Geneseo	Win	35	0	
Livonia	Win	35	14	
LeRoy	Win	28	20	
Honeoye Falls-Lima	Win	34	0	
Clyde-Savannah	Win	26	20	Section V Class B championship; OT; monumental meeting
		277	63	#1 in NYS small school poll

1980: 10-0-0

Opponent	Result	PF	PA	Notes
Albion	Win	14	6	Goal-line stand wins the game
Avon	Win	21	13	
Dansville	Win	34	0	
LeRoy	Win	47	12	
Livonia	Win	14	13	
Wellsville	Win	32	20	
Honeoye Falls-Lima	Win	33	0	
Notre Dame	Win	21	6	
Lyons	Win	34	0	
LeRoy	Win	26	21	Section V Class B championship; Ron Poles TD at end of game; monumental meeting
		276	**91**	#1 in NYS small school poll

1981: 7-2-0

Opponent	Result	PF	PA	Notes
Albion	Win	19	13	Goal-line stand wins the game (again)
Avon	Win	21	7	
Dansville	Win	34	8	
LeRoy	Win	21	20	Zimmer to Bowers and Goodburlet wins it
Livonia	Win	17	14	Hamilton Field crowd helps bring the win
Wellsville	Win	34	24	
Honeoye Falls-Lima	Win	34	6	
Notre Dame	Loss	0	16	"The Great Streak" ends; monumental meeting
Livonia	Loss	14	35	Section V Class B semifinals
		189	**146**	

Appendix A: Game-by-Game Scores, 1925-2011

1982: 7-2-0

Opponent	Result	PF	PA	Notes
Notre Dame	Win	35	0	
Dansville	Win	20	6	
LeRoy	Loss	14	34	
Livonia	Win	19	0	
Honeoye Falls-Lima	Win	19	0	
Wellsville	Win	29	0	
Bath	Win	49	6	
Avon	Win	12	0	
LeRoy	Loss	6	29	Section V Class B semifinals
		204	75	

1983: 9-1-0

Opponent	Result	PF	PA	Notes
Notre Dame	Win	40	0	
LeRoy	Win	20	9	
Livonia	Win	24	6	
Honeoye Falls-Lima	Win	18	0	
Wellsville	Win	34	0	
Bath	Win	44	0	
Avon	Win	21	19	
Dansville	Win	33	12	
Letchworth	Win	36	0	
Avon	Loss	0	27	Section V Class B semifinals
		271	73	

1984: 6-3-0

Opponent	Result	PF	PA	Notes
Notre Dame	Win	19	0	
Honeoye Falls-Lima	Win	20	14	
Newark	Win	25	6	
Livonia	Win	35	12	
Avon	Win	7	6	The "fog game"
Dansville	Win	28	6	
Greece Olympia	Loss	14	20	
LeRoy	Loss	6	33	
Red Jacket	Loss	7	27	Section V Class B semifinals
		161	**124**	

1985: 7-1-1

Opponent	Result	PF	PA	Notes
Notre Dame	Win	20	14	
Honeoye Falls-Lima	Win	20	0	
Livonia	Tie	20	20	
Avon	Win	7	0	
Dansville	Win	26	0	McAlee's 100th win
Marshall	Win	21	8	
LeRoy	Win	28	14	Roland Poles runs for 297 yards
Avon	Win	6	0	Section V Class B semifinals
Red Jacket	Loss	0	6	Section V Class B championship
		148	**62**	

Appendix A: Game-by-Game Scores, 1925-2011

1986: 5-2-2

Opponent	Result	PF	PA	Notes
LeRoy	Win	26	7	
Avon	Loss	0	10	
Honeoye Falls-Lima	Win	14	0	
Dansville	Win	14	0	
Livonia	Tie	6	6	
Hornell	Win	14	6	
Elba	Win	37	7	
Avon	Tie	0	0	Section V Class B semifinals
Avon	Loss	7	10	Section V Class B playoff
		118	**46**	

1987: 9-1-0

Opponent	Result	PF	PA	Notes
York	Win	25	0	
Avon	Win	19	0	
Honeoye Falls-Lima	Win	46	0	
Hornell	Loss	14	15	
Oakfield-Alabama	Win	39	0	
Dansville	Win	42	22	
Livonia	Win	20	14	
LeRoy	Win	21	14	
LeRoy	Win	28	7	Section V Class B semifinals
Avon	Win	21	11	Section V Class B championship; Coach McAlee's last game
		275	**75**	

1988: 2-6-0

Opponent	Result	PF	PA	Notes
Geneva	Loss	15	34	Mike Monacelli's first game
Dansville	Loss	26	27	
Elba	Loss	12	22	
LeRoy	Loss	6	34	
Honeoye Falls-Lima	Win	28	13	
Oakfield-Alabama	Win	38	0	
Livonia	Loss	6	28	
Avon	Loss	6	13	
		132	**171**	

1989: 4-4-0

Opponent	Result	PF	PA	Notes
LeRoy	Loss	0	7	
Alexander	Win	38	0	
Elba	Loss	16	38	
Perry	Win	30	0	
Notre Dame	Win	30	18	
Pembroke	Win	28	20	
Avon	Loss	7	14	
Warsaw	Loss	24	29	
		172	**121**	

Appendix A: Game-by-Game Scores, 1925-2011

1990: 8-2-0

Opponent	Result	PF	PA	Notes
LeRoy	Win	19	0	Monacelli's first win over LeRoy
Oakfield-Alabama	Win	22	20	
Notre Dame	Win	49	0	
Pembroke	Win	14	7	
Attica	Win	32	6	
Geneseo	Win	28	12	
Elba	Win	22	18	
York	Loss	0	20	
Oakfield-Alabama	Win	36	12	Section V Class C semifinals
Clyde-Savannah	Loss	14	20	Section V Class C championship; OT
		236	**115**	

1991: 10-1-0

Opponent	Result	PF	PA	Notes
Attica	Win	14	13	
Warsaw	Win	40	7	
Letchworth	Win	57	0	
Perry	Win	24	21	
Honeoye Falls-Lima	Win	29	7	
York	Win	29	6	
LeRoy	Win	22	18	Two goal-line stands win the game
Pembroke	Win	34	3	
Lyons	Win	52	6	Section V Class C semifinals
East Rochester	Win	27	9	Section V Class C championship
Silver Creek	Loss	8	13	NYS Class C western regional finals
		335	**103**	

1992: 11-0-0

Opponent	Result	PF	PA	Notes
Avon	Win	36	6	17-game winning streak begins
Attica	Win	18	0	
Alexander	Win	38	12	
Dansville	Win	38	20	
Barker	Win	55	8	
Honeoye Falls-Lima	Win	51	0	
Perry	Win	63	0	
LeRoy	Win	42	14	
East Rochester	Win	28	0	Section V Class C semifinals
Avon	Win	32	0	Section V Class C championship
Windsor	Win	16	8	NYS Class C western regional finals
		415	**68**	#1 in NYS small school poll

Appendix A: Game-by-Game Scores, 1925-2011

1993: 11-1-0

Opponent	Result	PF	PA	Notes
York	Win	34	6	
Dansville	Win	57	6	
LeRoy	Win	27	7	
Avon	Win	54	13	
Honeoye Falls-Lima	Win	22	0	
Attica	Win	78	0	Most points scored in C-M history
Livonia	Loss	22	25	17-game winning streak ends
Barker	Win	60	6	Section V Class C semifinals; 35 game winning streak begins
Warsaw	Win	54	0	Section V Class C championship
Salamanca	Win	27	0	NYS Class C western region quarterfinals
Windsor	Win	34	0	NYS Class C semifinals
Rye	Win	38	19	NYS Class C championship; Rowcliffe runs for 174
		507	**83**	#1 in NYS Class C

1994: 13-0-0

Opponent	Result	PF	PA	Notes
Barker	Win	2	0	forfeit
Dansville	Win	31	0	
LeRoy	Win	29	0	
Perry	Win	42	6	
Livonia	Win	37	0	
Attica	Win	34	7	
Honeoye Falls-Lima	Win	32	6	
Avon	Win	2	0	forfeit; Section V Class DD quarterfinals
Lyons	Win	55	6	Section V Class DD semifinals
Red Jacket	Win	42	0	Section V Class DD championship
Pine Valley	Win	23	7	NYS Class D western regional quarterfinals
Deposit	Win	23	7	NYS Class D semifinals
Rensselaer	Win	36	20	NYS Class D championship; Rowcliffe sets several game and season records
		390	58	#1 in NYS Class D

1995: 13-0-0

Opponent	Result	PF	PA	Notes
Elba	Win	45	19	
Dansville	Win	30	0	
LeRoy	Win	20	6	
Notre Dame	Win	43	6	
Attica	Win	29	0	
Honeoye Falls-Lima	Win	49	8	
Livonia	Win	51	8	
York	Win	27	6	Section V Class DD quarterfinals
Clyde-Savannah	Win	50	0	Section V Class DD semifinals
Red Jacket	Win	36	6	Section V Class DD championship
Pine Valley	Win	18	3	NYS Class D western region quarterfinals
Deposit	Win	27	6	NYS Class D semifinals
Rensselaer	Win	41	0	NYS Class D championship
		463	**67**	#1 in NYS Class D

1996: 10-3-0

Opponent	Result	PF	PA	Notes
Oakfield-Alabama	Win	36	0	
Attica	Win	30	0	
Livonia	Win	34	14	
Letchworth	Win	34	13	
Honeoye Falls-Lima	Loss	22	23	35-game winning streak ends
Dansville	Win	40	0	
LeRoy	Loss	14	35	
Bolivar-Richburg	Win	36	0	Section V Class D quarterfinals
York	Win	26	0	Section V Class D semifinals
Dundee	Win	30	0	Section V Class D championship
Maple Grove	Win	30	28	NYS Class D western region quarterfinals
Hamilton	Win	40	6	NYS Class D semifinals
Valhalla	Loss	8	12	NYS Class D championship
		382	**131**	#2 in NYS Class D

Appendix A: Game-by-Game Scores, 1925-2011

1997: 10-2-0

Opponent	Result	PF	PA	Notes
York	Win	26	7	
Livonia	Win	16	14	
Honeoye Falls-Lima	Win	22	0	
Geneseo	Win	40	0	
LeRoy	Loss	14	21	
Dansville	Win	35	6	
Alexander	Win	2	0	forfeit
Bishop Kearney	Win	48	8	Section V Class C quarterfinals
Letchworth	Win	20	9	Section V Class C semifinals
LeRoy	Win	20	15	Section V Class C championship
Gowanda	Win	30	8	NYS Class C western region quarterfinals
CBA	Loss	20	40	NYS Class C semifinals
		293	**127**	#7 in NYS Class C

1998: 8-1-0

Opponent	Result	PF	PA	Notes
Dansville	Win	27	0	
Hornell	Win	41	14	
LeRoy	Win	30	15	
Livonia	Win	28	19	
Honeoye Falls-Lima	Win	26	6	
Bath	Win	49	8	
Geneseo	Win	59	16	
Pembroke	Win	36	7	Section V Class C quarterfinals
LeRoy	Loss	6	28	Section V Class C semifinals
		302	**125**	#11 in NYS Class C

1999: 8-1-0

Opponent	Result	PF	PA	Notes
Wayland-Cohocton	Win	20	0	
Geneseo	Win	40	6	
Hornell	Win	22	16	
York	Win	27	0	
Avon	Win	57	6	
Warsaw	Win	55	0	
LeRoy	Win	14	6	
Letchworth	Win	40	0	Section V Class C quarterfinals
LeRoy	Loss	0	21	Section V Class C semifinals
		275	55	#7 in NYS Class C

2000: 9-3-0

Opponent	Result	PF	PA	Notes
Letchworth	Win	35	0	
Warsaw	Win	50	6	
Honeoye Falls-Lima	Win	26	20	
York	Win	47	12	
Perry	Loss	16	17	
Avon	Win	48	0	
LeRoy	Loss	0	24	
Bishop Kearney	Win	26	12	Section V Class C quarterfinals
LeRoy	Win	24	17	Section V Class C semifinals
East Rochester	Win	8	6	Section V Class C championship
Cleveland Hill	Win	14	6	NYS Class C western regional quarterfinals
Walton	Loss	24	34	NYS Class C semifinals
		318	154	#4 in NYS Class C

Appendix A: Game-by-Game Scores, 1925-2011

2001: 6-3-0

Opponent	Result	PF	PA	Notes
Warsaw	Win	49	0	
LeRoy	Lose	0	28	
Perry	Win	41	0	
Letchworth	Win	34	0	
York	Win	30	12	
East Rochester	Win	28	15	
Avon	Lose	28	30	
Pembroke	Win	26	0	Section V Class C quarterfinals
Avon	Lose	28	34	Section V Class C championship
		264	119	

2002: 8-2-0

Opponent	Result	PF	PA	Notes
Warsaw	Win	66	0	
LeRoy	Loss	0	21	
Avon	Win	34	12	
Letchworth	Win	37	0	
Wellsville	Win	36	0	
Cuba-Rushford	Win	36	0	
Perry	Win	56	6	
Letchworth	Win	26	0	Section V Class C quarterfinals
Pembroke	Win	49	6	Section V Class C semifinals
LeRoy	Loss	8	12	Section V Class C championship
		374	57	#6 in NYS Class C

2003: 13-0-0

Opponent	Result	PF	PA	Notes
LeRoy	Win	21	0	
Letchworth	Win	56	0	
York	Win	20	0	
Wellsville	Win	52	6	
Avon	Win	20	0	
Perry	Win	50	12	Section V Class C quarterfinals
Hornell	Win	20	0	Section V Class C semifinals
Perry	Win	48	0	Section V Class C championship
Avon	Win	42	0	NYS Class C western regional quarterfinals
Pembroke	Win	46	7	NYS Class C semifinals
Portville	Win	12	7	NYS Class C championship
General Brown	Win	48	7	Section V Class C quarterfinals
Hoosick Falls	Win	30	26	Section V Class C semifinals
		467	**65**	#1 in NYS Class C

2004: 4-4-0

Opponent	Result	PF	PA	Notes
York	Win	6	0	
Geneseo	Win	30	20	
LeRoy	Loss	8	14	
Cuba-Rushford	Win	58	16	
Canisteo	Win	26	16	
Hornell	Loss	14	35	
Bolivar-Richburg	Loss	34	55	
Elba	Loss	12	20	Section V Class C semifinals
		188	**176**	

Appendix A: Game-by-Game Scores, 1925-2011

2005: 6-3-0

Opponent	Result	PF	PA	Notes
Canisteo	Win	26	0	
LeRoy	Loss	0	26	
Avon	Loss	14	36	
Warsaw	Win	46	6	
Way-Co	Win	28	14	
Letchworth	Win	8	0	
Wellsville	Win	44	21	
Bishop Kearney	Win	44	18	Section V Class C quarterfinals
LeRoy	Loss	14	17	Section V Class C semifinals
		224	132	

2006: 4-4-0

Opponent	Result	PF	PA	Notes
Hornell	Loss	6	35	
LeRoy	Loss	12	13	
Perry	Win	36	14	
Avon	Win	30	7	
Letchworth	Loss	6	12	
Wellsville	Win	57	8	
Dansville	Win	50	20	
Letchworth	Loss	0	6	Section V Class C quarterfinals
		188	176	

2007: 5-3-0

Opponent	Result	PF	PA	Notes
Cuba-Rushford	Win	44	7	
Wellsville	Win	51	6	
Avon	Win	35	0	
Letchworth	Win	48	20	
Canisteo-Greenwood	Win	61	0	
LeRoy	Loss	6	21	
Bath	Loss	14	34	
Letchworth	Loss	6	10	Section V Class C quarterfinals
		269	**94**	

2008: 6-2-0

Opponent	Result	PF	PA	Notes
Cuba-Rushford	Win	29	6	
Wellsville	Win	41	6	
Avon	Win	24	19	
Letchworth	Win	23	13	
Canisteo-Greenwood	Win	35	0	
LeRoy	Lose	20	27	
Lyons	Win	2	0	forfeit; Section V Class DD quarterfinals
Avon	Lose	26	41	Section V Class DD semifinals
		119	**112**	#19 in NYS Class D

Appendix A: Game-by-Game Scores, 1925-2011

2009: 6-3-0

Opponent	Result	PF	PA	Notes
Canisteo-Greenwood	Win	48	6	
Letchworth	Loss	3	7	
Warsaw	Win	47	7	
Geneseo	Win	39	6	
Avon	Loss	8	36	
LeRoy	Win	14	0	
Oakfield-Alabama	Win	30	28	Section V Class DD quarterfinals
Clyde-Savannah	Win	17	14	Section V Class DD semifinals
Avon	Loss	16	37	Section V Class DD championship
		222	**141**	#15 in NYS Class D

2010: 11-2-0

Opponent	Result	PF	PA	Notes
York	Win	36	6	
Letchworth	Loss	0	13	
Avon	Win	16	8	
Warsaw	Win	42	0	
Perry	Win	52	0	
LeRoy	Win	42	0	
Perry	Win	48	0	Section V Class DD quarterfinals
Lyons	Win	51	0	Section V Class DD semifinals
Avon	Win	54	14	Section V Class DD championship
Dundee	Win	36	15	Section V Class DD/D play-in game
Silver Creek	Win	20	13	NYS Class D western regional quarterfinals
Walton	Win	24	10	NYS Class D semifinals
Tuckahoe	Loss	0	27	NYS Class D championship; Coach Monacelli's last game
		421	**104**	#2 in NYS Class D

2011: 5-3-0

Opponent	Result	PF	PA	Notes
Geneseo	Win	28	0	John Walther's first game
Letchworth	Loss	12	16	
Warsaw	Win	47	0	
York	Win	28	6	
Avon	Loss	22	27	
Perry	Win	36	6	
LeRoy	Win	35	13	
Letchworth	Loss	7	35	Section V Class DD quarterfinals
		215	103	

Appendix B:
Season Records, 1925-2011

Year	Record	PF	PA	Coach	Captain(s)
1925	6-0-1	83	9	McPherson	John Buckley
1926	4-3-0	80	73	Summers	Robert Miller
1927	6-2-1	108	14	McPherson	Earl Stone
1928	9-0-0	138	18	McPherson	George McPherson
1929	9-0-0	274	0	J.A. Matthews	Ed Davies
1930	6-2-0	177	12	J.A. Matthews	Roy MacDonald
1931	6-1-1	195	25	J.A. Matthews	Eugene Pullyblank
1932	8-1-0	304	24	Reynolds	Bob Freeman
1933	4-2-1	109	48	Reynolds	Duncan Cameron
1934	4-1-1	69	31	Flaitz	Frank Shaw
1935	4-2-0	83	26	Flaitz	Al Caesar
1936	5-1-0	157	21	Flaitz	----------------
1937	1-3-0	38	39	Flaitz	----------------
1938	2-3-0	51	38	Wasicek	Frank Balonek
1939	3-2-0	38	58	Freeman	----------------
1940	4-2-0	63	85	Freeman	William Thompson
1941	4-1-1	89	38	Freeman	John Callan
1942	WW II	-------	-------	No Football	----------------
1943	4-2-0	64	67	Brown	George Grattan/Dan Pangrazio
1944	3-3-0	47	52	Brown	Bill Reid, Jake Abbot

Year	Record	PF	PA	Coach	Captain(s)
1945	1-2-2	49	40	Freeman	Carl Fisher, Jack Sickles
1946	5-2-0	154	52	Freeman	George Smith
1947	7-0-0	239	33	Freeman	Jimmy Smith
1948	6-1-0	154	46	Freeman	Tony Bartalo
1949	5-2-0	152	70	Freeman	Rotated by game
1950	7-0-0	206	48	Freeman	Pete Coppini
1951	5-3-0	114	79	Freeman	Anthony Merola
1952	5-3-0	149	90	Freeman	Dick Cullinan
1953	4-2-1	106	70	Freeman	Vic Cappotelli
1954	7-0-0	155	38	Freeman	David Connor
1955	6-1-0	216	25	Freeman	Bernie Fagan/Archie Cappotelli
1956	4-2-0	142	59	Freeman	Don Robertson
1957	3-3-1	51	69	Collins	Joe Reid/Mike McDonald
1958	4-3-0	119	92	Cameron	Robert Poles/John Loomis
1959	2-3-2	51	89	E. Matthews	Don Sheffer
1960	0-6-1	40	154	E. Matthews	Bob Grattan
1961	2-5-0	51	127	E. Matthews	Joe Fisher
1962	4-3-0	66	84	E. Matthews	Don Oltman/Joe Wild
1963	5-2-0	101	96	Holland	Greg Connor/John Cannon
1964	4-3-0	130	88	Holland	Don Ranous/Bob Krenzer
1965	7-1-0	176	49	Holland	Mike Cannon/Bob Krenzer
1966	5-3-0	111	80	Ruane	Don Krenzer/John Niedzwick
1967	7-1-0	180	32	Ruane	Sam Seava/Don Krenzer
1968	7-1-0	206	61	Ruane	Bob Brown/Louie Kingsbury
1969	7-1-0	136	45	Ruane	Tom Bonacquisti/Tom Krenzer
1970	5-2-1	143	45	Ruane	Jim Price/Dennis Covey
1971	4-4-0	134	161	Ruane	Bob Sullivan/Gary Nichols
1972	3-5-0	146	124	Ruane	Don Brown/Dan Harmon
1973	8-0-0	389	67	McAlee	Bob Chiverton/Mark Reid

Appendix B: Season Records, 1925-2011

Year	Record	PF	PA	Coach	Captain(s)
1974	8-0-0	308	30	McAlee	Mike Tucci/Randy Grattan/Don Carpenter
1975	8-1-0	277	76	McAlee	Mike Pullyblank/Mike Mooney
1976	7-1-0	226	71	McAlee	Jim Freeman/Paul Brandes
1977	8-0-0	233	47	McAlee	Chris Wyatt/Jeff Sweet
1978	9-0-0	288	32	McAlee	Junior Poles/Dave Trojanski
1979	9-0-0	277	63	McAlee	John Freeman/Mark McGrath
1980	10-0-0	276	91	McAlee	Ron Poles/Bill Bernard
1981	7-2-0	189	146	McAlee	Jim Laubach/Mike Grattan
1982	7-2-0	204	75	McAlee	Dave Betz/Mark Streb
1983	9-1-0	271	73	McAlee	Don Wade/Cordie Greenlea
1984	6-3-0	161	124	McAlee	Any Wilcox/Russ Loughry
1985	7-1-1	148	62	McAlee	Roland Poles/Ray Dearcop
1986	5-2-2	118	46	McAlee	Rick Dearcop/Don Ryan
1987	9-1-0	275	75	McAlee	Tony Cicoria/Mike Edwards
1988	2-6-0	132	171	Monacelli	Gary Cicoria/Chad Baker
1989	4-4-0	172	121	Monacelli	Tige Monacelli/Trent Morris
1990	8-2-0	236	115	Monacelli	Matt Moyer/Gary Raymond
1991	10-1-0	335	103	Monacelli	Jason Reid/Dave Donaghue
1992	11-0-0	415	68	Monacelli	Gary Hartford/Adam Paladino/Josh Randall
1993	11-1-0	507	83	Monacelli	Carl Covey/Pete Moyer/Eric Thurley
1994	13-0-0	390	58	Monacelli	Tony Monacelli/Jeremy Peet/Eric Williams/Ron Stephany
1995	13-0-0	463	67	Monacelli	Dominic Monacelli/Kevin Donaghue/Aaron Edwards/Jamie Vokes/Tim Seifert/Louie Kingsbury
1996	10-3-0	382	131	Monacelli	Brian Grattan/Rich Simeone/John Beaumont
1997	10-2-0	293	127	Monacelli	Matt Brand/Matt Cappotelli/Kevin Sayers

Year	Record	PF	PA	Coach	Captain(s)
1998	8-1-0	302	125	Monacelli	Josh Hayes/Chris Jones/Dustin Preston
1999	8-1-0	275	55	Monacelli	Adam Cappotelli/Dan Coyle/Mike Fox/Tim Vink
2000	9-3-0	318	154	Monacelli	Chris Brown/James Beaumont/Justin Rodger
2001	6-3-0	264	119	Monacelli	Rotated by game
2002	8-2-0	374	57	Monacelli	Joe Greer/Jon Harrington/Craig Pullyblank/John Zelinski
2003	13-0-0	467	65	Monacelli	Jamie Fitch/Paul Keeley/Kyle Minter/Ryan Sherman
2004	4-4-0	188	176	Monacelli	Zach Nothnagle/Chad Pieri/Bob Toland/Justin Walsh
2005	6-3-0	224	132	Monacelli	Pat Combo/Aaron Hallett/Adam Schultz
2006	4-4-0	188	176	Monacelli	Dan Riggi/Jim Garland/Steve Lauffer
2007	5-3-0	269	94	Monacelli	Tom Gorrow/Nate Scheidel/Tim Sullivan
2008	6-2-0	119	112	Monacelli	Tom Gorrow/Dave Fox/Brian Sinclair/Jeremy Wilson
2009	6-3-0	222	141	Monacelli	Sean Ancher/Mike Anderson/Trevor Haut/Dan Whiteside
2010	11-2-0	421	104	Monacelli	Tyler Lauffer/Trevor Haut/Matt Riggi/Dan Whiteside
2011	5-3-0	215	103	Walther	Kyle Sickles/Jon Cappotelli/Mike Johnson/Colin Callan

Cal-Mum Red Raiders, 1925-2011

Overall record: 532-162-17
Winning percentage: .748

Total PF: 16,683 (23.46 avg. per game)
Total PA: 6,459 (9.08 avg. per game)

Appendix C: Cumulative Coaching Records, 1925-2011

Coach	Years	Record	WP
Summers	1926	5-3-0	.625
McPherson	1925, 1927-1928	21-2-2	.875
J. A. Matthews	1929-1931	21-3-1	.750
Reynolds	1932-1933	12-3-1	.750
Flaitz	1934-1937	14-7-1	.636
Wasicek	1938	2-3-0	.400
Brown	1943-1944	7-5-0	.583
Freeman	1939-1941, 1945-1955	75-24-4	.728
Collins	1957	3-3-1	.428
Cameron	1958	4-3-0	.571
E. Matthews	1959-1962	7-17-3	.259
Holland	1963-1965	16-6-0	.727
Ruane	1966-1972	38-17-1	.690
McAlee	1973-1987	117-14-2	.879
Monacelli	1988-2010	186-50-0	.788
Walther	2011-	5-3-0	.625

Appendix D:
The Undefeated Teams

NOTE: Caledonia was also undefeated in 1904, although evidence is scarce for the details of that season. Nonetheless, when added to the following undefeated teams, Caledonia/Cal-Mum ranks in the top ten of all high school football programs in the country in this category.

1928: Chet Hardman, Jimmy Jackson, Eddie Davis, Pete McPherson, Roy MacDonald, Charles Carson, John Harvey, Ronnie Wilson, Everett Youngs, Carl Gibson, Bob Johnson, Gene Pullyblank, Earl Stone.

1929: Ed Coots, Arlie Burkhart, Earl Stone, Jim Jackson, Ed Davis, Bob Johnson, Bill Miller, Tony Angelo, Pete McPherson, Charles Carson, Ronnie Wilson, Gene Pullyblank, Felix Balonek, Dunc Cameron, Roy MacDonald, Preston Sinsanick, Mason Ashford, George Ball, Stuart Griffin, Chet Hardman, Bill Jackson, Bob Freeman, Jack Skivington, Stuart Grant.

1947: James R. Smith (Captain), Robert Washburn, William Donegan, Tony Bartalo, Laverne Thompson, Robert Steedman, James Hank, Leslie Callan, Stewart Campbell, Charles Waters, Richard McKay, Edward Keenan, William Goodburlet, Murray Cohen, Robert Sickles, Ronald Greene, Joe Fagan, Gerald Callan, Gene Mooney, Howard Nelson, Dean Fisher (note: roster incomplete)

Appendix D: The Undefeated Teams 191

1950: George Henry, Richard Wall, John Vink, Robert Darling, Gary Hone, Anthony Coppini, Tom Shaughnessy, Richard Cullinan, Philip D'Angelo, Gerald Swanger, Robert Minster, Anthony Merola, Loren Geer, Ralph King, Harold Sickles, Peter Coppini (Captain), Howard Nelson, Dean Fisher, Ira Geer, Richard Sisson, James Walker, Donald Smith, Donald Pullyblank, Truman Clements, Robert Sheffer, Thomas Robinson, Lawrence Bonacquisti, Robert Beyer, John Ball, James Wall, John Poles, Robert Pullyblank, Everett Vail, Melvin Nelson, Joseph Tallo, Victor Cappotelli, Francis Fisher, David Cargill, Richard Fagan, Clement King.

1954: Robert Hanna, Lawrence Loomis, Richard Mack, William McQuilken, Richard Fisher, Michael MacDonald, Stanley Latko, Allan Sickles, Assistant Manager William McKernan, Manager Donald Hobbs, Peter Coureen, John Keenan, Mark Robinson, Archie Cappotelli, Roger Hill, Harold Connor, Charles Daniels, James Vokes, David McKay, Robert Loomis, Gordon Henry, David Connor (Captain), Frank Ianiro, Joseph Latko, Richard Feeley, Jon King, Bernard Babcock, Paul Janowski, Maurice Hill, Gerald Majors, Albert Blaker, James Jackson, Donald Robertson, Albert Poles, Louis Ward, Richard Wilkins, Arthur Kretschmer, Bernard Fagan, Thomas Brew, Washington Williams.

1973: Manager Donald Cameron, James Harrington, Charles O'Donnell, Robert Perhamus, Richard Brown, Joseph Rapone, Thomas Lauffer, Michael Pullyblank, Steve Kissell, Manager Paul Mooney, Robert Poles, Ronald Beach, Timothy Harrington, Randy Grattan, Gary Mattice, Thomas Sullivan, Timothy Nothnagle, Robert Freeman, Paul Day, Manager Steve Pullyblank, Timothy Lauffer, Edward Peet, Robert Chiverton (Captain), Donald Carpenter, Mark Reid (Captain), Michael Tucci, Thomas Cook, Charles VanGorder, Jonathan Barnes, James Craw, Timothy Balonek, David Mancuso, Clifford Anderson, Christopher Batzing, Steve Cameron, Scott Weitzel, Kevin Geer, Donald MacIntyre, Coach Roger House.

1974: Chris Wyatt, Ron Grant, Joe Rapone, Tom Shaughnessy, Jim Freeman, T.R. Harmon, Terry Nothnagle, Jim Sackett, Tom Lauffer, Don Carpenter (Captain), Frank Saeva, Mike Tucci (Captain), Rich Brown, Don MacIntyre, Steve Kissel, Ron Beach, Ron Grattan (Captain), Gary Mattice, Tom Cook, Steve Cameron, Jim Craw, Kevin Geer, Mike Kelley, Dave Mancuso, Chris Batzing, Scott Weitzel, Ken Troyer, Duaine Priestly, Toby Weitzel, Mike Pullyblank, Steve Krenzer, Jim Harrington, John

Garnes, Jim Goodburlet, Mark Seefried, Mark Rothrock, Don Miller, Mike Mooney, Chip Day, Rob Perhamus.

1977: Chris Ennis, Paul Toland, Justin Randall, Paul Mooney, Larry Anderson, Scott Fisher, John Freeman, Bill Clements, Frank Fisher, Jeff D'Angelo, Pat Randall, Mark Meyer, Tom Warters, Mark Seefried, Steve Pullyblank, Chris Wyatt (Captain), Jeff Sweet (Captain), Bill Donegan, Pat Harrigan, Steve Burger, Jim Wood, Dave Krenzer, Bob Loomis, Terry Donegan, Dan Keenan, James Pullyblank, Steve Sickles, Bob Cesare, Dick Thomas, Tom Matthews, Mark Callan, Dale Wyone, Junior Poles, Steve Balonek, Dave Trojanski, Mark Pullyblank, Rick Riggi, Kevin O'Dell, Doug Nothnagle, Dave Nailos, Dave Reeves.

1978: Terry Donegan, Tom Ball, Paul Toland, Justin Randall, Billy Clements, Frank Fisher, Jeff D'Angelo, Chris Ennis, Paul Mooney, Pat Randall, Mark Callan, Steve Riggi, Jimmy Grant, Danny Keenan, Billy Dollard, Steve Balonek, Robert Poles, Jr. David Trojanski (Captain), Doug Nothnagle, Dave Nailos, Bob Cesare, Richard Thomas, Dale Wynne, Rick Riggi, Pat Shaughnessy, Kevin O'Dell, Mark Stella, Doug Clements, Tim Grant, Bob Sinclair, Ron Poles, Mark McGrath, Bill Bernard, Chris O'Dell, Charlie Sisson, Jim Pike, Dan Romano, John Freeman, Brian Robinson, Adam Wightman, Richard Shelton, Larry Anderson, Richard Bierbrauer.

1979: Steve Grant, Roger House, Mark Sickles, Mickey Cappotelli, Steve Carpino, Michael Keenan, Leonard Hall, Daniel Parnell, Gregory D'Amico, Jim Grant, Charles Sisson, Douglas Clements, Mark Stella, Richard Shelton, Larry Anderson, John Freeman (Captain), Mark McGrath (Captain), Dan Romano, Terry McGinnis, Richard Bierbrauer, Brian Robinson, Steve Riggi, Tom Ball, Mike Grattan, Chris O'Dell, Scott Saunders, Brian Phillips, Tim Grant, Mike Connelie, Bill Bernard, Bob Sinclair, Joe Gustainis, Larry Riggi, Jim Laubach, Tom Pierce, Dwayne Wynne, Adam Wightman, Eric Sheffer, Scott Favreau, Tim MacDonald.

1980: Gary Heuer, Scott Saunders, Mike Keenan, Tim MacDonald, Ron Poles (Captain), Steve Carpino, Adam Wightman, Bob Sinclair, Bill Bernard (Captain), Brian Phillips, Mark Sickles, Craig Chadderdon, Steve Grant, Mike Grattan, Bill Day, Jim Pullyblank, Kevin Zimmer, Joe Gustainis, Richard Goodburlet, Jim Laubach, Eric

Appendix D: The Undefeated Teams

Sheffer, Greg D'Amico, Len Hall, Roger House, Francis Krenzer, Doug Grant, Larry Riggi, Colin MacKay, David Reeves, Andy Hodge, John Limner, Dwayne Wynne, Tom Pearse, Bob Clements, Brian Bowers, Dan Parnell, Scott Moran, Jerome Phillips, Barry Robinson.

1992: Brain Schneider, Brian Kissel, Adam Paladino (Captain), Josh Randall (Captain), Tom Martin, Bill McNelis, Tom Whiteside, Gary Hartford (Captain), Robert Drummond, Carlton Covey, Pat Ball, Eric Thurley, Jamie Vokes, Todd Smith, Dave Day, Pete Moyer, Paul Curts, Matt Grattan, David Steele, Aaron Cappotelli, Wade Rowcliffe, Josh Cummings, Jason Brooks.

1994: Jerrod Dunlap, Tony Monacelli (Captain), Aaron Edwards, Joe Bienko, Stash Merritt, Kevin Kissel, Eric Williams (Captain), Matt Emens, Matt Cappotelli, Bob Middleton, Don Peet, David Holler, Tim Davis, Mike Leach, Louie Kingsbury, Tim Keeley. Brian Gilman, Matt Hallett, Patrick Hammond, Kris Pangrazio, Tim Seifert, Dominic Monacelli, Jamie Vokes, Wade Rowcliffe, Ron Stephany (Captain), Jeremy Peet (Captain), Kevin Donaghue, Brendan Donlon.

1995: J.D. Baldeck, Rich Simeone, Kris Mitchell, Matt Cappotelli, Joe Kingsbury, Brad McCreedy, Stash Merritt, Bryan Grattan, Phelps Beardsley, Paul Swartzmeyer, Josh Bienko, Joe Hughes, John Beaumont, Jerrod Dunlap, Don Peet, Aaron Edwards (Captain), Mike Leach, Kevin Donaghue (Captain), Jamie Vokes (Captain), Mike Combo, Matt Loomis, Jeremy Dietchler, Tim Seifert (Captain), Dominic Monacelli (Captain), Tim Keeley, Louie Kingsbury (Captain).

2003: Chris Tomasso, Paul Keeley (Captain), Nathan Rogers, Justin Walsh, Rick Riggi, Ryan Sherman (Captain), Chris Harmon, Jeremy Darron. Middle: Mitch Atwell, Evan Scheidel, Jeff Boop, Tom Lauffer, Bob Toland, Joe Darron, Kyle Mynter (Captain), Jamie Fitch (Captain), Jeff Grattan, Jeff Williams, Chris Paladino, Zack Nothnagle, Tim Chriscaden, John Truscott, Tom Shepard, Chad Pierri, Chris Parker, Tim Gorton, Mike Atwell.

Appendix E:
25 Memorable Victories,
10 Forgettable Losses

Victories

1929: Caledonia 6, LeRoy 0 (The Raiders feted by the HF-L marching band)
1929: Caledonia 48, Dansville 0 (most points scored that season; tied for fewest points allowed)
1932: Caledonia 43, Aquinas 6 (Jimmy Jackson runs wild against the Little Irish)
1947: Caledonia 34, Avon 7 (Raider revenge after a 1-5-1 stretch against the Braves; tied 7-7 at halftime)
1950: Cal-Mum 33, York 12 (first game under the lights at Hamilton Field)
1973: Cal-Mum 42, LeRoy 16 ("Remember!")
1974: Cal-Mum 22, LeRoy 14 (LeRoy—"the undefeated underdog")
1976: Cal-Mum 28, Livonia 18 (The Great Streak begins)
1977: Cal-Mum 19, LeRoy 0 (Who's Number One? Coach McAlee's most memorable game)
1978: Cal-Mum 42, Lyons 0 (Run, Super-flea, run! Cal-Mum's first Sectional title)
1979: Cal-Mum 26, Clyde-Savannah 20, OT (Thriller at Fauver)
1980: Cal-Mum 26, LeRoy 21 (Ron Poles' winning run at Holleder)
1981: Cal-Mum 21, LeRoy 20 (Kevin Zimmer's miracle passes to Bowers and Goodburlet)
1985: Cal-Mum 28, LeRoy 14 (Roland Poles gets 297 yards worth of revenge at Hartwood Park)
1987: Cal-Mum 21, Avon 11 (Coach McAlee says farewell with a Section V title)
1990: Cal-Mum 19, LeRoy 0 (Monacelli's first big win)

Appendix E: 25 Memorable Victories, 10 Forgettable Losses

1991: Cal-Mum 27, East Rochester 9 (Return to Section V glory)
1992: Cal-Mum 16, Windsor 8 (Return to NY State glory)
1993: Cal-Mum 38, Rye 19 (We're Number One, twice!)
1994: Cal-Mum 36, Rensellaer 20 (Three in a row!)
1995: Cal-Mum 41, Rensellaer 0 (Fourth in a row!)
1997: Cal-Mum 20. LeRoy 15 (Seventh straight Section V championship; Matt Cappotelli beats his nemesis)
2003: Cal-Mum 30, Hoosick Falls 26 (Thriller in the Dome)

Defeats

1932-LeRoy 18, Cal-Mum 7 (worst loss from 1927-1932)
1958/59/60: Avon 68 (combined), Cal-Mum 0 (Al least it wasn't LeRoy…)
1972: LeRoy 48, Cal-Mum 0 (Coach Ruane's last game at Cal-Mum)
1975: Livonia 14, Cal-Mum 6 (Rain and mud at Saunders Field)
1976: LeRoy 28, Cal-Mum 7 (The night the lights went out at Hamilton Field)
1981: Notre Dame of Batavia 16, Cal-Mum 0 (The Great Streak ends)
1984: LeRoy 33, Cal-Mum 6 (Embarrassment at Hamilton Field)
1986: Avon 10/0/10, Cal-Mum 0/0/7 (Twelve quarters of futility)
1996: Valhalla 12, Cal-Mum 8 (The NYS streak ends)
2002: LeRoy 12, Cal-Mum 6 (So-close at Fauver, but wait 'til next year!)

Appendix F:
The Cal-Mum Red Raider Football Hall of Fame

(* indicates member of the 1929 undefeated, untied, unscored-upon team)

Troy Anderson
Mason Ashford*
Anthony Bartalo Jr.
Neil Barton
James Beaumont
William Bernard Jr.
Chris Brown
Arnold Burkhart*
Mark Callan
Pete Cameron
Adam Cappotelli
Arch Cappotelli
Chris Cappotelli
Matt Cappotelli
Steve Cappotelli
Don Carpenter
Charles Carson*
Tony Cicoria
David Connor
Greg Connor
Totsy Cook

Ed Coots*
Dick Cullinan
Ed Davies*
Ray Dearcop
Rick Dearcop
Dave Donaghue
Kevin Donaghue
Bill Donegan
Les Eaton
Aaron Edwards
Mike Edwards
Stu Edwards
Joe Esposito
Bernie Fagan
Dean Fisher
Mike Fox
Gary Fredericks
Jim Freeman
Robert Freeman*
Stuart Grant*
Brian Grattan

Michael Grattan
Randy Grattan
Cordie Greenlea
Harold Griffin*
Joe Gustainis
Tim Harrington
Dan Hartford
Gary Hartford
Roger House
Billy Jackson*
James Jackson*
Jim Jackson
Wright Johnson*
Robert Johnston*
Louis Kingsbury
Louis Kingsbury Jr.
Don Krenzer
Robert Krenzer
Jim Laubach
Mike Leach
Roy MacDonald*

Appendix F: The Cal-Mum Red Raider Football Hall of Fame

Tim MacDonald	Dan Pangrazio Sr.	Bob Steedman
Tom Martin	Dan Parnell	David Steele
Ed Matthews	Dave Parnell	Mark Stella
Gary Mattice	Robert Poles Jr.	Earl Stone*
Bill McAlee	Roland Poles	Jeff Sweet
Paul McGinnis*	Ron Poles	Eric Thurley
Mark McGrath	Bob Pullyblank	Paul Toland
Dave McNelis	Eugene Pullyblank*	Dave Trojanski
George McPherson*	Mark Pullyblank	Ken Troyer
J. Duncan McPherson	Mike Pullyblank	Mike Tucci
Roy McWilliams*	Josh Randall	Tim Vink
Tony Merola	Gary Raymond	Don Wade
Tom Micheaux	Bill Reid	Bob Washburn
Harold Miller*	Justin Rogers	Andy Wilcox
Dominic Monacelli	Wade Rowcliffe	Jamie Vokes
Tige Monacelli	Tim Seifert	Eric Williams
Tony Monacelli	Harold Sickles	Chris Wyatt
Mike Mooney	Steve Sickles	Francis Yopp*
Pete Moyer	Bob Sinclair	Everett Young*
Howard Nelson	Preston Sinzenich*	Kevin Zimmer
Tim Nothnagle	Jim Smith	
Chris O'Dell	Ron Smith	
Don Oltmann	Todd Smith	

Appendix G:
Cal-Mum Versus LeRoy, 1900-2011

Year	Result	Cal-Mum	LeRoy	Notes
1900	Win	16	5	LeRoy known as the "Monarchs"
1900	Lose	0	16	
1900	Win	16	0	
1902	Lose	0	11	
1902	Lose	0	11	
1904	Win	16	0	
1905	Lose	5	6	
1905	Win	11	10	
1911	Win	10	6	
1911	Win	19	0	
1927	Lose	0	2	
1929	Win	6	0	Lowest Caledonia point total of 1929
1930	Lose	0	6	
1931	Tie	6	6	
1932	Lose	7	18	Only Caledonia loss in 1932
1948	Win	18	2	
1949	Lose	6	25	
1950	Win	31	6	
1951	Lose	6	25	
1952	Lose	13	19	

Appendix G: Cal-Mum Versus LeRoy, 1900-2011

Year	Result	Cal-Mum	LeRoy	Notes
1953	Lose	0	12	
1954	Win	20	0	
1965	Loss	7	12	
1966	Loss	0	39	
1967	Win	31	0	
1968	Win	7	0	
1969	Win	6	0	
1970	Tie	0	0	
1971	Loss	0	32	
1972	Loss	0	48	Coach Ruane's last game at Cal-Mum
1973	Win	42	16	
1974	Win	22	14	
1975	Win	22	6	Coach Ruane's first season in LeRoy
1976	Loss	7	28	The lights go out at Hamilton Field; last loss before the 49 game "Great Streak"
1977	Win	19	0	Before the game—LeRoy #1 in NYS, Cal-Mum #7
1978	Win	13	3	
1979	Win	28	20	
1980	Win	47	12	
1980	Win	26	21	Section V Class B championship at Holledar Stadium; Ron Poles' last minute TD run
1981	Win	21	20	Zimmer's last minute TD pass to Bowers and PAT to Goodburlet
1982	Loss	14	34	
1982	Loss	6	29	
1983	Win	20	9	
1984	Loss	6	33	
1985	Win	28	14	Roland Poles runs for 297 yards
1986	Win	26	7	
1987	Win	21	14	

Year	Result	Cal-Mum	LeRoy	Notes
1987	Win	28	7	
1988	Loss	6	34	
1989	Loss	0	7	
1990	Win	19	0	Coach Monacelli's first varsity win over LeRoy
1991	Win	22	18	
1992	Win	42	14	
1993	Win	27	7	
1994	Win	29	0	
1995	Win	20	6	
1996	Loss	14	35	
1997	Loss	14	21	Overtime thriller at Hartwood Park
1997	Win	20	15	Section V Class C championship; Matt Cappotelli's last second TD wins it
1998	Win	30	15	
1998	Loss	6	28	Section V Class C semifinals
1999	Win	14	6	
1999	Loss	0	21	Section V Class C semifinals
2000	Loss	0	24	
2000	Win	24	17	Section V Class C semifinals; big upset win for Cal-Mum
2001	Loss	0	28	
2002	Loss	0	21	
2002	Loss	8	12	Section V Class C championship; thrilling late TD for LeRoy wins it
2003	Win	21	0	The road to a state championship begins here
2004	Loss	8	14	
2005	Loss	0	26	
2005	Loss	14	17	Section V Class C semifinals
2006	Loss	12	13	
2007	Loss	6	21	

Appendix G: Cal-Mum Versus LeRoy, 1900-2011

Year	Result	Cal-Mum	LeRoy	Notes
2008	Loss	20	27	
2009	Win	14	0	
2010	Win	42	0	
2011	Win	35	13	

Cal-Mum Red Raiders, 1900-2011

Overall record vs. LeRoy: 41-35-2

Index to Players and Coaches

NOTE: This index covers only the main narrative text of this book and does not include the acknowledgments, photo captions, or appendix material. The photo and appendix sections are chronological or alphabetical by design, and the reader should find those sections easy to navigate and reference without an aid. This index includes not only Cal-Mum players and coaches, but those from competing teams as well. There can be no doubt that the participants from both sides of the field contributed greatly to the history of Cal-Mum Red Raiders football.

Alena, Dave 50, 51
Anderson, Larry 51-54
Anderson, Troy 126, 127
Angelo, Tony 12
Ashford, Mason 12
Ashley, Pat 123
Ausher, Justin 123-125
Ball, George 25
Ball, Tom 67, 68, 70
Batzing, Chris 38, 42, 44
Beaumont, James 127
Bernard, Bill 56, 57
Betz, Dave 62
Bezon, Joe 111
Blair, Max 114
Bonacquisti, Dave 7, 8
Boop, Jeff 10, 129, 131
Bowers, Brian 55, 61-63
Bradley, Gene 115
Brandes, Paul 45
Brown, Chris 127
Brown, Rich 42-44
Bundy, John 66

Burger, Steve 6, 8
Burke, Ken 60
Caccamise, Phil 8
Cannon, Mike 31
Cappotelli, Adam 124-126
Cappotelli, Chris 62, 120
Cappotelli, Matt 25, 114, 123-126
Caraher, Dan 112
Caraher, Jeff 112
Carnevale, Derrick 96, 97
Carpenter, Don 41-44, 50
Cesare, Bob 51
Chiverton, Bob 41-43, 109
Cicoria, Tony 71, 74, 75, 95
Clark, Chad 123
Clements, Bob 60
Coots, Ed 12, 22, 29, 109, 120
Coppini, Pete 30
Cox, Mike 125
Cullinan, Dick 30
D'Angelo, Jeff 6, 8
D'Angelo, Phil 30
Darron, Jeremy 129, 131

Index to Players and Coaches

Dearcop, Ray..71
DerCola, Nick...............................53, 54, 96
Dixon, Germaine..128
Dollard, Bill...50, 53
Donaghue, Dave..............................95-98, 100
Donaghue, Kevin..............................110-115
Donegan, Bill..116
Drahms, David...113
Edwards, Aaron..............108, 110-113, 115
Edwards, Mike...74
Edwards, Stuart..74
Fagan, Bernie...28, 30
Fagan, Dick...41
Falgenhauer, Chris......................................70
Farrell, Joe..20
Fellows, David......................................20, 26
Fitch, Jamie..131
Fox, Mike..126
Fredericks, Gary..59, 95, 103, 107, 112-114, 124, 125
Freeman, Bob.......20-23, 25-28, 30, 103, 117
Freeman, Jim...45, 46
Freeman, John.........................22, 51, 53, 54
Fulmer, Brendan..............................129, 130
Geer, Kevin...45
Geer, Loren...30
Gibson, Carl..16
Goodburlet, Jim...45
Goodburlet, Rich...................................59, 61
Grant, Tim..51, 53
Grattan, Brian..115
Grattan, Matt.................101, 102, 106, 108
Grattan, Mike..55, 60
Grattan, Randy..............................38, 41-43
Griffin, Stuart...12
Gustainis, Joe...62
Hanna, Paul..70
Harmon, Chris...131
Harmon, Dan..97, 101
Harmon, Tom.......................................97, 101
Harrigan, Pat..6, 8
Harrington, Jon..129
Harrington, Tim...................................41-43
Hart, Mike..130
Hartford, Gary...................................100-102
Haugh, Mike............................45, 61, 66
Hayes, Josh..125
Hicks, Scott...41
Hildebrandt, R.J..96
Holland, Chuck..31
Holt, Jim..55
House, Roger.....................8, 31, 41, 47, 59
Jackson, Jimmy....12, 16, 19-23, 55, 109, 110
Johnson, Earnest..25
Johnson, Shannon......................................97
Johnson, Steve......................................53, 54
Jones, Chris..125
Keeley, Paul....................................130-132
Keifer, Bill...52
Kelley, Mike..45
Kelly, George..58
Kerr, Andy...20, 23
Kingsbury, Louie...........108, 110, 111, 113
Krenzer, Bob..31, 114
Krenzer, Francis..62
Krenzer, Gus...119
Krenzer, Steve..45
Laubach, Jim..62
Leach, Mike....................110-113, 115, 116
Loomis, Bob..8
Loughery, Russ.....................................68, 70
MacDonald, Tim....................................55-57
Maestre, Jesse..53
Marble, Todd..74
Martin, Tom............................101, 106, 108
Mathews, Jim..56
Matthews, Ed....22, 30, 31, 40, 41, 47, 59, 73
Matthews, J.A..16, 22
Mattice, Gary...42, 43
McAlee, Bill. 3, 4, 7, 8, 10, 11, 15, 22, 31, 36-47, 49-56, 58-75, 94, 95, 103, 108, 117, 122
McClenny, Scott..66

McClinton, Joe...............................113
McGrath, Mark..........................51, 53
McIlwayne, Jeremy.......................123
McMillan, Wayne............................72
McNeil, Ken......................................60
McPherson, George.........................16
McPherson, J. Duncan.....................16
McQuilken, Don..............................62
Monacelli, Dominic 108, 110, 111, 113, 115, 116
Monacelli, Mike....15, 31, 42, 47, 58, 59, 67, 71, 94-99, 101-109, 111-117, 120-125, 130, 131
Monacelli, Tony.............................108
Montemorano, Tim.........................53
Mooney, Mike..................................45
Moran, Brian............116, 120, 121, 127, 130
Moran, Scott....................................60
Morris, Trent...................................74
Moyer, Ken......................................70
Moyer, Matt....................................96
Moyer, Pete..............97, 101, 102, 106, 108
Mynter, Kyle..................................131
Nelson, Howard..............................30
Nothnagle, Tim................................41
O'Dell, Chris....................................57
Paladino, Andy..............................125
Parnell, Dan................................55-58
Parnell, Dave..............................95-98
Pearse, Tom.....................................55
Peet, Ed..41
Peet, Jeremy..................................108
Phillips, Jerome...............................60
Piazza, John.....................................57
Pike, Tracy.....................................7, 8
Pilznicnski, Mike.............................41
Poles, Robert "Junior"........3, 6, 8, 47, 50-53, 103, 109, 110, 120
Poles, Roland.........10, 11, 35, 68-73, 98, 122
Poles, Ronald.............................51-58, 124
Price, Bundy....................................31

Priestley, Duane..............................43
Pullyblank, Bob..........42, 44, 49, 60, 61, 109
Pullyblank, Craig...........................129
Pullyblank, Don..............................21
Pullyblank, Eugene................11-13, 18
Pullyblank, Jim................................62
Pullyblank, Mark...............................6
Pullyblank, Mike......................43-45, 50
Pullyblank, Steve...............................6
Ramsey, Sean..........................126, 127
Randall, Josh.................................101
Reid, Jason......................................97
Reynolds, George...............19, 20, 22, 23
Riddle, Ricky...........................129, 130
Riviello, Rick...................................54
Robinson, Barry......................55, 56, 60-62
Rodgers, Justin..............................127
Rodgers, Nate................................131
Roth, Josh......................................114
Rowcliffe, Wade.................101, 106-110
Ruane, Frank. 3, 7, 32-39, 46, 56, 67, 72, 94, 121, 122
Rucker, Ron....................................98
Sack, Jason....................................100
Santini, Don............................44, 122
Schuster, Bill.............................45, 61
Schuster, Bob.............................45, 61
Schuster, Kevin...............................61
Seefried, Mark..............................7, 8
Seifert, Tim........108, 110, 111, 113, 115, 116
Shaughnessey, Joe...................129, 131
Shaughnessey, Tom.......................125
Sheffer, Eric................................55-57
Sherman, Ryan........................129, 131
Sickles, Harold................................30
Simms, Gerry..................................31
Sinclair, Bob....................................57
Smith, Todd............................106, 108
Smith, Wes.................................96, 97
Snover, Chris................................102
Stauffer, Eric...................................96

Index to Players and Coaches

Steele, Dave..101, 102
Stephany, Ron..108
Stone, Earl..16
Sullivan, Johnny...19
Sutherland, Bill..63
Swarts, Milton..26
Sweet, Jeff.........................3, 7, 8, 11, 46, 50
Taylor, Matt...................................65, 66, 100
Thiele, Macky...6, 8
Thurley, Eric..106, 108
Toland, Bob...131
Toland, Paul..51
Trojanski, Dave..................51, 52, 103, 109
Troyer, Kenny..45
Tucci, Mike.....................41-44, 50, 109, 110
Van Gorder, Chuckr...42
Vilcheck, Brad...100
Vitticore, Ron..96, 113
Vokes, Jamie....101, 106, 108, 110, 111, 113-116
Vokes, Jim..28
Wade, Don..68, 70
Whiting, Jake..130
Whitman, D.J..115
Wightman, Adam..55
Wilcox, Andy...70
Wilson, Ronald..16
Wood, Jim..7
Wright, Dan...56
Wyatt, Chris...............................6-8, 45, 50
Wynne, Dale...51
Yarnes, Scott..45
Youngs, Everett...16
Zapada, David..109, 197
Zelinski, John..129
Zimber, Ryan...123
Zimmer, Kevin..................55, 57, 58, 60-63

About the Author

THOMAS E. PULLYBLANK, born and raised in a Caledonia football family, was the starting tight end on the 1985 Red Raider team. His grandfather played on the undefeated, unscored-upon 1929 team, his father and uncles played on the great Bob Freeman-led teams of the late 1940s and early 1950s, and his older brothers and cousins played on the McAlee powerhouse teams of the 1970s and 1980s. His mother baked Cal-Mum football cookies, his sisters led cheers, and now his nephews carry on the family tradition of wearing the maroon and white. A teacher, writer, pastor and farmer, Pullyblank lives outside Cooperstown, NY with his wife and son.

www.ingramcontent.com/pod-product-compliance
Lightning Source LLC
Chambersburg PA
CBHW080501110426
42742CB00017B/2963